Studies in the Short Stories of
WILLIAM CARLETON

ACTA UNIVERSITATIS GOTHOBURGENSIS

GOTHENBURG STUDIES IN ENGLISH 34

STUDIES IN THE SHORT STORIES OF WILLIAM CARLETON

BY
MARGARET CHESNUTT

ACTA UNIVERSITATIS GOTHOBURGENSIS
GÖTEBORG SWEDEN

ISBN 91-7346-027-3

(O

Distributors:
ACTA UNIVERSITATIS GOTHOBURGENSIS
Box 5096
S-402 22 Göteborg 5
Sweden

Printed in Sweden by Göteborgs Offsettryckeri AB 1976

CONTENTS

PREFACE

I wish to thank Professor Erik Frykman, University of Göteborg, for the patient kindness and sound advice which I have enjoyed during the writing of this work. His encouragement and guidance have been invaluable.

My thanks are also due to John Townsend, University College London, Margaret MacAnulla, secretary to the Anglo-Irish Committee of the Royal Irish Academy, and Martin Ryan of the National Library of Ireland for help in the compilation of the bibliographical appendix.

Dr. André Boué of the University of Paris IV very kindly placed a copy of his book on Carleton at my disposal. Johannes and Sigrid Hedberg, Göteborg, have also shown me much kindness.

This work is dedicated to Michael Chesnutt, University of Copenhagen, without whose constant support, criticism and great practical assistance it would never have been completed.

Aalborg Universitetscenter
November 1976

Margaret Chesnutt

ABBREVIATIONS

CE The Christian Examiner and Church of Ireland Magazine. Dublin 1825-69.

DUM The Dublin University Magazine. Dublin 1833-77.

IPJ The Irish Penny Journal. Dublin 1840-41.

Life David J. O'Donoghue, The Life of William Carleton: being his Autobiography and Letters; and an Account of his Life and Writings, from the Point at which the Autobiography breaks off. 2v., London 1896.

NM The National Magazine. Dublin 1830-31.

TS William Carleton, Traits and Stories of the Irish Peasantry. First series (TS^1), 2v., Dublin 1830; second series (TS^2), 3v., Dublin 1833.

Works The Works of William Carleton. 2v., New York 1880. Reprinted Freeport, N.Y. (Short Story Index reprint series) 1970.

INTRODUCTION

The literature of nineteenth century Ireland concerned itself to a high degree with the question of national identity. Culture, race, religion and politics were the to-
pics discussed throughout the century, and it was not until the literary revival of 1890-1920 that questions of
nationality were transcended and Irish literature written
in English became part of the mainstream of European literature.

From the eighteenth century onward the Gaelic
language and culture of Ireland declined. The defeat of
the Jacobite revolt in the last decade of the seventeenth
century and the consequent emigration of the Catholic
Irish aristocracy who patronized Gaelic literature had
dealt a hard blow to the professional literary classes,
who now had to depend upon the peasantry for their support. The Penal Laws of the eighteenth century and the
status of English as the language of commerce and the ruling class also contributed to the decline of Gaelic culture, which suffered irreversible setbacks in the 1840's
at the time of the Great Famine. Subsequent efforts were
made at revival, but the Gaelic language never regained
its leading position: it has been estimated that "The actual speakers of the old language, who numbered about four
million before the Famine, had become a mere hundred thousand by the end of the nineteenth century".[1] English had
been the language of the colonist and as such had been the
minority language of a minority culture. Writers in English had written mainly for an English public — it is only

---

1. Patrick C. Power, <u>A Literary History of Ireland</u> (Cork 1969),
    p. 110.

their birth which makes Richard Steele, Oliver Goldsmith
and Richard Brinsley Sheridan Irish, while Jonathan Swift,
exiled in Ireland, is very much part of the English neo-
classical movement.

In 1789 Charlotte Brooke published her <u>Reliques</u>
<u>of Irish Poetry</u>, translations of Gaelic songs which "help-
ed to build and form a literature in Ireland in the English language ... which was not just a reflection of English literature".[2] She had probably been influenced by
James Macpherson's Ossianic poems,[3] which had enjoyed
great popularity in Europe and in England and had captured
the imagination of Goethe. Despite the controversy about
his work, Macpherson had started a vogue for Celtic studies which increased throughout the nineteenth century.

While the heroic legends of Cuchulain, Deirdre
and Finn were being rediscovered by scholars, Irish fiction written in English was beginning to take shape. The
two greatest prose writers in early nineteenth century
Ireland were Maria Edgeworth and William Carleton. Maria
Edgeworth wrote of her own Anglo-Irish landlord class and
stands at the head of the nineteenth century tradition in
fiction which includes Charles Lever, Samuel Lover and Lady Morgan, and later Somerville and Ross. William Carleton wrote of peasant life and was a pioneer of the stronger, more vital native Irish prose tradition; Gerald Griffin and the Banim brothers were his lesser contemporaries.
In the introduction to the collected edition of his <u>Traits</u>
<u>and Stories</u> first issued in 1842/43, Carleton credits him-
self — not wholly justifiably — with having founded what
he calls a national literature with the publication of the
first series in Dublin in 1830. Up to that time Irish
writers had mostly published their work in London, but

> the publication of [these] two unpretending vol-
> umes, written by a peasant's son, established an
> important and gratifying fact — that our native
> country, if without a literature at the time, was
> at least capable of appreciating, and willing to

2. <u>ibid.</u>, p. 146.
3. James Macpherson, <u>Fragments of Ancient Poetry</u> (Edinburgh 1760);
    <u>Fingal</u> (London 1761); <u>Temora</u> (London 1763).

foster the humble exertions of such as endeavored to create one. Nor was this all; for so far as resident authors were concerned, it was now clearly established that an Irish writer could be successful at home without the necessity of appearing under the name and sanction of the great London or Edinburgh booksellers.[4]

Carleton was not alone in appreciating his own contribution. W.B. Yeats acknowledged the debt of Irish writers to Carleton when he said that with Traits and Stories "began modern Irish literature". He remarked further:

> William Carleton was a great Irish historian.
> The history of a nation is not in parliaments and battle-fields, but in what the people say to each other on fair-days and high days, and in how they farm, and quarrel, and go on pilgrimage. These things has Carleton recorded.[5]

CARLETON'S LIFE AND WORK

William Carleton, the son of an Irish-speaking tenant farmer, was born in Co. Tyrone in the north of Ireland in 1794. His career spans one of the most troubled periods in Irish history, a transition period in both social and literary terms, and his writings reflect the issues predominant in the period. The youngest of fourteen children, he was designated for the Roman Catholic priesthood and therefore encouraged in his pursuit of learning; a combination of circumstances led him, however, to a quite different career.

Carleton recounts in his autobiography,[6] which was written in his old age and left incomplete, how his participation in a pilgrimage to the Catholic sanctuary of

---

4. Works II, pp. 643-644.
5. Stories from Carleton, with an introduction by W.B. Yeats (London etc. n.d.), p. xvi.
6. The Autobiography of William Carleton, with a preface by Patrick Kavanagh (London 1968). Previously published in Life (1896), vol. I; cf. note 17 below.

Lough Derg opened his eyes to the faults of the Roman
Church, and it is clear both from his stories and from his
autobiography that the Catholic doctrine of exclusive salvation particularly disturbed him. It is also apparent
that he had a zest for life and a taste for female company which were incompatible with the contemplative and ce-
libate existence of a Roman Catholic priest.

    The fortunes of Carleton's family declined rapid-
ly after his father's death, and Carleton himself spent a
number of years in unsuccessful attempts to obtain an education and occupation commensurate with his talents and
ambitions. Finally, in 1819, having been rejected as a
lazy good-for-nothing by his relatives, he started out for
Dublin in the hope of making his fortune. He arrived penniless and starving, but with a wealth of rural experience
stored up in his memory. After many initial difficulties
he became tutor to the son of the Protestant evangelist
Fox; he married Jane Anderson, Fox's niece, and gave up
the Roman Catholic faith in favour of Protestantism.[7] He
became a schoolmaster through the agency of the Association for Discountenancing Vice, one of the institutions of
the "New Reformation", and taught for a time in Mullingar
and Carlow before returning to Dublin in 1826.

    It was at this time that Carleton met the Rev.
Caesar Otway, editor of The Christian Examiner,[8] and that
his career as a writer began. He had essayed short pieces
before[9] but had never contemplated earning a living for
himself and his family by his pen. Otway encouraged him
to set down his impressions of his pilgrimage to Lough
Derg and "A Pilgrimage to Patrick's Purgatory" was published in 1828; Carleton's association with Otway's journal continued until 1831. He wrote ten stories for The
Christian Examiner — most of them anti-Catholic propaganda — but broke with it on the publication of "Denis
O'Shaughnessy going to Maynooth".[10]

---

7. For further details on this period of Carleton's life see ch. I,
   p. 64.
8. Cf. ch. I, pp. 20-21.
9. Cf. The Autobiography of William Carleton, p. 204.
10. Cf. ch. I, p. 21.

4

The next and greatest stage of Carleton's career came when he published his Traits and Stories of the Irish Peasantry — the first series in 1830 and the second series in 1833. These are the stories for which he is most famous, and in them he captures the life and customs of the class which largely disappeared with the Great Famine. The Traits and Stories was an immediate success and Carleton found himself writing for the literary magazines which flourished in the Dublin of the 1830's. Even before Traits and Stories he had published in The Dublin Literary Gazette and The National Magazine but in 1833 he began to publish in a newly started journal, The Dublin University Magazine, a Tory publication edited by Isaac Butt. Carleton published in The Dublin University Magazine intermittently from 1833 to 1860; two of his greatest novels, Fardorougha the Miser, or the Convicts of Lisnamona and The Black Prophet. A Tale of Irish Famine, first appeared here in serial form.[11] The Dublin University Magazine was an important organ in the shaping of Irish culture and Carleton "attached himself ... firmly to its interests and was associated in the public mind with the political position of its editors". The aim of the magazine was "to establish an intellectual organ which could rise above the mean controversies of the day while remaining Ascendancy in tone and loyalties".[12] Such scholars as George Petrie, Eugene O'Curry and John O'Donovan, the novelists Charles Lever, Samuel Lover and Joseph Sheridan Lefanu, and the poets James Clarence Mangan and Samuel Ferguson also contributed to The Dublin University Magazine, which was widely read in its time. Carleton wrote a great variety of stories, sketches and novels during the 1830's and 1840's for the Dublin magazines, ranging from the sombre study of famine in The Black Prophet to sketches of Irish characters in The Irish Penny Journal (edited by George Petrie), the sentimental "Jane Sinclair or the Fawn of Springvale" and the light-hearted extravaganza "Moll Roe's Marriage or the Pudding Bewitched".

---

11. For Carleton's publications see Appendix II.
12. Thomas Flanagan, The Irish Novelists 1800-1850 (New York 1959), pp. 301-302.

In 1840 Daniel O'Connell turned his energies to securing a repeal of the legislative union between England and Ireland. During the struggle for Catholic Emancipation O'Connell had stood at the head of a popular movement but now he found himself isolated. However, in October 1842 The Nation newspaper appeared for the first time. The Nation was dedicated to achieving Irish independence and its leading associates were Charles Gavan Duffy and Thomas Davis. Both were influenced by the ideas of nationalism and liberalism widespread in the Europe of the time and for a while they joined forces with O'Connell. Carleton also wrote for The Nation, and encouraged by Duffy and Davis he produced Valentine M'Clutchy, the Irish Agent; or, Chronicles of the Castle Cumber Property, a novel which viciously satirizes the land system and which aroused the fury of his previous patrons when it appeared in 1845. Under the influence of The Nation Carleton adopted a Nationalist tone but he was never himself a Nationalist. He wrote condemning the landlords in as strong language as he had condemned Catholicism in The Christian Examiner; and four years later he condemned those who took part in the tithe war -- that is, the very same Catholic peasantry whom he had defended in Valentine M'Clutchy — in The Tithe Proctor: a Novel. Being a Tale of the Tithe Rebellion in Ireland. Indeed he served all parties and shades of opinion during his career: in 1848 he was writing for The Irish Tribune, a revolutionary journal, though he protested that he had no knowledge of "its intended object".[13] And his biographer suggests that his "drastic references" to agitators in his novels at the height of the repeal movement were motivated more by his desire to obtain a literary pension than by dislike of repeal.[14]

In 1848 Carleton was at long last awarded a government pension. The purpose of the pension would seem to have been to sever him from the revolutionary cause; if this was indeed the object it was fulfilled. O'Donoghue writes that from the time he acquired his pension Carleton

---

13. Life (1896) II, p. 124.
14. ibid., p. 43.

deserted the peasant cause and his works became artificial. "The sooner most of these later works are forgotten,
the better for Carleton's fame".[15] Thomas Flanagan sums
up as follows: "He fought with his creditors, appeared
and reappeared in bankruptcy court, steered clear of politics, wrote gentle folksy sketches for pious Catholic periodicals".[16] Carleton died poor and embittered in 1869.

REVIEW OF PREVIOUS SCHOLARSHIP

Carleton scholars have inevitably tended to adopt a biographical approach. Indeed the first major study of
Carleton was undertaken by D.J. O'Donoghue when he completed Carleton's autobiography.[17] O'Donoghue's work covers
Carleton's life in Dublin from 1828 onwards, principally
in terms of his writing career. His method is bibliogra-
phical/biographical, but apart from impressionistic comments on Carleton's writings there is no attempt at evaluation and the bibliography itself is not entirely reliable.
        Carleton's place in the literary history of Ire-
land is somewhat ambiguous. In his early Celtic period
W.B. Yeats credited him with being "the greatest novelist
of Ireland, by right of the most Celtic eyes that ever
gazed from under the brows of storyteller. His equals in
gloomy and tragic power, Michael and John Banim, had nothing of his Celtic humour".[18] Yeats also regarded Carleton as a historian of the peasantry, an opinion shared by
Horatio Sheafe Krans who characterized him as "the cre-
ative genius among the Irish novelists".[19] Krans gave the
following description of Carleton's relationship with his
people: "All that characterized the peasant was reflected
in his work — the imperfect education, the easily roused

15. ibid., p. 123.
16. The Irish Novelists, p. 329.
17. The Life of William Carleton: being his Autobiography and Let-
     ters; and an Account of his Life and Writings, from the Point
     at which the Autobiography breaks off, 2v. (London 1896).
18. Stories from Carleton, p. xvi.
19. Irish Life in Irish Fiction (New York 1903), p. 316.

passions, the intense affections, the prejudices, the strength, the weakness, and the besetting sins".[20] Carleton is thus regarded by Yeats and Krans as a living embodiment of the Irish peasantry.

Thomas MacDonagh represents early twentieth century Nationalist criticism of Carleton. MacDonagh, who was one of the executed 1916 leaders, considered that "Carleton made the mistake, during one part of his career at least, of writing for a foreign audience ... Carleton knew Irish, and might possibly, some think, have been the Gaelic Mistral — if he had been a patriot. As it was he fell between two stools".[21] MacDonagh thus applied the criterion of patriotism in evaluating Carleton. However, most early twentieth century criticism of Carleton in Ireland focused more on his change of religion than on his patriotism, though he was condemned on both counts.[22]

English literary historians writing on Carleton, or for that matter any of the early nineteenth century Irish novelists apart from Maria Edgeworth, tend to misunderstand him completely. He is discussed in E.A. Baker's The History of the English Novel, where he is judged to be "greater than any of his native rivals".[23] His failings are a lack of invention, a tendency to "stage Irishness", racy but sometimes overdone dialogue, wordiness and an excess of moral lectures. He is a great writer in his own way but "like the Banims and Griffin, he owed more than he knew to Scott ...".[24] Like Baker, Walter Allen[25] and Donald Davie[26] regard Scott as the touchstone of evaluation when commenting on early nineteenth century Irish fiction. Walter Allen dismisses these writers with the observation that they "found their exemplars in Maria Edgeworth and Scott ... Their natural

20. ibid., p. 320.
21. Literature in Ireland: Studies Irish and Anglo-Irish (London n.d. [1916]), p. 33. Actually it is impossible to imagine Carleton writing when he did for a purely "native" audience.
22. Cf. ch. I, pp. 24-27.
23. Vol. VII (London 1936), p. 31.
24. ibid., p. 34.
25. The English Novel: A Short Critical History (1954; reprinted Harmondsworth 1968).
26. The Heyday of Sir Walter Scott (London 1961).

talents were smaller and their interpretation of life crude".[27] Davie makes the same mistake as Allen in that he takes up only one of Carleton's works, compares it with Scott's production and finds it wanting; he remarks that although Carleton comes close to Maria Edgeworth "in his tendentiousness ... His model ... is Scott, and he is one of the multitude of writers who aspired to be the Irish Scott".[28] Davie reveals his own literary prejudices when he writes of Traits and Stories that "the very title ... reveals the double motive behind their writing, the two stools they are to fall between; are these indeed 'stories' or pieces of reportage?" He answers his own question when he admits that "it would be a sort of pedantry to ask whether the value of these astonishing productions is anthropological or literary".[29] His concluding statement that "Carleton ... fails to be an Irish Scott because he is himself a character out of Scott, he is part of Scott's subject-matter"[30] is meaningless. His insistence on dealing with Carleton in terms of the Scott tradition blinds him to what is both different and unique about Carleton. There can be no doubt that Carleton admired Scott, but to assert that he took Scott as his model and failed to live up to him does not help to evaluate his contribution. Carleton, who himself charged John Banim with imitating Scott,[31] wrote of the Ireland of his own day and concerned himself with the present state of the peasantry, whereas Scott wrote historical novels.

Vivian Mercier includes Carleton in the "Irish comic tradition", finding that the Swiftian tradition of macabre humour flourishes in his work.[32] However, Carleton is similar to many native Irishmen of the time in that he does not "make use of the opportunities for political satire" open to him. The most important reason for this failing is said to have been a "deep emotional involvement in the miseries" of Ireland. Another reason for

---

27. The English Novel, p. 131.
28. The Heyday of Sir Walter Scott, p. 80.
29. ibid., pp. 98-99.
30. ibid.
31. Life II, p. 60.
32. The Irish Comic Tradition (London 1962), p. 67.

these writers' neglect of the genre was that "Satire, especially when it employs irony, perhaps demands greater sophistication than they or, especially their audience, possessed in the new language".[33] Mercier assumes that satire of the Swiftian variety was the most suitable instrument of protest. Be that as it may, Carleton was perfectly capable of writing satire, as "An Irish Election in the Time of the Forties"[34] ably demonstrates.

Like Mercier, Frank O'Connor also takes up the question of Carleton's language, but his disapproval of it is based on aesthetic considerations. "His English is leaden, his judgement is dull, and he simply has no ear for speech".[35] While O'Connor is in no doubt as to Carleton's intrinsic ability, he bewails the circumstance that his "giant talent was ... rent asunder by faction-fighters who wished him to write from one distorted standpoint or the other".[36] This verdict, though true up to a point, is a little exaggerated as it bypasses Carleton's own search for a solution to the various ills of the Ireland of his time.

Benedict Kiely has written the first major study of William Carleton, a literary biography tracing Carleton's life from his birth in Tyrone to his death in Dublin.[37] Kiely takes social and political history into account, emphasizing Carleton's involvement with the sufferings of the people, but he is mainly concerned with Carleton the man. He is a little ambivalent about Carleton's change of religion: on the one hand he claims that Carleton betrayed "part of himself and part of his people"[38] when he became a Protestant; on the other hand he admits that to Carleton religion was more an emotional than an intellectual matter and that feeding his family — for he

---

33. ibid., p. 185.
34. Published in DUM XXX (1847).
35. The Backward Look: A Survey of Irish Literature (London etc. 1967), p. 148.
36. ibid., p. 140.
37. Poor Scholar: A Study of the Works and Days of William Carleton (1794-1869) (New York 1948).
38. Poor Scholar, p. 65.

could procure an income by changing his religion — was an understandable motive.[39]

The American scholar Thomas Flanagan examines "the works and careers of the principal Irish novelists of the early nineteenth century" in an attempt "to define the 'tradition' of the Irish novel".[40] As with Kiely, Flanagan's approach to Carleton is biographical. He agrees with O'Connor when he remarks that Carleton's "was the richest talent in nineteenth-century Ireland and the most prodigally wasted".[41] He takes issue with those who regard Carleton as a social historian: "it is this very general notion of Carleton as 'the historian of the peasantry' which has worked against an understanding of all that was hard and unique in the man ...".[42] However, Flanagan himself admits that "Carleton rendered the life of a peasant Ireland with a fullness, a passion, and an accuracy which no other writer has approached".[43]

Kiely and Flanagan write largely of Carleton's shorter stories. Eileen Ibarra's unpublished dissertation[44] is a historical and biographical evaluation of four of the novels, Fardorougha the Miser, Valentine M'Clutchy, The Black Prophet and The Emigrants of Ahadarra. The novels are read in terms of Carleton's aesthetic theory which, Ibarra claims, equated beauty with moral imagination. Ibarra remarks that Carleton was an extremely realistic author who in a search for "serenity" wrote for all political parties. She believes, however, that Carleton was merely acting in accordance with the essentially apolitical nature of the peasantry, an opinion which seems a little romantic.

A major contribution to Carleton studies has been made by André Boué in a dissertation presented in 1973.[45] Boué's work is divided into three sections, a biography,

39. ibid., p. 104.
40. The Irish Novelists, pp. viii-ix.
41. ibid., p. 255.
42. ibid., p. 263.
43. ibid., p. 262.
44. "Realistic Accounts of the Irish Peasantry in Four Novels of William Carleton", diss. Gainesville [Univ. of Florida] 1969.
45. William Carleton 1794-1869: Romancier Irlandais, diss. Paris 1973.

an analysis of Carleton's fiction and an extensive and valuable bibliography. He considers Carleton to have been a
realist with an extensive knowledge of his subject and a
desire to instruct his readers. By painting a faithful
picture of the life of the peasantry he gave them their
just place in the national literature of which he was the
founder. He was a "Propagandiste incorrigible, écrivain
négligent" but also "un admirable conteur", and his propa-
gandism is defended thus:

> Si sa conception utilitaire de la littérature
> l'entraîne trop souvent vers la polémique ou la
> prédication morale, il dénonce efficacement les
> abus, et s'il sert tour à tour des propagandes
> opposées, il refuse toute allégeance incondition-
> nelle à un parti. Son patriotisme est sincère,
> mais il se soucie moins de théorie que du bien-
> être des individus.[46]

John Wilson Foster adopts a relatively original
approach to Carleton, treating him thematically and finding that the major "thematic motifs" of "the blighted
land", "bad blood" and "lost fields"[47] are present in Ulster fiction from Carleton to the present day. Far from
considering Carleton to be a realist, he adds that "Of any
Ulster writer writing about the land, Carleton has the
most elaborate and effective disguise for the absence of
deep thought and a realistic vision. This disguise takes
the form of generic and stylistic richness ...". It is
also suggested that "in the light of contemporary fiction
criticism ... most Carleton criticism has been misdirected
by an insistence on treating Carleton as an autobiographer
or social historian or political polemicist rather than as
a fiction writer with his own lively theories of fiction
writing". The generic and not the social should be emphasized in order "to restore the balance in Carleton criticism". He should "be studied first and foremost as a comic writer".[48] This approach might indeed be fruitful if

---

46. William Carleton ..., pp. 489-490.
47. Forces and Themes in Ulster Fiction (Dublin etc. 1974), pp. 3-6.
48. ibid., pp. 16-17.

the critical point of departure were aesthetic; as it is, much groundwork remains to be done on the social aspects, not least on the relationship between Carleton and the reading public.

THE PRESENT STUDY

In this book I have adopted a socio-historical standpoint in dealing with Carleton and have concentrated my attention on his short stories. Despite John Wilson Foster's claim that Carleton has for too long been regarded as a social historian or polemicist, no thorough examination of his work from the point of view of social or religious content exists. In Chapters I and II I have attempted to make such an examination, reading Carleton's stories against the background of his own society, and in Chapter III I have examined Carleton's didacticism in terms of narrative structure and characterization.

Carleton is a talented but uneven writer viewed in relation to the English literary tradition. It is however a mistake to judge him merely by the standards of a tradition with which he had but scant acquaintance; and in interpreting his ever-changing political sympathies and the nature of his didacticism it is well to remember that he was greatly influenced by his social position as a writer in a troubled country that had long been a colony, and that while he tried to improve the lot of the Irish people he was at the same time desperately loyal to the English connection. In the following pages an attempt will be made to apply these and other previously neglected considerations to a similarly neglected body of material.

CHAPTER I.
THE DEPICTION OF PEASANT RELIGION

A. INTRODUCTORY

The earliest stories of William Carleton concern themselves almost exclusively with the religious condition of
the Irish Roman Catholic peasantry in the early nineteenth
century. They are written from the point of view of an
Evangelical proselytizer and are therefore polemical and
anti-Catholic. Since a knowledge of the religious question is necessary if these stories are to be placed in
their cultural and social context, I shall here attempt to
give an outline of the relations between Catholic and Protestant in Ireland from the late seventeenth century until
Carleton's own time.

The social, economic and cultural condition of the great
mass of Irish people in the early nineteenth century was
miserable indeed. George Berkeley's query, "Whether there
be upon earth any Christian or civilized people so beggar-
ly, wretched and destitute as the common Irish?"[1] applied
just as much in Carleton's youth as it had some three
quarters of a century earlier. The greater part of the
cultivated land had been transferred already in the seventeenth century from Catholic to Protestant hands, and the
majority lived as tenants on land which their ancestors
had owned. They were aware of this fact, and it contributed to their bitterness.

---

1. The Querist (1735-1737), Query 132; quoted by Constantia Maxwell,
    Country and Town in Ireland under the Georges (1940; revised edi-
    tion Dundalk 1949), p. 113.

Apart from ensuring that they remained landless, the Penal Laws enacted in the late seventeenth and early eighteenth centuries had excluded Catholics from political life and greatly hindered them in their religious, educational and economic progress. One of the enduring results of the Penal Laws was to inflict on the Irish people a sense of national inferiority which to some extent has lasted to this day. In Sybil, or the Two Nations,[2] Disraeli speaks of the young Queen Victoria as ruling on the one side a nation of property owners, and on the other a nation of dispossessed workers. These two nations rarely came into contact with one another and had no conception of each other's way of life or scheme of values. The analogy with Ireland is obvious: the Ascendancy who formed one fifth of the population ruled over the lives and fortunes of the other four fifths. After the Act of Union in 1800 a third tier was added to this social hierarchy; this was the English establishment who despised the Irish Ascendancy almost as much as the latter despised their peasant fellow-countrymen.[3]

The majority of the Penal Laws were passed by the Ascendancy in the Irish Parliament. King William III, after his defeat of the Irish armies who had fought for James II, had let it be known that he did not wish revenge to be taken on his defeated opponents. Accordingly, the civil articles of the Treaty of Limerick granted to Irish Roman Catholics among other things such freedom of religion as was "consistent with the laws of Ireland, or as they did enjoy in the reign of King Charles II"; and they further provided that "their majesties will summon a parliament ... [which] will endeavour to procure the said Roman Catholics such farther security in that particular, as may preserve them from any disturbance upon the account of their said religion".[4] But the terms of the treaty were

---

2. London 1845.
3. The superior attitude of the English to the Irish aristocracy is illustrated in such works as Maria Edgeworth, The Absentee (London 1812).
4. "The Civil Articles of Limerick" (1691), Article I, in: Irish Historical Documents 1172-1922, ed. Edmund Curtis and R.B. McDowell (London 1943), p. 172.

not fulfilled: the Irish Ascendancy feared the defeated Catholic majority, and four years later came the first bill directed towards curbing the freedom of Irish Catholics. Others followed in quick succession, until the high point of reaction was reached in the "Act to prevent the growth of Popery" passed in Dublin in 1704. The laws of 1695, 1697 and 1703 had forbidden Catholics to send their children abroad to be educated; they had forbidden them to carry weapons of any kind; they had also banished the Catholic bishops and regular clergy, while the secular clergy who remained were required to register themselves and to swear oaths of good behaviour. The "Act to prevent the growth of Popery" went even further, as a brief resumé of its provisions will show.

In 1704 there were still some Catholic aristocrats whose lands had escaped the earlier confiscations. Now legal action was taken against them by enacting that Catholic-owned land might only be inherited by gavelkind (that is, by equal division among the owner's sons); if, however, the eldest son was a Protestant, he could make his father a tenant upon his own estate in his lifetime and inherit the entire property after his death. No Catholic might inherit land owned by a Protestant. Clause six of the Act, forbidding Catholics to buy land or to take out a lease of more than thirty-one years' duration, affected aristocracy and peasantry alike, as did clause four which, in order to ensure that children be brought up in the Church of Ireland, forbade any Catholic to be guardian or tutor to a child under twenty-one. Further, to qualify for civil office Catholics must take the oaths of abjuration and allegiance which it was morally impossible for them to do; and "for the preventing papists having it in their power to breed dissention amongst protestants by voting at elections of members of parliament" it was enacted that these same oaths be administered to them before they could vote.[5] This was tantamount to depriving Catholics of the franchise, and 1 George II c.9 (1727) comple-

---

5. "An act to prevent the further growth of Popery", Clauses III-XXIV (Irish Historical Documents, pp. 189-194).

ted the process by formally excluding them from voting at parliamentary elections.[6]

It has been sagely remarked that the purpose of the Penal Laws "was not to destroy Roman Catholicism, but to make sure that its adherents were kept in a position of social, economic, and political inferiority".[7] This purpose was attained; and although the few remaining Catholic aristocrats managed to retain their estates by a policy of prudent silence, the rest of the native population were rendered utterly powerless. There was no incentive to obey the law, which for Catholics was an instrument of oppression rather than of justice. There was no point in thrift or hard work, as it was impossible to buy land, and the tenant majority were completely at the mercy of the landlord or — even worse — of his agent. The fact that there were good landlords and just magistrates, as Constantia Maxwell points out,[8] does not change the overall picture which emerges.

By the middle of the eighteenth century, the Penal Laws relating to worship and the Catholic clergy had been allowed to fall into abeyance, and between 1771 and 1793 many of them were repealed. In 1793 the right to vote was extended to Roman Catholics on the same terms as Protestants. This did not, however, have much immediate effect, as the votes of the famous "forty shilling freeholders" were now exercised by their landlords, tenants being driven to the polls like so many cattle and cajoled, bullied or terrorized into voting for the landlord's candidate.[9] Nor did the 1793 legislation give Catholics the right to stand for election themselves; this barrier, which excluded eighty per cent of the population from their own legislature, was only broken down in 1829 after popular agitation so intense that it drove the Government into concessions.

6. Irish Historical Documents, p. 194, footnote 1.
7. J.C. Beckett, The Making of Modern Ireland 1603-1923 (1966; reprinted London 1969), p. 159.
8. Country and Town in Ireland under the Georges, ch. IV. Carleton gives a graphic description of these abuses in "An Irish Election in the Time of the Forties" DUM XXX (1847), pp. 176-192, 287-297.
9. The Emancipation act of 1829 deprived the "forty shilling freeholders" of the franchise they had obtained a generation earlier.

In 1800 the Act of Union uniting the legislatures of Great Britain and Ireland was passed and in January 1801 it came into force. However, it did not fuse the two countries, and Ireland was "governed as a half-alien dependency".[10] But by 1820 those Irish Protestants who had been opposed to the Union, and who had voted for it because they were bullied and bribed, had come to support it as their only protection against the Roman Catholic majority. Religious tension was accordingly increased, and any British attempt to reconcile the majority automatically alarmed the minority. Before 1800 the "Protestant nation" had asserted its rights against the constitutional encroachments of Westminster. Its citizens had lived in the second city of the Empire and to a great extent on their own estates, and they had repealed most of the Penal Laws passed by their ancestors. Now, deprived of effective political power, they could only maintain their identity by standing openly as an English garrison in Ireland, and many became absentee landlords, draining the country of the income derived from rents and causing great hardship to their tenants.

In the north of Ireland particularly, where there was a large Protestant population, sectarian strife had increased throughout the eighteenth century to reach its peak in 1795. After a battle between Protestant and Catholic societies in Co. Armagh, the Orange Society (later the Orange Order) was established to protect the immediate interests and maintain the power of the Protestant population. In a couple of months the Society was joined by members of the middle and upper classes who proceeded to take over its leadership, and it quickly spread all over Ireland. It is obvious that it fulfilled a political need. Catholics were persecuted violently in Armagh, and it was commonly believed among the peasantry that the Society enjoyed Government support. In his autobiography, written at the end of his life, Carleton passes the following comment on this period in the north:

---

10. Beckett, The Making of Modern Ireland, p. 287.

18

the country was in a state sufficient, in the
mind of every liberal and thinking man, to fling
back disgrace and infamy upon the successive ad-
ministrations which permitted it. This was the
period of Protestant, or rather of Orange, ascendancy ... To find a justice of the peace not an
Orangeman would have been an impossibility ...
There was then no law against an Orangeman, and
no law for a Papist.[11]

Religious tension added to great agrarian strife
and the political agitation of the United Irishmen culmi-
nated in the abortive rebellion of 1798. This rebellion
was brutally repressed and for many years after it the
peasantry were leaderless. Secret societies were active,
and violence broke out sporadically, but these disturbances were isolated and of no national importance. At this
time the peasantry came to look upon themselves very much
as a degraded caste, and they therefore seized upon Emancipation as a symbol of their equality and freedom. To
the great mass of the people, the admission of a few landlords to Parliament could make no practical difference, but

in the popular mind Emancipation had come to mean
far more than this. The Irish peasant saw himself as the victim of injustice in almost all the
relations of life: the landlord and the parson
oppressed him; the magistrate refused him justice; his protestant neighbour, simply as a protestant, had the advantage of him at every
turn.[12]

The battle for Emancipation was a long and bitter one, and
in the course of their struggle the Irish learned the
principles of political organization which they used to
further their national and religious claims throughout the
nineteenth century. As time went on, Catholic demands for
religious equality and an end to the Protestant Ascendancy
developed into an attack on the Union itself: "The claim
to national independence, abandoned by the protestants,

11. The Autobiography of William Carleton (London 1968), pp. 36-37.
12. Beckett, p. 300.

became almost the distinctive political characteristic of the Roman Catholics; and the age-old connection between political and religious affiliations became stronger than ever".[13]

B. CARLETON AND "THE CHRISTIAN EXAMINER"

Between the years 1828 and 1831 Carleton wrote a number of stories for The Christian Examiner, a Dublin periodical edited by the Rev. Caesar Otway. The Christian Examiner and Church of Ireland Magazine, to give it its full title, ran from 1825 until 1869. It was "Almost purely religious and controversial in character and contents, but a small proportion being devoted to general literature".[1] It had been founded by Otway and others as a mouthpiece of the Evangelical "New Reformation" movement within the Church of Ireland. The editor was a talented writer, as can be seen from his Sketches in Ireland (Dublin 1827) or A Tour in Connaught (Dublin 1839). However,

> on the subject of the Church of Rome ... he was quite literally mad, a condition for which his vocation afforded a perfect disguise. Beneath theological and social objections to papist theory and practice lay a mind obsessed by the celibacy of priests, the virginity of nuns, and a hundred other objects of furtive sexual speculation. These thrust themselves to the surface of his books with frightening regularity.[2]

When Otway met Carleton, as the latter relates in his preface to "The Lough Derg Pilgrim",[3] he realized that he had found the perfect controversialist for his magazine. Carleton on the other hand was impressed with Otway and — more important — was relieved to have some means

13. ibid., p. 288.

1. Stephen J. Brown, S.J., Ireland in Fiction: A Guide to Irish Novels, Tales, Romances and Folklore[2] (1919; reprinted Shannon 1968), p. 336.
2. Thomas Flanagan, The Irish Novelists, p. 277.
3. Works II, pp. 796-797.

of earning a living for himself and his growing family. Accordingly a most unlikely partnership was entered into between the erstwhile Catholic peasant from Tyrone and the Evangelical clergyman from Dublin. For three and a half years Carleton wrote stories for The Christian Examiner; and as his reputation grew, so did the notoriety which has lasted into the twentieth century.[4] With these stories[5] Carleton introduced himself to the Dublin public. Thomas Flanagan comments on the paradoxical situation which now arose: "In the pages of this infuriate little periodical, from the pen of an embittered apostate had come stories beneath whose coating of polemic lay a deep persuasive love for the peasants of whom he wrote, and a great though ungauged power".[6]

These stories were for the most part intended as proselytizing material and were indeed published as such by Caesar Otway. However, they are not all uniform in style and subject matter and they reflect a development and change in Carleton's attitude to priests and people, culminating in "Denis O'Shaughnessy going to Maynooth" (1831). What should presumably have been an exposé of how young men are trapped into taking Holy Orders — a theme exploited in the earlier story of "Father Butler" and con- sistent with the editorial policy of The Christian Exami- ner — became a highly complex story in which irony and hu- mour predominate. There is a good deal of criticism of Roman Catholicism, but it centres on the social pressure on a young man to seek ordination rather than on the priestly state itself.[7] "Denis O'Shaughnessy" shows in this respect a marked contrast to the other stories which

---

4. See for example the pseudonymous review article "A Contrast in Public Values. The Catholic Statesman: The Apostate Man of Let- ters" in The Catholic Bulletin [Dublin] XXI (1931), pp. 583-587.
5. "A Pilgrimage to Patrick's Purgatory" (subsequently retitled "The Lough Derg Pilgrim"), "The Broken Oath", "Father Butler" (1828); "The Station", "The Death of a Devotee" (1829); "The Priest's Funeral", "The Brothers", "Lachlin Murray and the Blessed Candle", "The Lianhan Shee", "The Illicit Distiller or the Force of Con- science" (1830); "History of a Chimney Sweep", "The Materialist", "Denis O'Shaughnessy going to Maynooth" (1831).
6. Flanagan, p. 279.
7. See below, pp. 77-79 and ch. III, section C, pp. 156-162.

Carleton published in The Christian Examiner. Nevertheless, the majority of these early stories were intended to
serve the specific purpose of the proselytizer by whom
they were commissioned, and an examination of them must be
based on this premise. This is confirmed by the explicit
statement of the author's intentions in his preface to
Tales of Ireland,[8] a collection which includes some of the
stories previously published in The Christian Examiner
("The Death of a Devotee", "The Priest's Funeral", "The
Brothers", "The Illicit Distiller or the Force of Conscience" and "Lachlin Murray and the Blessed Candle"), together with two stories of a completely different character, "Neal Malone" and "The Dream of a Broken Heart" (both
originally published in The [Dublin] University Review and
Quarterly Magazine[9]). The substance of the Tales of Ireland preface will be reproduced here, because it is vital
to an understanding of Carleton's aims and of his attitude
to the Irish peasantry at this stage in his career.

First and foremost, Carleton claims that his stories "will be found to illustrate, more clearly than any I
have yet written, the religious prejudices and feelings of
the Irish people". This statement of intent may be said
to hold true for all the stories which he published in The
Christian Examiner. He claims that he has written only
for the welfare of the Irish people. They were, he had
found, "a class unknown in literature", unknown by landlords and by "those in whose hands much of their destiny
was placed". His didactic aim appears clearly in his attempt "to delineate their moral, religious, and physical
state". No one had attempted this before; and those who
should understand the character of the peasantry, but do
not, should know them in order to "teach them to know themselves and appreciate their rights, both moral and civil,
as rational men, who owe obedience to law, without the necessity of being slaves either to priest or landlord ...".
The latter remark points not only to Carleton's overall
aim in his stories, but also to the audience for whom they

8. Tales of Ireland (Dublin 1834). The preface was written after the
    stories and is thus a summary of what Carleton considered he had
    demonstrated in them. See below pp. 27-28.
9. Dublin 1833.

were intended — comprising the literate public in Ireland
and Britain who were the landlords and lawgivers of the
Irish peasantry, and who for the most part shared the prevailing combination of anti-Irish and anti-Catholic prejudice.[10]

A constant element in the earliest stories is the
hostility they display towards the Roman Catholic clergy.
Some light is thrown on this hostility in the preface,
where Carleton realizes that he may be censured for his
portraits of the clergy but defends himself by stating
that he would be lacking in honesty if he suppressed "moral truth, in the delineation of national manners, from a
dastardly reluctance to offend those in whom, or in whose
system, abuses detrimental to the freedom and welfare of
the community exist ...". He advises Catholics to love
and honour their clergy, but not slavishly. Priests, for
their part, should not exact "degrading homage" from their
people out of mere pride or because it has been customary
to do so in times past. He issues the following instruc-
tions which Roman Catholic priests should follow if they
wish to be described in a more complimentary fashion.
They should base their influence over the people on "reason, intelligence, and true liberty"; they should "discard
the spirit, since they cannot abrogate the letter, of barbarous dogmas concocted in barbarous ages, rather with a
view of subjugating the mind, for the sake of political
power and personal aggrandizment, than of training it to
habits of an ennobling nature ..."; and finally they
should "treat the body of the people as they do educated
and intelligent men of their own creed ...".[11]

Carleton's biographer D.J. O'Donoghue reports that Tales
of Ireland "deeply offended some of [Carleton's] Catholic
well-wishers, and the charges of intolerance and rank bigotry brought against the work are amply justified".[12]
Tales of Ireland followed directly after the immensely

---

10. Anti-Irish and anti-Catholic prejudice are discussed in section E
     below.
11. Tales of Ireland, pp. viii-xi.
12. Life II, p. 30.

popular Traits and Stories of the Irish Peasantry[13] and
must certainly have surprised that section of Carleton's
public who had not read him in his Christian Examiner
phase. Charles Gavan Duffy, friend of Carleton and co-
founder of The Nation, the mouthpiece of the Young Ireland
movement, remarked that Carleton's name remained "odious
to Catholic publishers"[14] until he redeemed himself more
than a decade later with the novel Valentine M'Clutchy.[15]

   This is perhaps the appropriate point at which to
consider critical reaction to Carleton's change of religion, which has in turn puzzled and angered his commentators right up to the present day. Many reasons have been
given for his conversion. His contemporary, Samuel Hall,
who prefaced his remarks on Carleton with the sarcastic
statement that he had "not much to say of Carleton, and
very little that is good", considered that he changed religion as it suited him. "He was a Catholic to-day and a
Protestant to-morrow, turning from one religion to the
other as occasion served or invited".[16] This pronounce-
ment on Carleton may have had something to do with the ri-
valry between Carleton and Hall's wife, Mrs. S.C. Hall,
for the position of delineator par excellence of the Irish
peasantry. Carleton wrote an article on John Banim in The
Nation (23 September 1843) which compares Mrs. Hall unfa-
vourably with Banim. It is written in his usual rash and
vehement manner. Unlike Mrs. Hall, Banim "does not give
us for the conversation of our countrymen and countrywomen
a monstrous and sickening repetition of the same emascula-
ted verbiage, studded here and there with a bit of Irish
phraseology, stolen from writers who knew Irishmen and
their language thoroughly".[17] This was not calculated to
please; but it was manifestly impossible for a writer with
Carleton's energy of expression and capacity for throwing

---

13. Published 1830-33.
14. Life II, p. 571.
15. Cf. introduction, p.6.
16. Life II, p. 135.
17. ibid., p. 60. In his introduction to the collected TS Carleton
    praises Mrs. Hall particularly for her "female creations" and for
    helping to "[set] right the character of Ireland and her people"
    (Works II, pp. 642-643). This is a good illustration of Carle-
    ton's critical inconsistency.

himself headlong into what he wrote to please all in Dublin literary circles of the day, although he tried to please all in turn. The country was divided religiously and politically and sectarian and party feeling ran high. Carleton wrote for several of these sects and parties in the course of his career, composing "stern Evangelical tracts for Caesar Otway; denunciations of the landlords for Thomas Davis; patronizing sketches for The Dublin University Magazine; unctous Catholic piety for James Duffy; a few sketches for Richard Pigott, the sinister mock-Fenian ..." and much more besides.[18] From the very beginning he was marked out for fame and notoriety. In 1829 "The Lough Derg Pilgrim" and "Father Butler" were published in one volume, and in Gerald Griffin's The Rivals (1832) a copy of this book is placed on the library table of one of the characters. Griffin "does not bother to describe [the book], nor was there need";[19] the title spoke for itself to his readers. Yet when Carleton many years later (in 1845) wrote three propagandist novelettes for the Young Irelanders (Art Maguire, Rody the Rover and Parra Sastha), a review in the Dublin University Magazine accused him of sycophancy with regard to the Roman Catholic clergy, and failure to blame them for the degraded moral condition of the people.[20]

In our own century, critical comment on Carleton's change of religion and anti-Catholic writings has been divided. The Rev. Stephen J. Brown S.J. characterized Tales of Ireland as "full of rank bigotry" and judged that Carleton was indifferent to religion for most of his life.[21] A pseudonymous review of Rose Shaw's Carleton's Country[22] in The Catholic Bulletin for 1931[23] likewise expresses the official Catholic view of Carleton in the earlier part of this century, calling him a "self-willed and self-sufficient apostate". He had been brought

18. Flanagan, The Irish Novelists, p. 256.
19. ibid., p. 279.
20. "The Didactic Irish Novelists — Carleton, Mrs. Hall" DUM XXIV
     (1845), pp. 737-752.
21. Ireland in Fiction² (1919), p. 54.
22. Rose Shaw, Carleton's Country (Dublin 1930).
23. Cf. note 4 above.

up decently by excellent parents, but "elected the path of the pervert". The reviewer writes in language as full of bile as anything Carleton himself ever produced: "Miserable, indeed, in all its petty malignity and abuse, is the record, set down by himself, of how he contrived, in every line that he wrote in the proselytizing press for many years, to vilify and misrepresent his own Catholic origins and the Church that he so deliberately and persistently contemned". His writings were "amorphous and sinister outpourings" and his imagination "turbid, conceited, demoniac".[24] In order to place this review in its proper perspective, it should be added that it was written at a time of Ultramontanism in Ireland, when as Austin Clarke justly says "The new Penal Age had begun". The censorship board of the Free State "became as ferocious as that in Spain or Russia". Catholic nationalism was so strong and so bigoted in this period that it was a mark of distinction in a writer to have his work placed on the banned list.[25] Irish sectarian feeling was in fact as marked in the 1930's as it had been when Carleton published his Christian Examiner stories a century earlier; it is therefore reassuring to record that such sentiments, though exceedingly common, were not quite universal. In 1938 Roger McHugh, a well-known Republican who subsequently became Professor of English at University College Dublin, published an article in which he called the Christian Examiner stories "graphic pen-pictures" with "sectarian bias laid on with a trowel",[26] but he considered Carleton's apostasy to proceed from circumstance rather than malicious conviction.

Recently a more reasoned, less emotional tone has been apparent in discussions of Carleton's change of religion. Lionel Stevenson ascribes it to his desperate search for a solution to the woes of his country, rejecting the notion that he was "a religious or a patriotic

---

24. Catholic Bulletin XXI, pp. 583-586.
25. Austin Clarke, A Penny in the Clouds: More Memories of Ireland and England (London 1968), p. 62.
26. "William Carleton: A Portrait of the Artist as Propagandist" Studies [Dublin] XXVII (1938), p. 52.

fanatic";[27] and Flanagan echoes McHugh in asserting that Carleton's "conversion to Protestantism was ... accidental and issuing from his circumstances".[28] John Montague, Carleton's fellow Northerner, passes no judgement whatever on the conversion, observing only that it raised a barrier between Carleton and his people. He goes on to remark pertinently:

> Carleton was prepared to begin his career by writing something like anti-Catholic propaganda as another writer in present-day Ireland might be prepared, for a time, to write Catholic propaganda. Now the reverse pays best: we have advanced little enough, only reversed our positions in the pointless jig that is Irish sectarian history.[29]

And one of the most recent commentators, Patrick C. Power, sums up the matter by saying that "Carleton's case is instructive. When he spoke uninhibitedly of his people, he was reviled as much for his private religious practice as for his sometimes unflattering portrait of the Irish peasantry".[30] An important function of the religious attacks was to undermine his credibility as a social reporter.

Carleton's conversion to Protestantism and his anti-Catholic outpourings early in his career formed the basis for critical judgement for many years. The reasons for his conversion have been lost in the mists of time — too much has been written about why he converted and very little about the works themselves. There is no critical analysis of any of the early Christian Examiner stories apart from "The Lough Derg Pilgrim", and in my opinion these stories must be examined together, from the point of view of aim and content as well as attitude, before any judgement can be passed on them — literary, social or religious. It should be remembered in this connection that the 1834 preface was written three years after Carleton had published

27. The English Novel: A Panorama (London 1960), p. 255.
28. Flanagan, The Irish Novelists, p. 275.
29. "Tribute to William Carleton" The Bell [Dublin] XVIII (1952), p. 18.
30. A Literary History of Ireland, p. 150.

his last Christian Examiner story, and after he had written the tales of peasant life which appear in the two series of Traits and Stories of the Irish Peasantry; his reputation as a delineator of national manners was established, and he never again returned to the tone of his contributions to The Christian Examiner. He may perhaps have regretted his own harshness, but even in 1834 he could defend himself by claiming that all he had written was written for love of his countrymen: "With the welfare of the Irish people my heart and feelings are identified, and to this object, in all its latitude, have my pen and my knowledge of their character been directed".[31]

Carleton tried to identify abuses in order that they might be corrected.[32] An element of spite may have sullied the purity of his motivation,[33] but there is no doubt that the abuses to which he pointed did exist. It is therefore essential to keep the preface to Tales of Ireland in mind when reading the stories printed in The Christian Examiner.

Three avenues of approach to the stories suggest themselves: to ascertain Carleton's view of the Irish peasant in relation to religious beliefs and practice; to consider his specific objections to Roman Catholic doctrine; and finally to assess the significance of the sto-

---

31. Tales of Ireland, p. x.
32. Carleton continued all his life in both novels and stories to point out the abuses and anomalies of Irish political and social life. Some examples: in Valentine M'Clutchy (1845) he deplores on the one hand Irish absentee landlords and their agents, and on the other sectarian strife. In The Black Prophet (1846) he shows the evil effects of famine on the physical and moral state of the peasantry, and in The Tithe Proctor (1849), for which he was reviled by the Nationalists, he shows the violence provoked in the Catholic peasantry who were forced to pay tithes to a Protestant parson.
33. This is the opinion of André Boué, who concludes that Carleton became "a turncoat out of spite for having been debarred from the priesthood — his bishop had apparently considered him unfit for it — and he let his talent serve the worst kind of religious propaganda" ("William Carleton and the Irish People", Clogher Record VI,1 [1966], p. 67). That his bishop had prevented Carleton from entering the priesthood is pure conjecture on Boué's part. There is no evidence to support this statement in Carleton's Autobiography or in contemporary writing about him.

ries against the background of contemporary social and cultural conditions. Such an examination may make it possible to undertake a fresh evaluation of Carleton in his propagandist phase.

C. POPULAR RELIGIOUS PRACTICE

The people whose way of life Carleton chose to explain to others are the Roman Catholic population of the Tyrone-Monaghan border area of the north of Ireland. These are the peasants among whom Carleton had grown up,[1] and he was therefore in a better position than any other writer of the time to transmit a knowledge of their customs and beliefs. He had, for example, a far greater direct knowledge of the peasantry than Maria Edgeworth, and because he was himself a peasant, a native Irishman and originally a Roman Catholic, his approach was totally different from hers. Maria Edgeworth belonged to the landlord class, was English by birth and Anglo-Irish by domicile, and was a Protestant. She looked at the peasantry from the point of view of a well-intentioned landlord, and her natural preoccupation was with the duties of her own class. Thady Quirk of Castle Rackrent[2] speaks dialect and acts as a seemingly uncritical commentator on the abuse of power by the Rackrent family and their lack of responsibility. However, he does not come alive as a character in his own right, and the peasants in the novel remain largely in the background. In his early works Carleton is not very complimentary about the Irish peasantry; but even here they are by no means so passive and acquiescent as Thady Quirk and the peasantry of Castle Rackrent. In the later Christian Examiner stories, where Carleton's main object is to portray the peasantry in their daily lives and where the exposure of Roman Catholic practice is a secondary object, the people are shown in a more favourable light; and in the stories from Traits and Stories of the Irish Peasantry

---

1. Cf. the account of Carleton's youth in his autobiography.
2. London 1800.

onwards, although their faults are not hidden, the peasantry emerge as a class to be known and loved, whose failings are not innate but are rather due to political instability and a lack of moral education.

The first three stories which Carleton published in The Christian Examiner show a uniformly hostile attitude to peasant religion and peasant life.[3] In "A Pilgrimage to Patrick's Purgatory" this attitude is not as pronounced as it is in "The Broken Oath" or "Father Butler", but it is nevertheless implicit. One of the reasons why it is not so apparent in "A Pilgrimage" is perhaps that the narrator is one of the pilgrims, a self-important, self-ironic "young priest" from a peasant family, who has been intended from boyhood for the priesthood and has been treated with veneration by parents and neighbours alike. He has learnt Latin, has never worked like his brothers and sisters, and makes the pilgrimage to Lough Derg because he has "a character of piety to sustain".[4] The narrators of "Father Butler" and "The Broken Oath" are both gentlemen, landlords, Protestants, ignorant of peasant life and customs and hostile to their manifestations; it is therefore technically easier for them to be explicit in their criticism.

"A Pilgrimage to Patrick's Purgatory" relates the story of a young man's journey to Lough Derg, an ancient site of pilgrimage (still attended) in Donegal in the north of Ireland. The intention of the story as stated in the introduction[5] is to expose the grossly superstitious practices of the Catholic pilgrims who went there, and to this end the narrator describes both the devotions carried out on the island and the behaviour of the priests and pilgrims. But in spite of this intention the story maintains for the most part a humorous tone, only slipping into polemic shrillness now and again.

---

3. References to these and other stories are as far as possible to the reprints in the collected Works, the orthography and punctuation of which have been followed here; in all other cases reference is made to the earliest edition which has been available to me.
4. Works II, p. 799.
5. This introduction (reproduced below in Appendix I) preceded the story in CE but was removed from all later editions.

"A Pilgrimage to Patrick's Purgatory" exists in two versions: the original Christian Examiner text, and a revised text entitled "The Lough Derg Pilgrim" which first appeared in a new edition of the Traits and Stories published in Dublin and London in 1842/43 (reissued 1843/44). It is the revised text which is reprinted in the collected Works. Carleton has not only renamed the story for the new edition but has also prefaced it with a tribute to Caesar Otway, who had died in 1842, and descriptions of the island of Lough Derg written by Otway[6] and Bishop Henry Jones. More interestingly, Carleton reports that Otway had offered to "dress up" the story before printing it. He further explains that the story originally printed in The Christian Examiner was "the Sketch of the Lough Derg Pilgrim as it now appears, with the exception of some offensive passages which are expunged in this edition".[7] Daniel J. Casey has compared the two versions and has concluded that:

> Taken together, the sources of mechanical differences, both major and minor stylistic changes, and numerous textual alterations and omissions raise serious doubts whether "A Pilgrimage to Patrick's Purgatory" and "The Lough Derg Pilgrim" are the same literary work. Carleton contributed the first as a propagandistic narrative to The Christian Examiner; it was a narrative that provided Otway a vehicle for extending the scope of his own Lough Derg essay ... That "A Pilgrimage to Patrick's Purgatory" is the source of "The Lough Derg Pilgrim" is undeniable, but to say without extensive qualification that it is "The Lough Derg Pilgrim" is outrageous.[8]

Casey claims that the version called "The Lough Derg Pilgrim" is to all intents and purposes the story which Carleton originally wrote for The Christian Examiner, and

---

6. Sketches in Ireland: Descriptive of Interesting and Hitherto Unnoticed Districts in the North and South (Dublin 1827), pp. 149-151.
7. Works II, p. 797.
8. "Lough Derg's Infamous Pilgrim" Clogher Record VII,3 (1972), p. 460.

that the passages which Carleton for many years has been criticized and reviled for writing were in fact largely the work of Caesar Otway.[9] He further speculates that all three stories which Carleton wrote in 1828, "A Pilgrimage to Patrick's Purgatory", "The Broken Oath" and "Father Butler", were touched up by Otway where the original manuscripts were too mild to meet his specification.

Casey's argument is far from conclusive. He has pleaded his case on stylistic grounds, but unfortunately gives no samples of Otway's style from any of the works which can definitely be attributed to him, merely quoting extracts from "A Pilgrimage to Patrick's Purgatory" and asserting that they were written by Otway. This procedure is methodologically inadequate. A systematic stylistic comparison of Otway's and Carleton's writings is the only basis on which such a claim could be made with any degree of certainty. After all, it is not impossible that Carleton wrote at least some of the offensive passages in question. He was a clever young man who was living on his wits, and he could very easily have pastiched Otway's style as he found it in Sketches in Ireland or in early numbers of The Christian Examiner. This was the type of material which would find a market, and it is clear from Carleton's autobiography at this point that he was in dire need of money. The fact also remains that Carleton nowhere says himself that Otway was the author of these passages. In the preface to the revised "Lough Derg Pilgrim" he merely states that "some offensive passages" have been "expunged". It is obvious that Casey would very much like to prove that Carleton did not write these passages, but the proof which he actually offers is unconvincing.

The account of the pilgrimage to Lough Derg is written to show two things: the nature of peasant super-

---

9. Casey quotes from a contemporary of Carleton, the literary critic Professor Patrick Murray of Maynooth, in which the latter argues against the prevailing criticism of Carleton. He says inter alia: "The great blemish in the tale ["A Pilgrimage to Patrick's Purgatory"] is from the 'suppressio veri', and the paragraphs written, not by Carleton himself, but by Caesar Otway". This information was supposedly obtained by Murray partly from Carleton himself, partly from Carleton's old school friend Father James Smith (Clogher Record VII,3 p. 453).

stition in Ireland, and the pilgrimage as it was in the
early nineteenth century. It begins on a polemical note:

> Superstition, that blind devotion, which draws
> the individual under its influence to the per-
> formance of external works, and unnecessary cere-
> monies, without being actuated by the spirit of
> pure religion, is as natural to the mind not en-
> lightened by true knowledge, as weeds are to a
> field that has ceased to be well cultivated ...
> The extent to which this kind of superstition
> prevails in Ireland, is inconceivable.[10]

The Lough Derg pilgrimage is taken as the most outstanding
example of Irish superstition, and of the power of the
Catholic church over the Irish:

> It is melancholy to perceive the fatal success to
> which the Church of Rome has attained, in making
> void the atonement of Christ by her traditions;
> and how every part of her complicated, but per-
> fect, system, even to the minutest points, seizes
> upon some corresponding weakness of the human
> heart, thereby to bind it to her agreeable and
> strong delusions.[11]

The story itself proceeds in a fairly light-hearted vein
with gloomier passages introduced only sporadically. The
pilgrims are of all ages and of all degrees of piety; the
one thing uniting them is their superstition. For the superstitious pilgrim the approach to Lough Derg is filled
with terror and gloom, and in the case of the rather self-
ironical narrator with "thick-coming visions of immortal-
ity, that almost lifted me from the mountain [mountainous
in the original Christian Examiner text] path I was

---

10. CE VI, p. 268.
11. ibid., p. 269. This is a familiar claim on the part of anti-
     Catholic writers. See for example the Rev. John Montgomery, Po-
     pery as it Exists in Great Britain and Ireland, its Doctrines,
     Practices, and Arguments (Edinburgh etc. 1854), passim.

ascending, and brought me, as it were, into contact with the invisible world".[12] The gloom of the place is mentioned frequently, as is the "superstitious awe" and religious melancholy which it induces in the pilgrims.

Two characteristics of Catholic devotion much stressed by proselytizers, including Carleton, are the mechanical nature of prayer and belief in the power of relics. In "A Pilgrimage to Patrick's Purgatory" these characteristics are dwelt on sometimes seriously and sometimes with amusement, whereas they are treated with uniform seriousness in "Father Butler" and "The Broken Oath". The beginning of "A Pilgrimage to Patrick's Purgatory" introduces us to a young man who regards praying as a game. He tells us of how he could out-pray and out-fast

> an old circulating pilgrim [bachelor uncle, who
> lived with us in original Christian Examiner
> text] ... a feat on which few would have ventur-
> ed; and I even arrived to such a pitch of perfec-
> tion at praying, that with the assistance of
> young and powerful lungs, I was fully able to
> distance him at any English prayer in which we
> joined.[13]

But he freely admits that he cannot keep pace with the professional when it comes to Latin.

The narrator is not always so ironical about mechanical praying, or about prayers in tongues not understood by the people. In describing the scene in the "Prison" or chapel at Lough Derg he gives an example of a man with a hare-lip who was leading the prayer. He presents a ludicrous picture, for "although Irish was his vernacular language, either some fool or knave had taught him to say his prayers in English". The narrator goes on to observe as a general rule "that the language which a Roman Catholic of the lower class [the tongue which a Romanist in original Christian Examiner text] does not understand,

---

12. Works II, p. 809; cf. CE VI, p. 344.
13. Works II, p. 799; cf. CE VI, p. 271.

is the one in which he is disposed to pray".[14] There is
a parallel instance in "Father Butler", where the devotee
Paddy Dimnick "formed the sign of the cross upon his
breast and forehead, repeating certain words that were
originally Latin, but which Paddy had stripped of that
useful character of language — intelligibility".[15]

Carleton remarks many times on the "insipid mum-
mery" of the pilgrims' prayers and on the self-inflicted
torture of the Lough Derg pilgrimage. These two elements
are illustrated by the account of the narrator's own "station" around the "Beds" — "sharp stones placed circularly
in the earth, with the spike ends of them up, one circle
within another ...". The pilgrims walk around these "Beds"
barefoot, and like the narrator repeat "fifty-five paters
and aves, and five creeds, or five decades".[16] But the
prayers do not come from the heart. They are set prayers
or formulae, and all of them in Carleton's eyes are mechanical mumbo-jumbo, intoned to induce a spirit of devotion rather than to reach God. There are indeed genuinely
pious people present, but these people do not interest
Carleton. He emphasizes instead those types of people who
go on the pilgrimage for unworthy motives. There is the
schoolmaster reading prayers in Latin to a circle of impressed pilgrims who do not understand the language. There
is the rake who comes to Lough Derg unrepentant: if he
goes through the motions of the pilgrimage, superstition
has it that he will be saved. The miser, the pharisee,
the hypocrite, the bigot — all take part in the pilgrimage
with the same belief in the efficacy of Lough Derg as a
means of attaining salvation. This peasant superstition
concerning Lough Derg is mentioned in many stories. In
"Father Butler" Paddy Dimnick openly asserts to the narrator's horror that the very act of going on the pilgrimage
shows repentance for sins: it is not necessary to have
true contrition, because God hears prayers better from
Lough Derg than from home, and will take the intention of

14. Works II, p. 813; cf. CE VI, p. 353.
15. CE VII, p. 117.
16. Works II, p. 810.

contrition for the state.[17] Similarly John Lynch, the
protagonist of "The Death of a Devotee", extracts a promise as he lies dying from his brother "to make three stations to Loughderg ... in my name".[18]

In "A Pilgrimage to Patrick's Purgatory" Carleton
gives many amusing descriptions of individual pilgrims,
one of whom is Nell M'Collum ("the most notorious shuler
[tramp] in the province"), who softens up the impression-
able and pompous young narrator by judicious flattery,
shames him into buying breakfast for herself and her companion, and in the end robs him of his money and clothes,
leaving him to slink home a sorry figure. Other comic
characters are the "religious tailor under three blessed
orders" and, best of all perhaps, the professional pilgrim
Sol Donnel, who offers to say a "gray profungus [De pro-
fundis] for the release of [his mother's] sowl out o' the
burning flames of purgathur". Reckoning that the narrator
is an easy bird to pluck, Sol Donnel swaps a prayer with
him, worms some money out of him and proceeds to another
victim.[19]

The professional pilgrim was a feature of Irish society
and recurs again and again in Carleton's stories, along
with that other individual remarkable for his piety, the
devotee or voteen. In "Father Butler" a workman defines
a pilgrim for the narrator; he is

> a blessed person that goes about from place to
> place, tachin' an' larnin' prayers an' hyms, an'
> goin' to Loughderg, an' holy stations, attendin'
> christenins an' weddins, an' wakes — where they
> say prayers, and sing rhans, an' may-be puts a
> pebble from Loughderg in the coffin, if they're
> well thrated ... a blessed an' holy crathur he
> is ...[20]

17. CE VII, pp. 192-193.
18. Quoted here from Tales of Ireland, p. 38. The story first
     appeared in CE IX (1829).
19. Works II, pp. 806-818.
20. CE VII, p. 429.

Owen Devlin, the pilgrim in "Father Butler", is not described, however, with the same indulgence as Sol Donnel
of "A Pilgrimage to Patrick's Purgatory" or another of
Carleton's pilgrims, Darby More of "The Midnight Mass".[21]
Devlin is a "man mountain", and he is vindictive. When
the narrator sees him he is a little afraid of him, but as
there are other people in the vicinity he plucks up courage to investigate "what kind of being he might be, or
whether he was tame or otherwise". Devlin preaches the
gospel and asserts that he has saved many souls in his
time. He asks the narrator for half-a-crown, gets a shilling, and tests it by putting it "under his fore tusk and
giving it a bend as if it were tin". The figure of Devlin,
his veniality and the respect with which he is treated by
the peasantry, causes the narrator to proceed on his way
lamenting the state of Ireland, "the state of ignorance
in which it is possible for a Christian country, in the
nineteenth century, to be placed, even within the reach
and influence of God's unsullied light".[22] This is a reflection on the extent to which the religious instruction
of the people was neglected by their own clergy; they were
the helpless victims of the pilgrims' exploitation.

The devotee shares with the pilgrim the quality
of praying mechanically, believing in relics and being
greatly respected by the people for piety. But in contrast
to the pilgrim, who rejects home and family and wanders
about from place to place, the devotee remains at home.
The pilgrim is therefore holier in the eyes of the people,
although the devotee enjoys a great local reputation and
is always consulted on matters pertaining to salvation. In
the parish he is second only to the priest. Paddy Dimnick
of "Father Butler" is an excellent example of this type.
He "attends the priest at mass every Sunday, and [is] under so many blessed ordhers -- from the scapular down to
the coard of St. Francis — [he] leads the Rosary and the
'stations' in the chapel — [he] goes to Lough Derg wonst
a year, and fasts every Friday and Wednesday ...". He

---

21. First published in TS^2 (1833); reprinted in Works II.
22. CE VII, pp. 428-429.

prays regularly, almost endlessly, and his favourite
place of worship is high above the earth in a tree, where
he rocks back and forth, repeating his prayers in a high,
loud voice while at the same time keeping an eye on his
farm, and interspersing his pious utterances with impre-
cations to his workmen. He is a consummate hypocrite: he
boasts to the narrator in the same breath of his feats of
prayer and of his humility. "I'm a vile worm, a crawlin'
raptile on the yearth ... and for that matter so is yourself ...".[23] He is ignorant of the Scriptures, and has
utter confidence in "the saints, marthyrs, confessors,
apoastles, innocents, evangelists, baptists, or divines"[24]
to intercede with God on his behalf — a feature of popular
Catholic belief to which objection is often made in these
stories. He is also a bigot. He suspects the narrator of
trying to convert Father Butler to Protestantism (or, as
he puts it, to "heresy"); and when he has been unable to
prevent Father Butler from meeting him, he and Owen Devlin
hamstring the narrator's cattle as a warning.

Belief in relics, scapulars and holy water are examples of
peasant superstition which occur repeatedly and point
to the peculiar mixture of superstition and orthodox religion which was peasant Irish Catholicism. In "The Death
of a Devotee" (cf. above, p. 36) a priest is called to give
Extreme Unction to a man who has lived as a devotee for
over fourteen years. Religious austerity, instead of giving him the serenity of true faith and trust in God, has
only made him "more dark, peevish, and repulsive": he is
terrified of death and damnation and clings to the relics
which he has about him. These include the Scapular of the
Blessed Virgin; the cord of the order of St. Francis;
written charms against sudden death; a blessed candle; and
some black paste "made of the ashes of the candles used at
Mass, mixed up with holy water", with which he makes the
sign of the cross upon his breast. "He could not give up,
even at the remonstrances of a priest, his scapulars, his

---

23. ibid., pp. 114-117.
24. ibid., p. 192.

cords ...". The point Carleton is making in examples of
this sort is one which many evangelical propagandists made
when denouncing Roman Catholic practice: "He knew his Redeemer, if he knew him at all, only as constituting one
among a crowd of intercessors";[25] and included among the
number of these intercessors was the priest.

Relics and the like were sold by pilgrims such as
Owen Devlin of "Father Butler" and Darby More of "The Midnight Mass", and belief in them was not confined to their
power of saving the soul. About midnight on Christmas Eve
Darby More is to be found holding "an immense torch formed
into the figure of a cross" and selling "blessed" carols
to the crowd who had come to Mass. "They're but hapuns a-
piece; an' anybody that has the grace to keep one o' these
about them, will never meet wid sudden deaths or accidents
...".[26] It was to beliefs like these that John Lynch, the
devotee, was hopelessly and ignorantly enslaved.

The peasantry also had a great belief in the efficacy of charms. Nancy M'Keown of "Ned M'Keown" has a
prayer which she had got from "Darby M'Murt the pilgrim
... if I only repeated it wanst, I mightn't be afeard of
all the divils in hell".[27] And in "A Pilgrimage to Patrick's Purgatory" a woman learns the following Latin
charm against colic:

> Petrus sedebat super lapidem marmoream juxta ædem
> Jerusalem et dolebat, Jesus veniebat et rogabat
> "Petre, quid doles?" "Doleo vento ventre". "Sur-
> ge, Petre [et sanus esto]". Et quicunque hæc ver-
> ba non scripta sed memoriter tradita recitat nun-
> quam dolebit vento ventre.[28]

The boundary between Christian and pagan superstition is of
course unclear in such cases; and that Carleton was fully
aware of this fact appears from many instances where Christian superstitions are mixed up with native Irish super-

25. Tales of Ireland, pp. 22-27.
26. Works II, p. 867.
27. ibid., p. 660. The story first appeared in TS¹ (1830).
28. Works II, p. 807; cf. CE VI, p. 284. The words in square
    brackets are not in CE.

stitions about the fairies. Mary Sullivan of "The Lianhan Shee", the epitome of the superstitious Irish peasant, has "the dust of what had once been a four-leaved shamrock, an invaluable specific 'for seein' the good people' [i.e. the fairies]" sewn in "the folds of her own scapular" — a juxtaposition of pagan and Christian in which she apparently saw no harm. When she hears crickets chirping behind the hearth-stone she shakes holy water over it, and mutters a prayer or charm against the evils which crickets are supposed to carry with them.[29] "The Donagh" similarly displays the superstition of the peasantry in such beliefs as that "If a man had a sick cow, she was elf-shot", and that "if his child became consumptive, it had been overlooked, or received a blast from the fairies ...".[30] These last examples are, however, of a kind which is not always directly related to Carleton's purpose of religious propaganda.

A very telling manifestation of the popular synthesis of superstition and religion is the attitude of the people to the chapel or "Prison" at Lough Derg. In addition to the physical rigours of fasting and walking barefoot on sharp stones, the pilgrims are summoned at midnight to spend the following twenty-four hours in the Prison. There is a "dim religious twilight" in the place, the pilgrims are exhausted from the journey and the devotions of the day, there are no special religious exercises to perform in the Prison, and the natural inclination is therefore to fall asleep. This desire is made even greater by "the deep, drowsy, hollow, hoarse, guttural, ceaseless, and monotonous hum, which proceeded from about four [six in original Christian Examiner text] hundred individuals, half asleep and at prayer ...".[31] Legend had it that the "supernatural tendency to sleep" which overcame the people when they entered the chapel was

29. Works II, pp. 963-964. The story first appeared in CE X (1830).
30. Works II, p. 888. The story first appeared in NM I (1830).
31. Works II, p. 812; cf. CE VI, p. 349.

an emblem of the influence of sin over the soul,
and a type of their future fate ... if they resist this they will be saved; but if they yield
to it, they will not only be damned [to the
flames of hell added in original Christian Examiner text] in the next world, but will go mad,
or incur some immediate and dreadful calamity in
this [but will go mad in this in original Christian Examiner text].[32]

Carleton criticizes the Prison in very strong
terms. "There is not on earth ... a regulation of a religious nature, more barbarous and inhuman than this". It
is "itself the monster which St. Patrick is said to have
destroyed in the place — a monster, which is a complete
and significant allegory of this great and destructive superstition". Many people have supposedly died in the chapel: the narrator himself witnesses the death of a young
man who, either because of "lethargic indifference" or because, having slept, he believes himself to be surely
damned, throws himself or falls from one of the galleries.
Carleton suggests that this superstition is encouraged by
the priests. It is the "policy" of the place to have no
set exercises in the Prison; calamities are "turned to account" and the superstition of the people is strengthened.
Many who succumb to the desire to sleep, but who do not
die, sink into "the incurable apathy of religious melancholy".[33]

Although Carleton deleted several "offensive"
passages from "A Pilgrimage to Patrick's Purgatory" when
editing the story in later years, it is worth noticing
that he stands by his general condemnation of Lough Derg,
a condemnation made explicit in such passages as the following:

As for that solemn, humble, and heartfelt sense
of God's presence, which Christian prayer demands, its existence in the mind would not only

---

32. Works II, p. 811; cf. CE VI, p. 349.
33. ibid.

be a moral but a physical impossibility in Lough
Derg. I verily think that if mortification of
the body, without conversion of the life or heart
— if penance and not repentance could save the
soul, no wretch who performed a pilgrimage here
could with a good grace be damned. Out of hell
the place is matchless, and if there be a purgatory in the other world, it may very well be said
there is a fair rehearsal of it in the county of
Donegal in Ireland.[34]

There is genuine outrage and genuine sympathy in these
words, and I see no grounds for supposing that either sentiment was spurious.

D. ROMAN CATHOLIC DOCTRINE

One of the tasks which Carleton set himself in the Christian Examiner stories was to explain the more serious doctrinal and social objections to Roman Catholicism to his
readers. Thus the Roman Catholic sacraments of Confession
and Extreme Unction, which were favourite targets for the
proselytizers, are included in the general condemnation of

---

34. Works II, pp. 809-810; cf. CE VI, p. 346. The passage has been
shortened in the revised edition by the omission of the following
remarks after the first sentence: "The terms of salvation, as offered in the word of God, and the simple, unencumbered views of
man's fallen nature, and of God's mercy in enabling him by faith
in Christ to raise himself from his natural state of sin, do not
belong to the place. If these doctrines were known, salvation
would not be made, as in the present instance, to depend on lo-
cality. There is nothing there but rosaries to the blessed Virgin — prayers and litanies to dead men and women, called Saints
— acts of faith, hope, and charity, economically performed by
repeating them from memory, or by reading them from books. There
is confession, penance to the eyes, and repetition of forms of
prayers; but seldom repentance or prayer. As I said before, they
could not be felt here. How could a creature, with feet spliced
and cut up, address the Almighty Father of the universe, limping
about, too, like a cripple, upon the villainous spikes above-
mentioned, without being guilty of impiety and insult to the Dei-
ty? But if it be not calculated to excite religion in the heart,
it is right well adapted to delude the sinner; and in a church
which, contrary to reason and Scripture, ascribes merit in the
sight of God to human works, it is no wonder that it has attained
such eminence. For (I verily think ...)".

Roman Catholicism which forms the introduction to "A Pilgrimage to Patrick's Purgatory", where they are classed
under the general heading of superstition.[1] In Carleton's
opinion there were three evils connected with these sacraments, especially with Confession. In the first place the
sinner could not feel true contrition for his sins. He
confessed and avowed his intention not to repeat the sin,
was absolved and then committed the sin again; and this
process continued until contrition became an empty formu-
la. The second evil was that the sinner did not place his
trust in God but came to believe that it was the priest
himself who absolved him from his sins. The priest, also
a sinner, thus became someone apart, more important in the
penitent's eyes than God; and in this way the priest acquired tremendous power over his flock, a power which he
could use for good or evil. The third defect of Confession
in a country in the political state of Ireland was that
the notion that sins could be wiped away by the mere act
of Confession could lead to the sinner's believing that he
might commit even murder with impunity. The same applied
to Extreme Unction, which is "a sacrament in which the
sick by the anointing with holy oil and the prayers of the
priest, receive spiritual aid ... [it] confers upon the
soul the sanctifying grace causing the remission of sin".[2]
Because of the belief that this sacrament — like Confession — automatically conferred remission of sin on the re-
cipient, it too was regarded as doctrinally and socially
objectionable. Carleton refers quite often to the lack of
true penance for sins shown by Irish Roman Catholics. But
he concentrates on the other two elements mentioned above:
the near-beatification of the priest by the peasants, and
the undesirable social consequences of believing that sins
could be wiped out by the physical reception of the sacraments.

   "The Broken Oath" is a much more virulently anti-
Catholic story than "A Pilgrimage to Patrick's Purgatory"
but has not been so much remarked upon by commentators.

---

1.   See the text in Appendix I.
2.   John O'Brien, 90 Common Questions about Catholic Faith (1962; re-
     printed London 1963), p. 191.

It first appeared in The Christian Examiner VI-VII and
has never since been reprinted. Because the text is not
easily obtainable I shall here give the main outlines of
the story, which in narrative form is an exemplum — a form
often used by propagandists and again employed by Carleton
in three novelettes which he wrote in 1845.[3]

In a prefatory note to "The Broken Oath", the
author remarks that it is "but too evident, that there
exists some deteriorating power at work amongst the people,
weakening the sanctions of God's moral code, and lowering
the standard of conscientious accountability".[4] The story
is intended to illustrate the "consequences attendant on
confession and absolution". It does not confine itself to
these points, however, but runs through the whole catalogue of ills that can be attributed to the practice of Roman Catholicism amongst the Irish peasantry, and that can
be exemplified in the person of the principal character,
Henry Lacy, who believes in virtually all the doctrines
and devotions designated as superstitious by the proselytizers. Lacy practises mechanical Confession without
ever experiencing true contrition; he trusts in the value
of good works as a means to salvation; he believes in the
infallibility of the Catholic Church, the power of the
priest and the exclusive salvation of Roman Catholics. He
is a scapularian and attends his devotions so regularly
that he is renowned for his piety. Like most of his co-
religionists he has never studied the Bible and relies on
his Church for direction in spiritual matters. Had he
been taken in hand in his youth and given true moral and
religious training, he might have grown up a good man.[5]
His reason causes him to doubt much of what he has been
taught, but his final stumbling-block is the infallibility

3. Art Maguire; or, the Broken Pledge, A Narrative (Dublin 1845).
   Rody the Rover; or, the Ribbonman (Dublin 1845). Parra Sastha;
   or, the History of Paddy-go-Easy and his Wife Nancy (Dublin
   1845). Cf. above p. 25.
4. CE VI, p. 425.
5. Lacy can be contrasted in this respect with Peggy Graham of "The
   Brothers", a story first published in CE X (1830). This woman's
   sound biblical upbringing stood her in good stead during the
   trials of her married life. See below pp. 56-60.

of his Church. These conflicts between his reason and his
habits of belief "relaxed his moral principles and increased his devotion". Life has treated him badly: he turns to
drink and becomes caught up in the activities of a secret
society, and ultimately he takes an oath not to drink for
fourteen years — the "last resource, which many Roman
Catholics, in the absence of better religious opportunities, are in the habit of imposing on themselves".[6] Later,
however, an irresponsible priest releases him from his
oath, and in a drunken fit he kills his eldest son.

The breaking of the oath is the moral fulcrum of
the story, and after the death of his son Lacy sinks into
utter gloom and depravity: "When principle and moral obligation are once broken down, every succeeding effort to
resist depravity becomes gradually more weak, until at
last they cease to exist, or to be felt as restraints". He
continues attending Confession, but his misunderstanding
of the nature of the sacrament means that he feels no motivation to stop sinning -- on the contrary, "sin and confession mutually re-produced each other".[7] Calamity follows upon calamity; he loses his best farm, and his wife
and second son die as a result of the shock sustained when
the house is raided for illicit spirits. Finally he is
evicted for non-payment of rent and reduced to living in a
hovel with no means of subsistence. He changes appalling-
ly in a couple of months: "the last remaining ties which
bound him to mankind and to principle"[8] have been broken
by the death of his wife and second son. It is worth noticing that the author's tone is characterized here by an
unsympathetic smugness which is never present in later
stories of peasant hardship and misfortune.[9] Lacy continues his religious devotions, the habits of which are
deeply ingrained, despite the fact that he has now lapsed
far into profligacy. Carleton explains this paradox by

6. CE VI, pp. 430, 432.
7. CE VII, p. 27.
8. ibid., p. 30.
9. E.g. "Tubber Derg, or the Red Well" and "The Poor Scholar" (both
    in TS² [1833] and reprinted in the collected Works; an extract
    from "Tubber Derg" entitled "The Landlord and Tenant" had appeared
    already in 1831 in NM II).

remarking that the more a Roman Catholic sins, "the greater necessity has he, according to his own notions, for practising a parallel course of external devotion. He thinks they neutralize each other, and that if his religious duties be equal to his crimes, he is safe".[10]

Lacy's brother-in-law Tom persuades him to join the Whiteboys[11] in taking revenge on the gauger (exciseman) who now occupies the farm from which Lacy has been evicted. Tom claims that the Whiteboys do not have murder in mind, but "even if we had ... when the sin can be removed, as blessed be God, who has given that authority to his church, it can, there is nothing we might be afraid of, but the law of the land ...". Implicit in Tom's words is the assurance that the priests are on the Whiteboys' side. Lacy joins in the planned revenge, is arrested for murder and sentenced to be hanged. While he is in prison he reads the Bible and gradually begins to realize his error. He rejects all help offered by the Catholic chaplain and ascribes his fate to the malign influence of Confession. An undisguisedly political element enters into the story when the priest is accused by Lacy of suppressing information about criminal activities which he had gained in the Confessional, despite the fact that he had sworn allegiance to the civil power of the king. Lacy, addressing the narrator, claims that "the state of Ireland is bad at present, but the disturbances so prevalent, are ascribed to the wrong causes". No man would commit an outrage were he not sure of secrecy and that his accountability for the crime would be removed by confessing it. "Here are the two principles, joined to a hereditary religious hatred which no circumstance can modify, from which the disturbances of Ireland proceed".[12] Father Butler similarly remarks: "to [Confession] may be attributed much of the bloodshed, crime, and misery which have disgraced religion, and shaken

---

10. CE VII, p. 31.
11. The Whiteboys were a secret society whose name came from the white shirts they wore. They agitated against rents and tithes. "Whiteboys" and "Ribbonmen" (yet another illegal organization) are terms used interchangeably by Carleton.
12. CE VII, pp. 33, 35, 36.

46

the frame of civil society ...".[13] Written in 1828, when the country was in the throes of the Emancipation crisis, these passages would have been received as powerful anti-Catholic propaganda.

Belief in the priest's power of absolution can also be seen in the case of the devotee John Lynch.[14] Lynch had on some occasion accompanied his parish priest, Father Moyle, to France, and while they were there the two men had been implicated in some mysterious crime, the nature of which we never learn. The remembrance of their crime haunts them, however, and when he is dying Lynch insists that Father Moyle be summoned to give him the last rites of the Church. He shrieks at the priest: "you're come, thank God; − now you _must_ save me; now you must keep your _promise_ − it mustn't rest upon my head, for you _said_ it".[15] The implication is that the priest had abused his power by offering his superstitious companion "immunity" for what he had done.

The role of the priest as intermediary is frequently discussed by Carleton. Father Butler reasons with Paddy Dimnick on this point. When asked why he accepts his religion from a man who is as liable to error as anyone else, Paddy replies that the Pope is infallible and that his line goes through the bishops to the priests. And Father Philip Dallaghy, the tragic hero of "The Lianhan Shee", asks the crowd of villagers who have seen him face to face with the consequences of his former sin: "what is it now, ye poor infatuated wretches, to trust in the sanctity _of man_? Learn from me to place the same confidence in _God_ which you place in his _guilty creatures_, and you will not lean on a broken reed".[16] Even the light-hearted Denis O'Shaughnessy remarks that he had mingled with priests whom as a boy he had looked upon as "men who held vested in themselves some mysterious and spiritual

---

13. _ibid._, p. 430.
14. In "The Death of a Devotee" (1829); see above, pp. 36, 38-39.
15. _CE_ IX, p. 26.
16. _CE_ X (1830); _Works_ II, p. 974.

power ... I find them neither better nor worse than those who still look upon them as I once did".[17]

Another matter which was hotly discussed by Catholics and Protestants at this time was the doctrine of salvation. As late as 1854, the Rev. John Montgomery charges Roman Catholics with intolerance on this issue and quotes from a contemporary Irish catechism[18] to prove his point: "Dr. James Butler, in his Catechism, having emphatically asserted that no one can be saved out of the true Church, proceeds to make his meaning quite clear, by informing us that the Church is called Roman, 'because the visible head of the Church is the Bishop of Rome, and because St. Peter and his successors fixed their see in Rome'".[19]

At the time when Montgomery published his book some Catholic theologians were actually writing rather liberally about salvation, but Montgomery explains this fact away by arguing that "Many Popish writers in this country [Britain], having written in part for Protestant eyes, and knowing how odious this doctrine is esteemed, have been much more cautious [than Butler] in their statement of it".[20] Cardinal Wiseman had pointed out that the exclusive rule applies only to those who culpably reject the doctrines of the Church.[21] The point was a fine one, and controversy raged over the definition of the "soul of the Church", outside of which "there can be no hope of salvation".[22] There were Roman Catholic theologians who still

17. CE XI (1831); Works II, p. 1024.
18. The Most Rev. Dr. James Butler's Catechism, Revised, Enlarged, Approved, and Recommended by the four R.C. Archbishops of Ireland, as a General Catechism for the Kingdom. Montgomery used the revised and enlarged thirty-first edition (Dublin 1845).
19. Popery as it Exists in Great Britain and Ireland, p. 593.
20. ibid., p. 594.
21. Lectures on the Principal Doctrines and Practices of the Catholic Church delivered at St. Mary's, Moorfields, during the Lent of 1836. By Nicholas Wiseman, D.D., now Cardinal Archbishop of Westminster. Quoted by Montgomery who uses the third edition (London 1851).
22. Montgomery, p. 595, quoting from the Rev. Stephen Keenan, Controversial Catechism; or Protestantism Refuted and Catholicism Established, by an Appeal to the Holy Scriptures, the Testimony of the Holy Fathers, and the Dictates of Reason; in which such Portions of Scheffmacher's Catechism as suit Modern Controversy are Embodied, second edition (Edinburgh 1849).

maintained that the Roman Catholic Church was the only
true Church and that it was necessary to salvation to accept it, while others held more radical views.[23] However,
it was the former attitude which generally prevailed among
the Roman Catholic people and clergy in Ireland. It is
significant that Carleton exhibits this peasant belief in
exclusive salvation not only in his earliest proselytizing
works but also in somewhat later stories such as "Tubber
Derg, or the Red Well",[24] which was written when his general attitude towards the peasantry had become more sympathetic. It was presumably one of the dogmas which he
calls "barbarous" in the Preface to Tales of Ireland (1834).

As we have already seen, the peasantry regarded
Protestantism and "heresy" as synonymous. In "A Pilgrimage
to Patrick's Purgatory" Carleton refers only fleetingly to
this in the introduction. He relates how in his youth he
had seen a Protestant woman being expelled from the house
where her Roman Catholic friend lay dying because the latter's son was afraid that "the presence of a heretic might
communicate a taint of sin to the departing spirit ...".[25]
Henry Lacy of "The Broken Oath" felt himself bound to believe that Protestants were damned. Lacy was a potentially rational man and was frequently "on the point of breaking the chain which bound him down to that curse of reason,
infallibility ...": he looked at his child and found difficulty in believing that the infant "if born in another
communion ... should for no other reason be doomed to the
eternal torments of a future life".[26] But his Church had

---

23. At the fourth Lateran Council in 1302, Pope Boniface VIII issued
    the Bull Unam Sanctam in which he stated: "Porro subesse Romano
    Pontifici omni humanae creaturae declaramus, dicimus, diffinimus
    et pronunciamus omnino esse de necessitate salutis" (Corpus Juris
    Canonici ed. E. Friedberg, II [Leipzig 1881], col. 1246). This
    question was taken up again after the Reformation and by the
    nineteenth century two trends were apparent. On the one hand,
    membership of the Catholic Church was declared absolutely neces-
    sary for salvation by Gregory XVI and Pius IX, in response to the
    claim of Indifferentism that one could be saved in any Church; on
    the other hand Pius IX in 1854 and 1863 made in this very connec-
    tion the first authoritative statements as to the possibility of
    salvation for non-Catholics.
24. Cf. note 9 above.
25. CE VI, p. 269.
26. ibid., pp. 429-430.

taught him so and he had to accept its teaching. Again, Father Butler tells the narrator of the story that his parents "certainly did not believe that it was possible to be saved outside their Church", and at a later point he elaborates the theory that the doctrine of exclusive salvation was based on a primitive and selfish pleasure in the prospect of others being damned: "Alas! this principle it is which is carried into the religion of the Church of Rome, because that religion is founded upon human passion, which it really draws out and nourishes, in order to strengthen its own influence over the heart".[27] But the most horrifying example of the consequences of believing in exclusive salvation is given in "The Brothers". It is because Dan Gallagher believes that both he and his wife will be damned if she does not become a Catholic that he acts as the creature of Father Dorneen in the latter's attempts to convert Peggy. The family, instead of finding a modus vivendi, is divided and destroyed.

In the somewhat later, more light-hearted stories this doctrine (or superstition) is often referred to as being a fixed element of Roman Catholic belief. Lachlin Murray's parents were, "like many poor Catholics, ignorant, scrupulously honest, sincerely devout, according to their knowledge, and brimful of simplicity and the choicest superstition. It is true, they believed, as in duty bound, that all Protestants, after death, were gifted with a prodigious 'alacrity at sinking'".[28] Father Neddy Deleery in "Ned M'Keown" announces regretfully to Andy Morrow the Protestant: "... you must go this way ... to the lower ragions; and, upon my knowledge, to tell you the truth, I'm sorry for it, for you're a worthy fellow";[29] and the same regretful note is struck in "Shane Fadh's Wedding", where Shane, addressing Andy Morrow, says of a good landlord that "... if ever one of yez went to heaven, Mr. Morrow, he did ...".[30] A not untypical, and certainly not humourless

---

27. CE VII, pp. 272, 365.
28. Tales of Ireland (1834), p. 335. The story of "Lachlin Murray and the Blessed Candle" first appeared in CE X (1830).
29. TS¹ (1830); Works II, p. 666.
30. TS¹ (1830); Works II, p. 702.

mixture of anger and pity is expressed in "The Poor Scholar", when Dominick M'Evoy, looking down from his poor land on the "sheltered inland which [was] inhabited chiefly by Protestants and Presbyterians" exclaims that St. Peter is "the very boy that will accommodate the heretics wid a warm corner; an' yit, faith, there's many o' thim that myself 'ud put in a good word for, afther all".[31] This story points out the comfort some poor Catholics could draw from belief in their own exclusive salvation: Dominick M'Evoy predicts that the devil will take Yellow Sam, the tyrannical middleman, because he is an evil man and a heretic.

Carleton very often brings up the fact that Catholics did not read the Bible as Protestants did, in order to emphasize how ignorant Catholics were of the true basis of religion. Mrs. Cashel Hoey, a friend of Carleton and an authoress of some fame in her day, wrote that Carleton never fully understood the tenets of the Catholic faith (and never understood why his countrymen should find his criticism so insulting).[32] An examination of Carleton's writings on this particular point shows Mrs. Cashel Hoey's statement to be correct. A Protestant apologist like the Rev. John Montgomery was acquainted with the Roman Catholic attitude to Bible reading, although he did not accept it himself: "... the Papist perpetually appeals to tradition and the authority of the Church, thus endeavouring to subvert the authority of Scripture ...".[33] The answer to this charge offered by Roman Catholic theologians was the same then as now. The Catholic Church regards the Bible as the inspired word of God; she assembled its various parts, determined what books were inspired by God, and herself declared it to be the inspired and authoritative word of God. "She is not the child of the Bible ... but its mother. She derives neither her existence nor her teaching authority from the New Testament ... she secured her

---

31. TS² (1833); Works II, p. 1075.
32. Life II, p. xxii.
33. Montgomery, Popery as it Exists in Great Britain and Ireland, p. 467.

being, her teachings, her authority directly from Jesus Christ".[34] The Catholic Church regards individual inter- pretation of the Bible as a source of strife, and she ac- cordingly reserves to herself the unique right of inter- pretation.

Whereas Carleton never mentions the different theological bases of the Protestant and Roman Catholic Churches, he picks up the last point mentioned above — private judgement — and argues that if Roman Catholics were allowed to read the Bible they would very soon become protesters. He maintains in the early stories that the Roman Catholic clergy, often ignorant and uneducated, ac- quire great power over their parishioners by the very act of interpreting the word of God, and he accuses them of exploiting their position to the full. Montgomery goes even further, roundly declaring that "In Ireland, in Italy, and over the whole world, Popish priests evince the strong- est anxiety to keep the minds of the people from any close and familiar contact with the Word of God".[35]

Carleton's Christian Examiner stories thus reflect the furious Bible controversy which raged in Ireland in the 1820's. Montgomery quotes the renowned Dr. Doyle, Catho- lic Bishop of Kildare and Leighlin, who in 1825 spoke of "the wild superstition which under the name of Bible read- ing or Bible distributing, is now disturbing the peace of Ireland, and threatening the safety of the State ...".[36] The evangelical reformers, "undertaking with the sponsor- ship of English and Irish Bible societies an intensive campaign for a 'New Reformation' in Ireland, were touring the country ... distributing religious tracts and pamphlets, holding revival meetings, and preaching, along with fervid Bible sermons, violent attacks on popish creed and ri- tual".[37] In "Father Butler", the narrator's workman Tom Garrett reports the outcome of one of these meetings. The priests and the "Biblemen" had had a public debate in

---

34. O'Brien, 90 Common Questions about Catholic Faith, p. 61.
35. Montgomery, pp. 524-525.
36. ibid., p. 524.
37. James A. Reynolds, The Catholic Emancipation Crisis in Ireland, 1823-1829 (New Haven etc. 1954), p. 66.

which the priests were worsted. The priests "... were bate in the argument, an' ... instead of argyin' soberly, they went outrageous an' spoke to the people an' egg'd them on, an' ... the people got mad when they seen the priests beaten, an' were goin' to ill-trate the Biblemen, an' ... then the Biblemen had to escape over a wall to save their lives".[38] Tom Garrett is here portrayed as a peasant who shows promise, and he is not as completely taken in by Paddy Dimnick and Owen Devlin as the other members of the community. Tending in the same direction though on a rather different intellectual level is the unfortunate Henry Lacy of "The Broken Oath", who wonders if there is "any standard ... amongst men, whereby we can fix the character of virtue and vice, or ascertain their intrinsic merits?",[39] but who remains confused and ignorant until it is almost too late.

In "Father Butler" we see the voteen Paddy Dimnick warning his workmen against reading in the Bible; more subtle and more sinister is Father A—, the Jesuit, who advises James Butler to stop reading the Scriptures because they ought not to be read "indiscriminately". When Father Butler questions Paddy Dimnick on his knowledge of the Bible and tells him to go to Father Driscoll, his parish priest, to aks for permission to read it, Paddy merely replies: "Why, what need I do that, when he made me burn the Bible that Blaney Irwin gave me, bekase it was a heretic book?".[40] In short, the peasants in these stories are extremely suspicious of the Bible. Their priests have told them not to read it by themselves, and they are ignorant of the difference between the "Protestant" and "Catholic" bibles, but they are sure that the former is pernicious. Dimnick has told Garrett about the "Protestant" Bible, and how "the lheaddhan wurrah [Litany of the Virgin] isn't in it, nor the salha-na-mharrho [Prayer for the Dead], nor nothin' about Purgathory; an' to crown it all, doesn't every one of their Bibles abuse the Pope?". Garrett is

---

38. CE VII, p. 199.
39. CE VI, p. 429. (For a discussion of the didactic structure of the Christian Examiner stories see ch. III, section B.)
40. CE VII, p. 362.

firmly told that the supposed heretical omissions do not appear in the "Catholic" Bible either; and the narrator deposits a Douai and a Protestant Bible with one of his tenants, so that all may see "... what tenets of their creed are in the word of God, and what are not — they can see also the difference between the two versions".[41] Thus he hopes to dispel Catholic prejudice. On another occasion Father Butler confronts Paddy Dimnick with the question why most priests are "so unwilling to allow you, and every layman like you, to read the word of God?".[42] Paddy is compelled to admit that the clergy must have something to hide, but he will not draw the logical conclusion that he should read the Scriptures for himself. Like Dan Gallagher of "The Brothers" he believes that only "the clergy ... has the larnin' to understand them".[43]

In the nineteenth century as in the twentieth religious hatred was a way of life in the north of Ireland,[44] and social as well as doctrinal factors entered into it. I shall deal with its social causes and manifestations in the next chapter. Here it will suffice to note that the tide of religious hatred swept many along with it, rich and poor, landlord and tenant, vicar and priest, and that imaginative literature naturally reflected the bitterness of contemporary sectarianism. Against the prevailing background of intolerance, conversion from Roman Catholicism to Protestantism was viewed as an extreme example of social and class disloyalty, and this must especially have applied to Catholic priests who deserted the Church in which they had been ordained. Among Carleton's characters are two priests who convert, Father Butler of the story of that name, and Father Moyle of "The Death of a Devotee" and "The Priest's Funeral". These instances may be examined for the light which they throw upon prevailing attitudes to the phenomenon of conversion.

---

41. ibid., pp. 198-199.
42. ibid., p. 361.
43. Tales of Ireland, p. 197.
44. See for example "The Funeral and Party Fight" TS[1] (1830), reprinted under a slightly modified title in Works II.

Father Butler is converted for many reasons. Catholicism is in his opinion "unscriptural", and Catholics are kept ignorant of the written word of God. The Bible implicitly condemns many of the doctrines of the Roman Catholic Church, her priesthood and many of her rites. Catholicism is not only an erroneous creed; it also encourages such dangerous beliefs as that "the withholding of our civil allegiance to the king could be resolved into a spiritual duty to the Pope or to the church".[45]

The conversion of Father Butler shocks the devotee, Paddy Dimnick; but far more violent is the reaction of the clergy to the conversion of Father Moyle. In "The Death of a Devotee" he is shown with his message of "Christian hope" and trust only in the Redeemer, contrasted to John Lynch, his erstwhile companion, who dies in the "delusive security" of the Church of Rome.[46] In "The Priest's Funeral" he refuses the last rites of the Catholic Church, defying even the bishop, who has gathered his clergy to the venerable old man's house to try to tyrannize him into dying within the faith which he has abandoned. He manages to smuggle a letter out to the Protestant rector, a letter in which he relates that he is dying and that his deathbed is guarded by his former fellow-priests: "I wish to testify before you — that I die trusting alone on the merits of Jesus Christ; I wish to receive the consolations of religion — according to the forms — of your Church — for it is due — to truth — that I should openly avow my principles —".[47] It was this last point, the wish to proclaim publicly that he died a Protestant, which terrified and provoked the bishop and his clergy into depriving the old man of warmth and food in his last days. According to the curate, Father John, it was "mortification and shame, added, probably, to a fear of evil from the influence of his example"[48] which made the clergy attempt to conceal Moyle's change of religion. The conversion of a parish priest, known and respected

---

45. CE VII, p. 279.
46. Tales of Ireland, pp. 28, 40.
47. ibid., p. 87. The story first appeared in CE X (1830).
48. Tales of Ireland, p. 61.

throughout the neighbourhood, would have as great an effect on the local level as the conversion of a bishop would have on the national, and Carleton willingly exploits the powerful psychological effect of this example.

Closer to the everyday reality of the layman (and perhaps not as uncommon as one at first might think) was the problem of mixed marriage. The narrator of "Father Butler" mentions in passing the experiences of a Protestant woman who was married to a Catholic man. Her life had been made a misery by the attempts of her husband to convert her, and in a footnote to "Father Butler" Carleton adds that he will write later at greater length on this particular form of domestic tyranny.[49] He fulfilled his promise less than two years later with "The Brothers" (published in The Christian Examiner in 1830), a story to which passing reference has already been made, and whose central theme is the unremitting efforts of a husband to convert his Protestant wife, who however, in spite of persecution, remains true to her own faith to the bitter end. It is worth observing that Carleton here essays yet another variant on the general theme of religion and society. In "A Pilgrimage to Patrick's Purgatory" and "Father Butler" the focus is mainly on Catholic practice and doctrine; "The Broken Oath" concentrates on the evil effects of confession on Irish society; "The Death of a Devotee" and "The Priest's Funeral" deal partly with peasant superstition and partly with the conversion of a Catholic priest; but in "The Brothers" Carleton introduces his readers to an Irish family of the class above the peasantry, and exhibits the progress and results of religious dissension and priestly interference on the lives of every member of that family.

In the Preface to Tales of Ireland Carleton claims that the "picture of the deplorable effects which too frequently proceed from marriages between Roman Catholics and Protestants" is one which he has "too often witnessed". He continues:

---

49. CE VII, p. 430.

The Roman Catholic clergy condemn the Protestants for proselytizing, and publicly disclaim it themselves. No sooner, however, do they get scent of a proselyte, than they commence a system of low, secret, and harassing perseverance, altogether unworthy of open honesty and truth. It is, however, in intermarriages, and conversion _from_ their own creed, that this gnawing and persecuting spirit operates with the most baleful and disastrous consequences.[50]

In accordance with his usual practice, Carleton associates in "The Brothers" a responsible moral upbringing, wise behaviour, honesty, good character, intelligence used for good ends, educated speech and restrained emotions with characters who profess the Protestant religion, while Catholics are brought up in darkness and superstition, are rash, dishonest, have weak or even bad characters, are stupid or cunning, speak in a very uneducated way and are wildly, even fatally, emotional. This set of contrasts is to be found in the Gallagher family, where the mother, the former Peggy Graham, and the elder son Tom are Protestant, and the father Dan and the younger son Ned are Catholic. Peggy is characterized as a girl who made only one mistake, that of eloping with Dan Gallagher, and it is a mistake which she spends the rest of her life paying for. As a young girl she had received careful training in the "moral and doctrinal truths of the Old and New Testaments". She was upright and honest, a good daughter, wife and mother. Her parents were not wealthy but they had been long established in the neighbourhood and were Godfearing and respectable. Dan, on the other hand, was the son of illiterate parents who had risen in the world by accident and circumstance. He was an ugly little fellow, whereas Peggy's beauty — as Carleton quaintly puts it — "was considerably beyond that of persons in her station of life".[51] Dan was malicious, offensive and uneducated, and "the principles on which he conducted his business were those

---

50. _Tales of Ireland_, pp. xi-xii.
51. _ibid._, pp. 147-148.

of avarice and extortion". He was persevering and knavish, and yet, "with all his worldliness, he actually affected to be religious". Like Paddy Dimnick of "Father
Butler" he was strongly superstitious and completely under
the sway of the parish priest, Father Dorneen. He was "a
man whose ill-temper, penuriousness, and bigotry, were
proverbial, even among those of his own creed".[52] Peggy
had married him out of a misguided desire to be comfortably established in life, and from their very wedding day he
used every means at his command to persuade her to adopt
his religion. But all his efforts failed, and he might
have given up but for the determination of Father Dorneen
to win a convert. Father Dorneen was not in fact very
successful with Peggy either. He engaged in frequent doctrinal debates with her, but as he grudgingly had to admit, she was "a tartar at the Scriptures".[53] Dan, in his
perverse way, was proud of his wife's ability in argument
but his superstitious fear of hell-fire and damnation led
him to continue trying to force her into the Catholic
Church. Their family life was made miserable, their sons
were used as pawns in the struggle and Peggy became ill,
but the parish priest would not relax his pressure on her
through the husband; and the final threat came when the
priest conceived a scheme to force Peggy and Tom to leave
their home if they would not convert to Catholicism.

The sons of the family and their respective careers are an object-lesson in misguided sectarianism: Tom
becomes a Church of Ireland clergyman while his brother
Ned ends up on the gallows.[54] His father had indulged Ned
and mistakenly expected him to grow out of his wildness.
When his wife attempted to give advice on the subject of
the boy's upbringing, the only answer she received was
this: "Where's the use in talking about what can't be
helped? If he had been born a Saint, or a Protestant, it

---

52. ibid., pp. 161-168.
53. ibid., pp. 171-178.
54. The same situation is exhibited in "History of a Chimney Sweep"
    (CE XI [1831]; never reprinted), where the one son, John, ends
    his life a felon, and his brother, Tom, who had been brought up
    with the Bible, becomes a respectable and respected clergyman of
    the Church of Ireland.

would have satisfied you, maybe; bad as he is, I wouldn't give his little finger for the whole body of that sober-faced dring upon your knee there [Tom], with his Bible and his preaching".[55] Ned attended the local hedge-school, a hot-bed of Ribbonism and immorality, whereas Tom, who had received his elementary education from the Protestant schoolmaster, finally left home without his parents' knowledge and became a student at Dublin University, where he was duly ordained as a Protestant clergyman.

There was a saying common among the Roman Catholic peasantry to the effect that "the clargy says, that whin a Roman Catholic girl marries a Protestant, if she doesn't get him to turn she sleeps in the arms of the divil ...". Yet the Roman Catholic clergy did not discourage intermarriage because, as one of Father Dorneen's flock sagaciously explains, "the Protestants mostly come over to the right place". Indeed the clergy of both sects are censured for neglecting their flocks in order to proselytize: "What throuble does our clargy take about us in religion or larnin'? Let a priest or a parson hear of a convert, an' he's at him ...".[56] Carleton nevertheless maintained that it was the Roman Catholic priests who deserved most censure on this account. He was always of the opinion that they had too much power over the people. When condemning Father Dorneen's influence over Dan, and Dan's toleration of the priest's interference in his marriage, he asks: "What man, what husband, possessing spirit or affection for his wife, would permit her to become a butt for the insolence and ignorance of a bigotted and illiterate priest?"[57] He here gives vent to that fundamental Protestant sentiment of individualism which distinguished and in his estimation divided the two communities.

Carleton expounds in thunderous tones the moral to be drawn from the story of "The Brothers":

Yet so it happens, and ever will happen, until
the grappling irons of this power are broken, and

55. Tales of Ireland, pp. 186-187.
56. ibid., pp. 152-157.
57. ibid., p. 205.

> our peasantry taught to think and act like men
> whom God has formed for nobler ends than to be
> the contented slaves of a subtle and ambitious
> class, who hang upon every religious and politi-
> cal movement among nations, to watch those mo-
> ments in which they may confirm their authority
> over mankind.[58]

He was never again to be so biased and hostile in his picture of the Catholic priest and his position in rural society. However, in his early stories he constantly reite-
rates the veniality and cunning of the priest, and his
excessive influence over the peasantry for good and evil,
and darkly hints at the political ambitions of the Catholic Church in Ireland and the threat which it represented
to civil security and the political stability of the United Kingdom. He maintains and sets out to prove from
"true" examples that rural Irish Catholicism is primitive
and reminiscent of pagan rites. Instead of improving the
moral and spiritual state of the peasants, it reinforces
their native superstition and in no way acts as a brake on
their worst excesses. Confession and Extreme Unction make
forgiveness of sins automatic, and the doctrine of exclusive salvation makes the peasantry arrogant where they
should be humble. This effect is deliberately encouraged
by the priests, who keep the peasantry in darkness for
their own ends, which are personal aggrandizement and the
furthering of the power of the Catholic Church. They prevent the peasantry from reading the Bible, where like Henry Lacy they might find rational truth, and they pursue
potential converts pitilessly, even going so far as to destroy a whole family in their efforts to win a single
soul.

E. EDUCATION, POLITICS AND PREJUDICE

Carleton wrote his most blatantly anti-Catholic stories
("A Pilgrimage to Patrick's Purgatory", "The Broken Oath"

---

58. ibid.

and "Father Butler") at the beginning of his literary career, a time when the debate on Catholic Emancipation was
at its height. The main purpose of these stories, as indeed of most of Carleton's Christian Examiner work, was
propagandistic, and "The Broken Oath" and "Father Butler"
in particular display specifically literary merit only in
small flashes of characterization or peasant dialogue.
Carleton's anti-Catholicism was not, however, by any means
an isolated phenomenon, and by placing his early work in a
broader context it may be possible to draw some new conclusions about its significance.

The situation outlined in the historical introduction to this chapter (pp. 14-20) is hardly if at all reflected in Carleton's early stories. No reference is made
to the history of the savage repression of Roman Catholicism in Ireland. When agrarian agitation is referred to
in "The Broken Oath" it is for the purpose of showing how
murderous the Catholic peasantry are, and "Confessions of
a Reformed Ribbonman (An Owre True Tale)"[1] is a violent
and terrifying report concerning the vengeance taken by
the Ribbonmen on a Catholic family who had refused to give
them arms. In "The Funeral and Party Fight",[2] however,
Carleton shows how sectarian strife operated on a local
basis when the Ribbonmen and Orangemen fought a long and
bloody battle with fists, stones, clubs and muskets. The
"party fight" is one of the old-established traditions of
Northern Ireland, and Carleton's story reflects intensely
the way in which resentment on the part of Catholics and
fear on the part of Protestants could spill over into violence and death.[3]

Catholic Emancipation was opposed strongly by
Irish Protestants because they rightly feared that it was
the beginning of a series of claims which would result in
a transfer of power and the dissolution of the Protestant
establishment. It was against the background of Prote-

1. This story first appeared in The Dublin Literary Gazette (1830);
   it was retitled "Wildgoose Lodge" in later editions including the
   collected Works.
2. See the reference in section D, note 44 above.
3. Cf. ch. II, section D for a discussion of violence in rural Ireland in the nineteenth century.

stant fears, and bitterness on the part of Catholics who after 1829 felt that they had wrenched Emancipation from the hands of an unwilling Government, that Carleton published his stories in The Christian Examiner.

For most Irishmen — paradoxical as it may seem — the nature of religious difference in their country had little to do with religion itself; religion functioned as a banner of identity for Catholics and Protestants alike. The Rev. Arthur Leary, addressing the House of Lords in 1800, explained the reason why the Penal Laws had not eradicated Catholicism in Ireland:

> The ancestors, my Lords, of the Catholic clergy
> of Ireland, had the religion which the Christian
> world professed, and the estates and castles of
> their fathers, ages before Tudors or Stuarts had
> ascended the British throne ... Amidst the vari-
> ous changes that happened in Europe, the descen-
> dants of those Catholics preserved their religion,
> which persecution contributed to rivet deeper in-
> to their minds; as, the more the wind attempted
> to strip the traveller of his cloak, the closer
> he held it.[4]

The Catholic religion was the peasantry's one link with their past, and they stuck to it tenaciously. Well-meaning Protestants made many attempts to convert them, but these attempts were resented and did not have any noticeable effect. The administration of charity in times of distress was "made subservient to the propagation of sectarian principles, generally speaking without much success, but not independent of annoyance and grief".[5]

Carleton wrote frequently of the lack of "moral education" amongst the Roman Catholic peasantry, and regarded the education they received in their hedge schools as morally and politically damaging for the country. The Penal Laws

---

4. Quoted in Constantia Maxwell, Country and Town in Ireland under the Georges, p. 314.
5. Anon., Proselytising the Irish: or the Struggles and Prospects of Protestantism (Edinburgh n.d. [1858]), p. 3.

had debarred Catholics from organized education, and the
hedge schools had emerged with the relaxation of these
laws in the course of the eighteenth century; but the quality of education offered by the schools varied considerably, and they did not serve the majority of the rural
poor.[6] In Carleton's country, Tyrone and Monaghan, the
1841 Census reports an illiteracy rate of fifty to seventy-
five per cent. Official education "was linked with the
Church and most of the pioneer educational societies included among their aims the spread of the Protestant religion".[7] The schools set up by these societies were in any
case few and far between and could in no way satisfy the
country's educational needs. There were endowed schools,
partly supported by lands granted by Charles I and Charles
II, and each diocese had in theory its own school, but endowed and diocesan schools only provided education for
Protestants. The infamous "Charter Schools" had been set
up in 1703 to teach "the poor Irish" the English language
and the Protestant religion; but until 1803 no Catholic
children were actually admitted.[8]

Among early nineteenth century educational societies, the Kildare Street Society (later Kildare Place Society) is perhaps the most famous. It had been founded in
1811 "to promote 'mixed' schools in which poor Catholics
and Protestants should be educated together, where, according to theory at least, only the general principles of
Christianity would be taught".[9] Its board was composed of
Catholics and Protestants, with the latter in the majority.[10] Although proselytism was supposedly prohibited it
was ruled that the scriptures should be read in the
schools. The Protestant Dean of Achonry pointed out that
this policy conflicted with the declared aims of the so-

6. The curriculum and organization of the hedge school can be stu-
    died in Carleton's "The Hedge School and the Abduction of Mat Ka-
    vanagh" (TS[1] [1830], reprinted in Works II).
7. T.W. Freeman, Pre-Famine Ireland: A Study in Historical Geography
    (Manchester 1957), p. 135.
8. Freeman, loc. cit.
9. Reynolds, The Catholic Emancipation Crisis in Ireland, p. 68.
10. 21 Anglicans, 4 Quakers, 2 Presbyterians and 2 Catholics. Cf.
    Gustave de Beaumont, L'Irlande: Sociale, Politique et Réligieuse
    (Paris 1839) I, p. 407.

ciety: "To insist upon the reading of the Scriptures as the only condition under which education will be given to the children of the Irish poor, is to exclude from the schools the Roman Catholic children almost universally".[11] For this reason alone the society schools made very little impact on the general level of education amongst the ordinary people.

Carleton was for a short time (c. 1826-1827) employed as a schoolmaster by one of these early educational societies, the Association for Discountenancing Vice, which was incorporated in 1800 and launched its educational programme in 1806.[12] His attitude to Catholicism at this period appears clearly from a letter to his friend William Sisson[13] dated 3 November 1826, in which he encloses a memorandum intended for Robert Peel.[14] He claims that only damnatory facts can defeat the Catholic fight for Emancipation. There is a close connection between the Catholic Association[15] and other illegal societies, and he can advance evidence to prove that many Roman Catholic schoolmasters are agents of such societies. Here we have an explanation of the fact that the hedge schoolmasters in Carleton's early stories are always Ribbonmen who initiate their pupils and the men of the district into the Ribbon society. This is the case for example with Nulty of "The Brothers", Mat Kavanagh of "The Hedge School" and the schoolmaster of "Confessions of a Reformed Ribbonman".[16]

---

11. Quoted by Freeman, Pre-Famine Ireland, p. 137.
12. "This society had 13,189 Protestant and 5,994 Catholic children under its care in 1828 but there was a decline from 1830, when the government grant was withdrawn" (Freeman, loc. cit.).
13. Librarian of Marsh's library, Dublin which was the meeting place for many Church of Ireland clergymen including Caesar Otway.
14. British Library Add. MS. 40,390 (Peel papers vol. CCX) ff. 29-35. Printed in André Boué, William Carleton (1973), pp. 495-500.
15. In 1811 the Catholic Board was set up to promote Irish Catholic interests. It was suppressed in 1812 and the Emancipation cause languished for many years. Eventually the Board was replaced by the Catholic Association, which progressed rapidly under the leadership of Daniel O'Connell. It too was suppressed in 1825 but re-established itself under a new name.
16. Cf. ch. III, section C, pp. 162-165 for the characterization of the hedge schoolmaster.

The peasantry were leaderless, propertyless and to a large
extent illiterate. Although in a numerical majority they
were impotent, and they had a more intangible enemy to
combat in their struggle for recognition. This was the
prevailing combination of anti-Catholic and anti-Irish prejudice which finds its reflection in the Christian Examiner stories. It will be recalled that Carleton states in
the preface to Tales of Ireland that he was concerned to
portray the people as they really were. They were "a
class unknown in literature",[17] and to give a true picture he had to reveal their bad as well as their good characteristics: "on one side, the generous humorous people
of the Clogher valley; on the other, the underlying violence and degradation of an oppressed people".[18] The early stories concern themselves only with the latter aspect
of peasant character, although Carleton was later to take
the reasons for the peasantry's degradation into account
in his Traits and Stories and in novels such as Fardorougha the Miser[19] and Valentine M'Clutchy. But the early, one-dimensional approach was, of course, eminently appropriate to the purposes of The Christian Examiner.

Carleton functioned in the beginning as one of
the literati of the Ascendancy élite, helping to "provide
the social system with a sophisticated and elaborate justi-
fication for its existence and continued survival".[20] As
he became conscious of what he was doing, his work took on
another aspect and he shifted from justifying the oppression of the peasantry by the élite to expressing sympathy
with the oppressed. This process of change does not show
an even development: "Father Butler", for example, is hostile to the peasantry, while "The Station", which appears
in the next number of The Christian Examiner, is sympathetic to them and "The Death of a Devotee" in the next number

17. Tales of Ireland, p. x; cf. pp. 22-23 above.
18. Margaret MacCurtain, "Pre-Famine Peasantry in Ireland: Definition
    and Theme" Irish University Review IV,2 (1974), p. 195.
19. Fardorougha the Miser, or the Convicts of Lisnamona (first pub-
    lished in DUM 1837-1838).
20. Gideon Sjoberg, "Folk and Feudal Societies" American Journal of
    Sociology LVIII (1952), p. 234. Quoted by Margaret MacCurtain,
    "Pre-Famine Peasantry in Ireland".

again is antipathetic to them from the point of view of race and religion. From "Denis O'Shaughnessy" onwards Carleton attempts to give a more rounded picture of the peasantry, adopting a sympathetic starting-point but maintaining his right to criticize and pronounce moral judgements. It cannot be denied, however, that in his early stories Carleton has steeped himself in the prejudices of the ruling élite. It may seem that he was an opportunist, merely writing what he knew would sell; and there is no doubt that he was extremely poor at the time. But the conviction apparent in his anti-Catholic pronouncements and in his letter to Sisson cannot be explained away either by accusing him of opportunism, or by claiming that Caesar Otway wrote the anti-Catholic parts.[21] In the late 1820's Carleton would seem to have rejected his origins, both religious and social,[22] and to have filled the vacuum by adopting a set of principles and attitudes utterly opposed to those with which he had been brought up. Faced with the incomprehensible, abject misery of the Irish Catholic people, he subscribed to what seemed for the time a satisfactory means of explaining it.

Anti-Irish prejudice[23] had a long history in both Britain and Ireland, and from the time of the original Anglo-Norman invasion there had been a tendency to differentiate in theory and law between native Irish and English patterns of behaviour. To the Tudors the Irish "were a turbulent, semi-nomadic, treacherous, idle, dirty, and belligerent lot",[24] and this view persisted after the English Reformation when antipathy towards the Irish as a race was joined to distaste for the religion professed by the majority. Curtis points out that English politicians dealt in terms of an Irish national character, far inferi-

---

21. Cf. pp. 30-32 above.
22. See Autobiography, chs. XIV and XV.
23. I use prejudice here as L.P. Curtis, Jr. does "to convey that cluster of negative and patronizing attitudes and beliefs which characterized the thinking of many Englishmen and not a few Scots, Welsh, and Anglo-Irishmen about the so-called native Irish" (Anglo-Saxons and Celts: A Study of Anti-Irish Prejudice in Victorian England [Bridgeport, Conn. 1968], p. 3.).
24. Curtis, Anglo-Saxons and Celts, p. 18.

or to their own self-image, and that in the nineteenth century there prevailed a notion of a deep gulf between Irish and English character and culture. He terms this English conviction of national superiority Anglo-Saxonism, and defines it as the specifically English and Victorian form of ethnocentrism:

> Ethnocentrism characterizes that nucleus of be-
> liefs and attitudes, cultivated and cherished by
> people who seek relief from some of their own
> anxieties and fears, which make for more or less
> rigid distinctions between their own group (or
> in-group) and some other collection of people (or
> out-group) with the result that the former are
> ranked far above the latter in the assumed hierar-
> chy of peoples, nations, or ethnic units which
> together make up the species of man.[25]

Thus Anglo-Saxonism explains the conviction that the great success of Britain in all fields was due to racial superiority, and that the failure of other nations, including the Irish, to match the British achievement was due to racial inferiority. Anglo-Saxonism was not a coherent system, but a collection of prejudices which permeated all classes and all shades of opinion in England. In literature it manifested itself in references in all genres to the unfitness of the Irish people for self-government, their incompetence in business and domestic economy, their deficiency in intellectual power, and the proverbial Irish faults of violence, indolence and intemperance.[26]

Three themes representing three kinds of prejudice based on race, class and religious differences make up the most active ingredients of Anglo-Saxonism as it affected the Irish Question. "These themes may be loosely translated into the negative statement that the real trouble with the Irish was that they were not Anglo-Saxon, upper class, or Protestant".[27] It would appear obvious from his

---

25. ibid., p. 7.
26. See W.M. Thackeray, The Irish Sketch-Book (London 1843) for one nineteenth century example.
27. Curtis, p. 19.

early stories that Carleton had imbibed a large dose of
Anglo-Saxonism, and it seems reasonable to assume that he
adopted what for an Irishman was a spurious form of ethnocentrism in order to "seek relief from his own anxieties
and fears" by identifying with the "in-group" — in this
case upper-class Protestants. The point may be illustrated from the description of peasant characters in "Father
Butler". Paddy Dimnick, the devotee of the story, is characterized as stupid and cunning. He has a "round, rosy,
fat, unmeaning face" and has married a little above himself. He is also spiteful, vengeful and a drunkard. (The
figure of the drunken devotee is a favourite with the early Carleton, recurring in Henry Lacy of "The Broken Oath"
and Darby More of "The Midnight Mass".) Dimnick is chosen
to have a theological debate with the narrator, where the
latter's superior intelligence and more graceful English
of course allow him to conquer this ignorant peasant with
one hand tied behind his back. The treatment meted out to
the pilgrim Owen Devlin is rather similar: he is a "colos-
sus" dressed in rags whom the narrator examines as he
would an animal in a cage.[28] In his characterization of
these men Carleton has gone beyond the "sturdy peasant"
convention of his day. Indeed, there is no doubt in any
of his early stories of the tremendous qualitative difference between the Anglo-Irish and the native Irish. There
are peasants who are rational and respectable, but the majority are presented as simpletons who need strong leadership, and who can easily be made the dupes of a demagogue.

Race and class are thus alluded to, but it is of
course religion upon which the greatest emphasis is laid.
The examples of Dimnick and Devlin are again appropriate:
Dimnick is a cunning hypocrite and Devlin monstrous mainly
because of their religion. In contrast, a remarkable
change comes over Henry Lacy as soon as he has rejected
Catholicism. He becomes upright and candid, and speaks
amazingly correct and fluent English. The most direct set
of contrasts in this regard is perhaps to be found in Ned
and Tom Gallagher of "The Brothers". Ned, the Catholic,

---

28. Cf. p. 37 above.

is a true Celt. He is highly emotional, laughing one minute and crying the next. He frequently gets drunk, and
when drunk he is violent. He has a very low intelligence,
and for want of a strong hand to guide him commits a crime
for which he is hanged. His manner of speaking is utterly
different from that of his brother Tom, whose English is
impeccable. Tom is a fine lad. Patient, well-balanced,
intelligent and rational, he is as much a credit to his
Protestant upbringing as Ned is a true product of his Catholic upbringing. The more a character is disapproved of
by the narrator, the more he conforms to the Irish stereotype; the more he is approved of, the more he conforms to
the civilized Anglo-Saxon ideal.[29]

Popular hatred of Catholicism was based on an ignorance of the real tenets of the Roman Church, and it
joined the more informed antipathy of the educated classes
to form a solid and complacent wall of bigotry.[30] Catholics were accused of superstition and moral corruption,
and the political aims of their Church were distrusted.
"Catholic beliefs, especially the sacerdotal nature of the
Christian ministry ... the primacy of St. Peter and the
See of Rome, the invocation of saints, veneration of the
Virgin, transubstantiation and so on, seemed to some Protestants mildly derisory, to others downright wicked, and
to some, even perverted". The claim of Papal infallibility seemed final proof of the "unenlightened condition of
the whole of Catholicism".[31] Carleton takes up most of
these points in his early stories. In this way, he may
have unconsciously striven to shake off his origins and by
writing in a tone approved of by the establishment have
hoped to be accepted among their ranks.

---

29. Carleton's later modification of his characterization of the
    peasantry is discussed in ch. III, section D.
30. The adjective bigoted is defined by The Shorter Oxford English
    Dictionary as "obstinately and blindly attached to some creed,
    opinion, or party, and intolerant towards others". Both creeds,
    Catholic and Protestant, were bigoted in this sense in nine-
    teenth century Britain and Ireland.
31. E.R. Norman, Anti-Catholicism in Victorian England (London 1968),
    p. 14.

Moral corruption was also an accusation frequently levelled against Catholics. The Gothic novel The
Monk[32] reflects the popular image, and in Carleton's "The
Lianhan Shee"[33] the theme of sexual relations between
nuns and priests is exploited. More seriously for the
Irish, however, "Catholics were imagined to be potential —
and sometimes (as in Ireland) even actual — subversives of
the Protestant constitution".[34] The Jesuits were connected in the popular mind with the Catholic plot to enslave
the free peoples of the world, and Carleton treats this
theme in "Father Butler". In Ireland the largest and
poorest section of the population was Catholic. The Act
of Union had brought this large population under the direct rule of the Westminster government, and throughout
the nineteenth century there was a whole series of Irish
demands for increased freedom of religion. These demands
included Catholic Emancipation, which was finally granted
in 1829; a demand for denominational education; a demand
for the disestablishment of the Church of Ireland, and for
the abolition of tithes paid by Catholics to Protestant
ministers; and a demand for the abolition of oaths for
holders of municipal and state office. A number of nineteenth century ministries fell because of the Irish question, "and although the causes of disaster were always
mixed, Protestant distrust of the Irish because they were
Catholics, and differences between Protestants over the
extent to which they were prepared to carry their distrust,
were prominent contributions to political instability".[35]
Catholicism was believed to be inimical to progress; Catholic countries were notoriously bad at trade and commerce
and their laws were oppressive and unenlightened. The
great problem for Victorians was therefore "how to maintain a safe balance ... in the formulation of policy towards those whose religious principles inclined them un-
avoidably to intolerance".[36]

---

32. By Matthew Lewis; first published 1796.
33. Cf. section C, note 29.
34. Norman, p. 15.
35. ibid., p. 18.
36. ibid., p. 19.

70

While Carleton's earliest work panders to Anglo-Saxonist prejudice, it must be emphasized that his anti-Irish and anti-Catholic tone is modified and has almost entirely disappeared by 1831. The course of this change can be seen most clearly from the way in which he treats the related issues of the figure of the priest and the involvement of the Roman Catholic Church in national politics. In his letter to Sisson[37] Carleton had insisted that the people were the dupes of their secular and spiritual leaders, who whipped them up into a fury over their "imaginary oppression"; these leaders, from motives of power and personal aggrandizement, "insolently charge the policy of the British Cabinet with that want of peace and prosperity in Ireland which is the consequence of their own secret intrigue and open licentiousness". The priests, burning for Ascendancy and revenge, have made hatred of Protestantism a religious duty. It is mostly the priests who are to be feared, and because they have the people under their power it would be madness to enter into a compact with their Church, which reserves to itself the right of dissolving "any obligation which political expediency may compel her to enter".

In the Christian Examiner stories Carleton treats people and priests as types rather than as individuals. There are the bullying, grasping and unscrupulous priests of "The Lough Derg Pilgrim", "The Broken Oath", "The Priest's Funeral" and "The Brothers", while the priests of "Father Butler" and "The Death of a Devotee", because they have converted to Protestantism, are represented as gentle, intelligent and pious. A more sympathetic priest is represented by the crafty but jovial Father Philemy of "The Station"; this type, which appears again in Father Finnerty of "Denis O'Shaughnessy going to Maynooth", was to recur in Traits and Stories in the persons of Father Ned of "Ned M'Keown", Father Corrigan of "Shane Fadh's Wedding" and Father Mulcahy of "The Geography of an Irish Oath".[38] The priests of the first group of stories are neither

---

37. See note 14 above.
38. The last-mentioned story appeared in TS² (1833).

very attractive nor very realistic, and the converts among them are stiff and lifeless, a little too good to be true. On the other hand, priests of the type of Father Philemy, despite their greed and their tyrannical rule over their flocks, have the best interests of the people at heart and are accepted as an integral part of the community. In his earliest stories Carleton attempts to lay the blame for the lawless state of Ireland at the door of the Catholic clergy, but no such blame attaches to them in his later work.

One constant element in the portrayal of the priest in the community is the veneration with which the people regard him. He has tremendous power and status, and one of the ambitions of most Catholic parents was for one of their sons to become a priest. It is obvious that a people whose traditional leaders had been dispersed, and who were not in a position to educate leaders of their own, would turn for leadership and inspiration to the class which had suffered with them and supported them. The great local power of the priests could be applied to political ends: this was evident during the Emancipation struggle, when the priests organized their parishioners in support of O'Connell, and it was the political power of the priests and the Church which was feared most. Carleton has Father Butler give a long exposition of the evil role of the Church of Rome in world history and the reasons why it should be thwarted in its obvious aim of taking over political control in Ireland: "wherever her influence is established, or has been established, knowledge, arts, science, industry, and civilisation have retrograded — the human mind has become dark and grovelling, and the character of mankind sunk into slavery on the one hand, or raised into an intolerable and arrogant oppression on the other".[39] The same note is struck in "The Priest's Funeral", where the Protestant rector Mr. S—, rebuking the priests for their maltreatment of the dying Father Moyle, expresses his suspicion that "the spirit which dictated such conduct, is only restrained by the free constitution under which we

_____

39. CE VII, p. 423.

live, from attempting to exercise the same unscriptural tyranny over both mind and body, which marks its existence whenever it wields the sword of temporal power".[40] Father Butler and Mr. S— both accuse the Roman Church of aspiring to political power in Ireland. It is left to Father A—, the "wily Jesuit" in "Father Butler", to formulate this ambition when he says that he and his brethren "are struggling with a heresy which has usurped our place, and striving, in the midst of our poverty, to plant a Christian colony here and there in secret and in silence, with a blessed hope of contributing in some degree to replace the church in her former power".[41] The same character also brings up the vexed question of allegiance, and equivocates in the best tradition of Jesuitical casuistry: "Now, if it ever happens, and it _has_ happened, that the exercise of the civil allegiance which they owe the king, should directly tend to overthrow or essentially injure the power and security of the church, then the withholding that allegiance would become a _spiritual_ duty".[42] "The Catholic Plot", and the Protestant establishment's fear that Ireland would be subordinated to the dictates of the Pope if Catholics assumed power, were issues often debated. By concentrating on the issue of religion, the Ascendancy could persuade itself that it was taking the morally correct course of action in denying a share of power to the general population. Political power could not be granted to those whose political allegiance was doubtful.

These questions occupy comparatively little space in Carleton's stories of religion although they very much underlie his attitude. He is more concerned with the local community and with the way in which the priest could exercize his political power for evil ends. Secret societies were a feature of Irish rural life, and in "The Broken Oath" Carleton directly accuses the priest of breaking his vow of allegiance to the king by encouraging these societies. The priest is held responsible both for socie-

---

40. _Tales of Ireland_, p. 81.
41. _CE_ VII, p. 275.
42. _ibid._, pp. 278-279.

ties which plot rebellion and for the more common secret societies and religious factions which were symptomatic of widespread civil disorder.[43] Henry Lacy, the principal character in the story, upbraids the priest for having led him astray: "You knew me to be a ribbonman, and why permit me to run into the jaws of destruction? Why not fulfil your duties to the state?".[44]

Some priests were actively involved in the disastrously unsuccessful 1798 revolution. Bishop Stock, reporting to the Plowden commission of inquiry, attempted to explain why: "The peasant will love a revolution because he feels the weight of poverty, and has often the sense to perceive that the change of masters may render it heavier. The priest must follow the impulse of the popular wave, or be left behind on the beach to perish".[45] And as late as 1845 Campbell Foster, correspondent of The Times, considered it "not wise and expedient for the peace and tranquillity of Ireland, and consequently for the prosperity and strength of the empire, that the clergy of three-fourths of the people of Ireland should thus be left dependent on the people".[46] Campbell Foster proposed that the Roman Catholic clergy should be paid by the state. If this were done they would not be disposed to bite the hand that fed them, and would accordingly support the Government more effectively. It thus appears that Bishop Stock and Campbell Foster on the one hand, and the early Carleton on the other approached the question from different standpoints — the former asserting that the priest was forced by economic necessity to follow popular opinion, the latter asserting that the people followed the priest.

It is only in the early Christian Examiner stories that Carleton ascribes such overwhelming influence to the priest, making the peasants appear mere instruments of his desire for power. In the later stories the peasant is

---

43. In his memorandum to Peel, Carleton had explicitly stated that the priests connived openly with illegal societies (Boué, William Carleton [1973], p. 499).
44. CE VII, p. 35 (cf. above, pp. 43-47).
45. Quoted in Thomas Campbell Foster, Letters on the Condition of the People of Ireland² (London 1847), p. 517.
46. ibid., pp. 517-518.

more the priest's equal in areas of life other than the purely religious. The priest, who after all came from the people, shared their general outlook and sympathies. This may be seen in "The Station", where Father Philemy refers enthusiastically to the overthrow of the Established Church, and in "Denis O'Shaughnessy going to Maynooth", where Denis dreams of the power which the Catholic Church will have when it is supreme; but in none of the later stories is there any hint of the priest colluding in violent rebellion. The priests share the dreams of the peasants for a better and more independent way of life, but they do not encourage them in thoughts of an armed uprising.

The full extent of Carleton's modified attitude towards the people and their religion can be studied in the story of "Denis O'Shaughnessy".[47] In "The Station"[48] the people had emerged as lively, kindly and witty, and the priest as the all-powerful leader, whose word and whip were feared, but who had the best interests of the community at heart. "Lachlin Murray and the Blessed Candle"[49] had reverted to the superstitious peasant whose credulity is rather amusing than otherwise. But "Denis O'Shaughnessy", partly by virtue of its greater length and inclusiveness, shows how completely Carleton had altered his former attitude and tone.

The Royal College of St. Patrick at Maynooth was established in 1795. Before that date, candidates for the priesthood had had to go abroad to continental seminaries and it was feared "that students educated abroad would now be exposed to the 'contagion of sedition and infidelity'" prevailing in Revolutionary Europe.[50] The establishment of Maynooth did not, however, conciliate Catholics as it had been intended to do, but instead produced an entirely new type of priest, a type which very often came from the peasantry and which shared their social and political out-

---

47. For this story see section D, note 17.
48. CE VIII (1829); reprinted in Works II.
49. Cf. section D, note 28.
50. Beckett, The Making of Modern Ireland, p. 256.

look and ambitions. For the peasant, the road to social advancement led through Maynooth to ordination, and consequently "The highest object of an Irish peasant's ambition [was] to see his son a priest".[51] Priests were respected for their vast learning as much as for their sacerdotal powers, and the parish priest occupied the highest position on the social scale in rural communities. The peasants, who had little respect for the law of the land, obeyed the priest, and in many of Carleton's stories and novels we see the priest keeping the community in order. When a fight breaks out at the festivities in "Shane Fadh's Wedding" it is brought to a speedy end by the priest, who by a combination of physical force and verbal threats terrorizes the combatants into quiescence. He commands them "... in the name of the Catholic church and the Blessed Virgin Mary, to stop this instant"; he threatens to "turn the heads around upon [their] bodies in the twinkling of an eye", and he orders the worst offenders to make a pilgrimage to Lough Derg for their sins.[52] Father Philemy of "The Station" likewise exercises a judicial role. He declares from the altar at Sunday Mass that if the Bradys and the O'Scallaghans continue their feud "I'll read them out from the altar".[53] To be "read out from the altar" was one of the worst punishments which could befall a member of a small rural community. It took the form of the offender standing up to face the congregation while the priest reprimanded him. Couples who eloped were forced to undergo this ordeal with its attendant shame and humiliation.[54] The priest's threat in "Shane Fadh's Wedding" also testifies to the peasant belief that the priest had magical powers, as does the following exchange in "The Station" between a son intended for the priesthood and his adoring father:

51. Works II, p. 977.
52. ibid., pp. 694-695.
53. ibid., p. 741.
54. The terror induced by this threat can be seen in Carleton's "Alley Sheridan. An Irish Story" NM I (1830), pp. 544-570. This story was reprinted several times in the first half of the nineteenth century but is not available in any modern edition.

"Well, I'll tell you what I'm thinking I'll be
apt to do, Phaddy, when I'm a clargy".
"And what is that, Briney?"
"Why, I'll — but, Phaddy, don't be talking of
this, bekase, if it should come to be known, I
might get my brains knocked out by some of the
heretics".
"Never fear, Briney, there's no danger of that —
but what is it?"
"Why, I'll translate all the Protestants into
asses, and then we'll get our hands red of them
altogether".
"Well, that flogs for cuteness, and it's a won-
dher the clargy doesn't do it, and them has the
power; for 'twould give us peace entirely".[55]

Education was a commodity highly valued by the Irish peasant, and those who possessed it were greatly respected.
Carleton relates that as soon as a boy is "designed for
the priesthood, he is, as if by a species of intuition,
supposed to know more or less of everything — astronomy,
fluxions, Hebrew, Arabic, and the black art, are subjects
upon which he is frequently expected to dilate";[56] and
when the priest raises his voice to give his opinion on
any subject, a respectful hush descends.

Denis O'Shaughnessy is a "young priest" and is
venerated in this capacity by his family and neighbours.
His parents' ambition for him is expressed by his mother's
dream, where she has seen Denis dressed like a Protestant
parson, eating and drinking regally, and telling her that
the Protestant clergy have been banished from Ireland and
the Catholics are in their place. The hopes of the family
are centred in Denis. He will make his parents comfortable in their old age and will be in a position to make
advantageous matches for his brothers and sisters. For
Denis also, it is not so much piety as visions of future
power and wealth which motivate him:

---

55. Works II, p. 744.
56. ibid., p. 981.

> To be, in the course of a few years, a _bona fide_
> priest; to possess unlimited sway over the fears
> and principles of the people; to be endowed with
> spiritual gifts to he knew not what extent; and
> to enjoy himself as he had an opportunity of see-
> ing Father Finnerty and his curate do, in the
> full swing of convivial pleasure, upon the ample
> hospitality of those who, in addition to this,
> were ready to kiss the latchet of his shoes --
> were, it must be admitted, no inconsiderable mo-
> tives in influencing the conduct of a person
> reared in a humble condition of life.[57]

The tone of "Denis O'Shaughnessy" is for the most part
humorous and ironical, and the figure of Denis in all his
bombast and innocent pride captures beautifully the es-
sence of peasant ambition. Denis is in love with the idea
of becoming a priest, but he is also in love with Susy
Connor. In his dilemma, he explains to her that "keeping
back such a - a - a - galaxy as I am from the Church ...
a _rara avis in terris_ ... is a sin that requires a great
dale of interest with the Pope to absolve". The great and
glorious Church

> thinks proper to claim your unworthy and enamour-
> ed swain as one of the brightest Colossuses of
> her future glory. The Irish hierarchy is plased
> to look upon me as a luminary of almost super-
> human brilliancy and coruscation: my talents she
> pronounces to be of the first magnitude; my elo-
> quence classical and overwhelming, and my learn-
> ing only adorned by that poor insignificant at-
> tribute denominated by philosophers unfathomabi-
> lity ...[58]

Notwithstanding these considerations, love wins in the end
and Denis marries Susy.

---

57. _ibid._, p. 997.
58. _ibid._, pp. 995-996.

Denis O'Shaughnessy only speaks of the pomp, power and glory of the Church in terms of his own private ambition. The thesis of the earlier stories had been that the priests of Ireland desired political power above all, and that they abused their special position to that end. This sinister aspect has been much muted in the later stories, and where political ambition is mentioned it takes the vague form of visions of great days ahead, when the Protestant Church will be disestablished and Catholics raised to social and political eminence. There is no mention of doubtful allegiance or of priests inciting to civil disorder, and the priests are not represented as monsters but as ordinary men who have their own faults and their own virtues.

Religion and the land are interrelated themes in Anglo-Irish literature, and Carleton treated both in the course of his career. However, in the beginning he chose to focus almost exclusively on religion, and it is only when he puts this subject in a broader perspective that he ceases to be a mouthpiece of establishment prejudice and releases the full range of his artistic ability. The anti-Catholic stories aroused such resentment among nationalistic Irishmen that they earned him the soubriquet of turncoat, which pursued him into the twentieth century and has blinded many critics to his talent. It might be said of Carleton that the main error of judgement which he committed in his early work was that in describing the "religious prejudices of the Irish" he exceeded his own intentions, exhibiting not only the prejudices of the Catholic poor but also, by his very manner of writing, the prejudices of the Protestant Ascendancy whom he was addressing.

CHAPTER II.

THE DEPICTION OF PEASANT SOCIETY

A. INTRODUCTORY

Misery, poverty and endemic famine were the grim realities
of life for the majority of Irish peasants long before the
great famine, and they lie beneath the surface gaiety of
many of Carleton's stories and sketches. The French republican Gustave de Beaumont, who was only one of many commentators, made the following observation on the Irish situation as he saw it in 1839: "La situation de l'Irlande
peut se résumer ainsi: indigence profonde parmi le peuple,
anarchie permanente dans l'État".[1] I shall here attempt
to outline the reasons for this state of affairs, an understanding of which is part of the necessary background
for reading and assessing Carleton's stories of Irish
life.[2]

From the time of the legislative union with England the
economy of Ireland steadily declined. The advocates of
Union had argued that prosperity would follow in its wake,
but for the great majority the situation grew worse and
1815 to 1850 were years of poverty and misery. The resentment of the peasantry at their steadily worsening conditions found expression in increased agrarian agitation,
and a vicious circle of outrage and repression was created. The Government, rather than enquiring into the fun-

---

1. L'Irlande: Sociale, Politique et Réligieuse II, p. 103.
2. For my account of the political situation I rely chiefly on the
    studies of J.C. Beckett, K.H. Connell, T.W. Freeman and J.E. Pom-
    fret.

damental causes of agrarian unrest, relied on coercive measures to stamp it out.[3]

A sense of insecurity prevailed in Ireland, discouraging to the investment of the English capital which the country so urgently needed; and in addition there were at least two factors which substantially contributed to the scarcity of native Irish funds. From 1800 to 1817 Ireland had to pay 2/17 of the total expenditure of the United Kingdom. Due to the European wars this expenditure was vast, and in order to meet its share Ireland was forced to borrow, in England, much of the money that was required. The payment of interest on these loans drew revenue out of the country and the Irish national debt rose by 250 per cent in these years (as compared with a rise of 50 per cent in the British national debt). Another economically damaging factor was the money drained out of the country in the form of rents paid to absentee landlords. Absenteeism was by no means a post-Union phenomenon,[4] but it increased greatly when Dublin ceased to be a seat of government and is indeed a problem which preoccupies Carleton greatly. Thus, much-needed capital was drawn out of the country in increasing volume at a critical period, and was not compensated for by British investment.

For a variety of reasons Irish industry did not thrive. Ireland had always had an agriculturally based economy, and the absence of mineral resources precluded any effective participation in the Industrial Revolution. The political ascendancy of England was also a limiting factor. Because of its colonial status Ireland had not been allowed to compete with England in the economic field until 1780, when permission was granted for trade in colonial and foreign markets, and it was not until 1800 that

---

3. "Among the earliest Irish measures of the union parliament was one for the continuation of martial law; and for more than thirty years the country was almost continually administered under special coercive legislation" (J.C. Beckett, The Making of Modern Ireland, p. 294).
4. In 1780 Arthur Young estimated that out of a total rental of c. £6m., more than £732,000 was spent abroad (A Tour in Ireland [London 1780] Part 2, p. 59), and in 1797 the figure given in the course of Irish parliamentary debates was £1,500,000 (Constantia Maxwell, Country and Town in Ireland under the Georges, p. 47).

trade with England was effectively countenanced. But this freedom came too late to be of any lasting value, since practically all the duties protecting Irish industry were abolished in the first quarter of the nineteenth century, and the majority of Irish manufacturers could not compete unaided with the more developed industries of Britain. The woollen and cotton industries had collapsed by 1820, and the linen industry which replaced cotton was confined to Ulster. Had capital been available at the right time industries such as wool and cotton might perhaps have been able to withstand British competition. However, it was only in the north-east of Ulster that industry prospered, and social and economic differences between Ulster and the rest of the country became more marked as the century progressed. This resulted, politically, in differing attitudes to the Union: "Ulster Protestants came to regard it as the essential basis of their prosperity, while to Irishmen in general it appeared the main barrier to economic progress".[5]

The Union and its political ramifications meant very little to the peasantry who were struggling to survive. Rural Ireland was facing a severe crisis at this period in the form of a population explosion which, unlike industrial Britain, it could not begin to absorb.[6] Indeed the pressure of population was the major social, economic and thus political problem of pre-famine Ireland. The rate of population growth is difficult to determine because of the imprecise nature of the source materials, but it has been estimated as at least 100 per cent from c. 1780 to 1841.[7] This would make it comparable with the rate of increase in England and Wales at the same time. The increase was due neither to a falling death rate nor to immigration. On the contrary, emigration was simultaneously on the increase: between 1780 and 1845 c. 1,140,000

---

5. Beckett, p. 291.
6. This is not to say that Britain did not have agrarian problems of its own; see for example E.J. Hobsbawm and G. Rudé, Captain Swing (London 1969).
7. K.H. Connell, The Population of Ireland 1750-1845 (Oxford 1950), estimates the population in round figures as numbering 4,753,000 in 1791; it had increased to 6,802,000 by 1821, 7,767,000 by 1831 and 8,175,000 by 1841.

people emigrated to the United States and Canada alone.[8]
K.H. Connell's thesis is that the "unusually rapid growth
of population must be attributed very largely to the increase of fertility that followed earlier marriage".[9] And
the possibility of marriage stood in direct relationship
to the availability of land.

Population explosion and the subdivision of tenant holdings went hand in hand. After 1793, with the ad-
vent of the forty shilling freeholder vote, landlords divided their property into small holdings "thereby increasing their rents and political influence".[10] Thereafter
subdivision gathered momentum up to the time of the great
famine, and small holdings had progressively to support
more and more people. In 1841, 45 per cent of all holdings were between one and five acres. The Devon Commis-
sioners made it clear that "almost all those with 7 acres
or less, which means over one-third of the farmers, had
too little land".[11]

The peasantry were the victims of economic circumstances over which they had no control. Two points
must be borne in mind in this connection: "practically all
were forced to eke a living from the soil and, furthermore, ... these peasants were not owners but merely occupiers".[12] Owing to the lack of industrial opportunity,
the peasant evicted from his holding had only two choices,
emigration or starvation. The desire to hold on to the
land and the pressure of population upon it were therefore
equally intense. From 1785 to 1815, when the grain trade
was very profitable, the peasants were permitted to lease
land and laws were passed to encourage tillage. It was in
this period that the middleman system expanded greatly:
many owners were absentees who rented their estates to
speculators, and these in turn let out their leaseholds in
small portions to the peasants. During the war years Ire-

8. W.F. Adams, Ireland and Irish Emigration to the New World from
    1815 to the Famine (New Haven, Conn. 1932).
9. Connell, p. 248.
10. T.W. Freeman, Pre-Famine Ireland, p. 15.
11. ibid., p. 58.
12. J.E. Pomfret, The Struggle for Land in Ireland 1800-1923 (Prince-
    ton, N.J. 1930), p. ix.

land remained comparatively prosperous, but after 1815 a decay set in. In the period when tillage was profitable there had been a tremendous increase in the number of small holdings, and a correspondingly rapid increase in population, but after 1815 a reconversion to arable land became necessary for the landlords. Grain prices went down, and when landlords refused to decrease their rents many well-to-do tenant farmers collapsed. The landlords did not escape in the general depression, but the peasantry were the main victims. As large farms were withdrawn from cultivation, many lost the employment which had supplemented the income from their small holdings and had paid their rent. In order to secure themselves an income landlords often had to lease their lands to graziers, which meant the consolidation of small holdings and the eviction from large estates of hordes of small tenants. From 1815 onwards, landlords and tenants thus had interests which were diametrically opposed. This conflict is reflected in the rise in agrarian outrage.

Agriculture in early nineteenth century Ireland was in a very primitive state. Exorbitant rents, the lack of encouragement to improve the land, and the nature of the leases between landlord and tenant "made it all but impossible for the average tenant to cultivate his holding properly".[13] Land was at such a premium that the landlord found it more profitable to let his land to the highest bidder than to negotiate with the tenant when a lease expired. Consequently, rack-renting caused increasing poverty and prevented income from being used to replenish the soil. Only in Ulster was it a custom to allow for improvements to a holding: in the rest of Ireland, far from receiving compensation for improvements, the tenant often found his rent increased at the expiry of his lease. Tenants therefore had no motive to improve the land, and many did not even manure or drain. Nor did the majority of landlords themselves attempt to introduce new agricultural techniques on to their estates.

---

13. _ibid._, p. 19.

As has already been indicated, the tenant was in a very disadvantageous position as far as the terms of his lease were concerned. Most tenancies went from year to year. In 1780 Arthur Young had suggested a reasonable tenancy of twenty-one years, a fair rent, and some compensation for improvements as the only way of bettering the state of agriculture in Ireland. Short tenancies made rack-renting possible and discouraged the implementation of improvements. But Young's sage advice went unheeded. The modern historian John E. Pomfret concurs fully in Young's analysis when he writes that the Irish land system "was an immediate cause of Irish poverty and from its toils the peasants could not escape. Rack rents reduced them to the margin of subsistence; the law in regard to improvements deprived them of hope; and the insecurity of their tenure kept them in a state of terror".[14]

At this stage the tenants had no champions. Daniel O'Connell utilized their massive numbers in his fight for Catholic Emancipation[15] but he never took up the land question; after 1829 he devoted his energies to fighting for repeal of the Act of Union. Emancipation, however, meant little or nothing to the tenants: in fact the 1829 act deprived freehold tenants of the vote, and as they no longer justified their existence they were unceremoniously, indeed brutally, cleared from the land. In 1828 they numbered 191,000; in 1830, 14,200.[16]

Added to the discontent caused by economic hardships was the burden of tithe. Tithe was paid to what the majority considered a heretical and alien church. Theoretically, tithe was a charge upon land which should have been included in the assessment of rent, but "in practice, most Irish landlords exacted the utmost that the land would bear, and, so far as the tenant was concerned, tithe was an unjust and additional burden".[17] Resistance to tithe was common in the early part of the nineteenth century but the "tithe war", organized resistance on a national scale,

14. ibid., pp. 22-23.
15. Cf. ch. I, p. 19.
16. Pomfret, p. 15.
17. Beckett, p. 295.

did not come until the 1830's. It came then because of
the sense of power felt by the Catholic clergy after the
successful Emancipation struggle. With the adoption of
reform legislation in 1838, tithe ceased to be a subject
of popular agitation.

The peasants were powerless to prevent their own
decline into further poverty. They organized themselves
in secret societies and revenge was taken on a local level;
but landlords and agents suffered less than those peasants
who leased land from which others had been evicted. Although they caused considerable damage, agrarian societies
could not and did not become a decisive factor in the determination of Irish affairs.

Meanwhile the landlord class exploited its political influence to secure legislation which strengthened it against
the peasantry[18] and ignored constructive measures. The
London Government was not unaware of the problems: between
1800 and 1833 it is said that "no less than 114 commissions
and 60 select committees had investigated the state of Ireland".[19] It would have been entirely feasible for the Government to intervene in order to increase the quality of
agriculture; this would have meant a redistribution of the
soil in the tenants' favour. However, the sacred rights
of property and the prevailing doctrine of laissez-faire
made this kind of intervention politically impossible, although significant steps were taken to help the landlords.
Another solution would perhaps have been to increase the
amount of land under cultivation, but this also remained
largely untried, and even Pitt's proposed scheme of assist-
ed emigration to Canada had been rejected by the Cabinet
in 1815. Some landlords did indeed encourage their tenants

---

18. Three acts passed between 1816 and 1820 actually helped to sim-
    plify the process of eviction.
19. Pomfret, p. 28.

to emigrate, but they failed to induce sufficiently large numbers to do so.[20]

The Government had, in short, no remedial policy and merely adopted measures at times of particular distress, distributing money through relief agencies (often suspected by the people of being Protestant proselytizing organizations), or advancing money for public works in order to provide employment. Current economic doctrine and attachment to the Malthusian thesis prevented the necessary radical measures from being implemented. Thus the rapacity of the landlords, the powerlessness of the peasants and the negligence of the Government, all added to the innate economic weakness of Ireland, caused misery and poverty to prevail in the country and made the great famine inevitable. The majority of Irishmen lived off the land, and in ever increasing numbers they lived on the brink of destitution. Most of them relied on the potato for food, and when the potato crop failed, as it had done already in 1817 and 1821, there was famine in certain areas. The great famine of the 1840's was, however, particularly harrowing in its effect because the crop failed all over Ireland and the failure was repeated in successive years.[21] The country had never been particularly peaceful or prosperous, but the great famine surely represents the lowest point in its history.

B. THE SOCIAL STRUCTURE

All classes and types of people in late eighteenth and early nineteenth century Ireland appear in Carleton's pages: landlord, agent and tenant, priest and parson, schoolmaster, politician, tailor and merchant. However, Carleton confines his description and analysis to the tenant family,

---

20. The tenants' reluctance to leave could have been due partly to a fear of leaving the land and partly to opposition from the Roman Catholic clergy. By and large the clergy opposed emigration schemes in the years of greatest distress (1845-49). See O. MacDonagh, "The Irish Catholic Clergy and Emigration during the Great Famine" Irish Historical Studies V (1946-47), pp. 287-302.
21. Beckett, pp. 336-337.

its relationships with society and with those placed in authority over it. It is important to emphasize that the individual and the family are always treated in the context of rural society as a whole, and that Carleton is interested in characterizing the typical Irish peasant rather than any single person or group; the same principle is also applied to the description of such other elements in the rural population as may appear.

Carleton's rural society is strictly hierarchically ordered, almost feudal, and although its members may move up a step or two like the Connell family,[1] or down a step or two like the M'Carthys,[2] the order of precedence is very rigid. At the top of the social scale stand the trinity of powers which most concern the peasantry in their daily lives. The priest and parson represent religious authority, magistrate and exciseman the civil authority, and the landlord and his agent a complex of powers which determine the livelihood of the peasant community. Next on the scale of being are those who are not attached to the land, government or church, but who are nevertheless held in great respect by the peasants. The schoolmasters and the well-to-do merchants and townspeople fit into this category. Then come the peasantry themselves, by far the most numerous, and although they are regarded by their overlords as one class, they see themselves as constituting several classes. However much their living conditions may vary, they are nevertheless bound together by the occupation rather than the ownership of the land.

Anthropologists have had difficulty in defining "peasantry", but Robert Redfield settles for a definition of this class as people who are "small producers for their own consumption ... who make a living and have a way of life through cultivation of the land" and for whom "their agriculture is a livelihood and a way of life, not a busi-

---

1. In "The Geography of an Irish Oath", first published in TS[2] (1833); reprinted in Works II.
2. In "Tubber Derg or the Red Well" (1833).

ness for profit".[3] It is in this sense that Carleton uses
the term "peasantry". Above them on the social ladder
stand the gentry and beneath them the landless labourers
and mendicants, but characters from either of these groups
appear only on the periphery of Carleton's stories and are
seen largely from the point of view of the middle group.
Furthermore, Carleton's principal personae and examples
are drawn from this middle group, which remains constantly
in place. The gentry may travel to Paris or London, the
landless labourers may migrate, but the tenant is the
backbone of society around whom everything seems to re-
volve in Carleton's world. When this group begins to emigrate in large numbers, to Carleton's mind the very fabric
of society is rent.[4]

Within the middle, landholding group Carleton describes several degrees of social circumstances. Pride of
place in the peasant hierarchy is enjoyed by the comparatively comfortable and wealthy tenant-farmer like Mr. La-
nigan of "The Poor Scholar". The next category consists
of those who work for a modest sufficiency, like Phaddhy
Sheemus Phaddhy in "The Station". Then come those peasants who have sunk into poverty and wretchedness through
their laziness and ignorance, like the family in "Larry
M'Farland's Wake",[5] or who are poor through no fault of
their own, like the families of "The Poor Scholar" and
"Tubber Derg or the Red Well". Lowest on the tenant scale
is placed the vast army of cottiers, represented by such
rogues as Phelim O'Toole, who hold small portions of land
at rents fixed by competition and whose lives are a constant
fight for survival. These various groups are very conscious of their status and anxious to preserve it. Generally speaking they do not socialize or marry outside of
their own "class".

However, the peasantry are by no means socially
isolated. As Redfield says, they "look to and are influ-

3. Peasant Society and Culture: An Anthropological Approach to Civi-
   lization (Chicago 1956), pp. 26-27.
4. Cf. "The Fair of Emyvale" Illustrated London Magazine I (1853);
   and The Emigrants of Ahadarra. A Tale of Irish Life (London and
   Belfast 1848), reprinted in Works II.
5. TS[1] (1830); reprinted in Works II.

enced by gentry or townspeople whose way of life is like theirs but in a more civilised form".[6] They are in fact peasants partly by reason "of their long-established interdependence with gentry and townspeople".[7] And in discussing Carleton's presentation of the Irish peasantry one must also take into account their colonial status, and the influence exerted upon them by the culture and way of life of the colonist. The latter added another element to the peasants' self-definition. They were unlike the gentry (and the townspeople) in that they rented and worked the land. They were also unlike the gentry in that many of the latter were of English or Scottish extraction and professed a different (heretical) religion.

The large town and the city play no direct part in Carleton's stories of the peasantry. The village or the country town with its shops and pubs is the focal point of the community's commercial life, where the people go to the fair to sell their produce, to drink and to engage in faction and party fights. To Barney Branagan Dublin is "the great metropolis of Ireland",[8] a city to which most of the peasantry never travel. It is a faraway place, full of evil and danger, where simple people like themselves would be cheated and regarded as fools. Barney himself once travelled to Dublin and inadvertently made his fortune there, and he beguiles away many of the long winter nights telling stories about the city. Dublin houses the magnificent residences of some of the landlords, but it is an alien world and when the peasants are forced to leave the land they travel to America or England rather than to Dublin. It is the small town, then, rather than the city with which the peasant has his dealings. Besides being the centre of commerce it houses the assizes and the gaol, and while the people are dependent on it they are also suspicious of it.

The gentry had much more power over the peasantry than the townspeople had, and indeed it is the gentry to

6. Peasant Society and Culture, p. 31.
7. ibid., p. 37.
8. "The Misfortunes of Barney Branagan" DUM XVII (1841), p. 598.

whom Carleton points as the potential leaders and protectors of the people; but his image of them is curiously imprecise. It has justly been said of Carleton that while his portraits of the peasantry are vivid and realistic, he was totally incapable of portraying the wealthier classes.[9] In his work they are presented in absolute terms, either very good or very bad, and their style of life and manner of speaking, insofar as they are represented, are thoroughly implausible. More refined and genteel than the peasantry, their actions are less motivated and less comprehensible. To the peasant Carleton, the gentry were indeed creatures from another order of being, and in this sense his representation of them is just. He saw them as the peasantry did and portrayed them from their tenants' point of view.

Sir Jonah Barrington was a typical representative of the class to which Carleton appealed. His father had been a landlord in pre-Union days, and in his Personal Sketches[10] Barrington reveals the attitude of the gentry of those days towards their peasantry. In this way he serves as an independent corroborator of Carleton's testimony. Barrington was a member of Parliament in the time of Grattan when the "Protestant Nation" was in its heyday. He took great pride in being "a sound Protestant, without bigotry; and a hereditary royalist, without ultraism".[11] His loyalties lay with the Protestant constitution, but he was typical of many aristocrats of the time in that he considered himself to be first an Irishman and second a staunch Protestant royalist. Therefore he resented any attempts by England to direct Irish affairs, and in landlord-tenant affairs he adopted a thoroughly patriarchal stance.

 In the golden days of Barrington's youth, before the Union, "a kind Irish landlord then reigned despotic in the ardent affections of the tenantry, their pride and pleasure being to obey and support him ...",[12] and "good

---

9. Baker, The History of the English Novel VII, p. 46.
10. Personal Sketches of his Own Times, 2v. (London 1827); I quote from the second (revised) edition, 2v. (London 1830).
11. Barrington I, p. xi.
12. ibid., p. 5.

landlords and attached peasantry were then spread over the entire face of Ireland ...".[13] Very much in Carleton's manner, Barrington finds the present state of Ireland wanting, and relations between the classes disturbing to say the least. In Barrington's youth the landlord had lived among his people, whom he loved and protected, and the peasantry in their turn offered him unadulterated affection and unquestioning obedience. The lord of the manor lived in a high rollicking style, he hunted recklessly and was hospitable and generous to a fault. This was accepted behaviour for the landlord, and a gentleman who did not live up to his role disappointed the peasantry. This can be seen from another recorder of the manners of the period, Maria Edgeworth, whose Thady Quirk is astonished at the meanness of Sir Murtagh.[14] The landlord's sense of honour was so delicate that he would "call out" any man he suspected of slighting him. As the tenant was the landlord's property, as it were, to injure a tenant was to injure the landlord.

But these days were long past, and now hostility prevailed between landlords and their tenants. Barrington lays the blame squarely on the landlords themselves: "If the landlords had continued the same, the tenantry would not have altered".[15] In the first place, "the grandsons of those joyous and vigorous sportsmen"[16] have become foppish and effete. Secondly, they live their dissipated lives in the salons and coffee houses of London or Paris and leave their estates in the hands of middlemen. The tenant now "has no master to employ, no guardian to protect him! — pining, and sunk in the lowest state of want and wretchedness, sans food, sans covering, sans every thing, — he rushes forlorn and desperate into the arms of destruction, which in all its various shapes stands ready to receive him".[17]

Unlike Carleton, Barrington was an opponent of the Union which he regarded as the ultimate cause of the

---

13. ibid., p. 43.
14. Castle Rackrent (London 1800).
15. Barrington I, p. 51.
16. ibid., p. 72.
17. Barrington II, pp. 62-63.

disturbed state of Ireland. The years since the Union had been years "of beggary and of disturbance", [18] not least because they had resulted in increased absenteeism. He strongly urges landlords to live upon their lands and not to employ middlemen. If they treat their tenants well but firmly they will be as tractable as lambs. This is very reminiscent of Carleton's advice. Being essentially a pragmatist and a politician Barrington displays no great faith in education: it is "a very good thing in its proper place, but a sorry substitute for food; and I know the Irish well enough to say they never will be taught peace upon an empty stomach". [19] He pronounces in a characteristically no-nonsense manner: "Neither honourable intentions, nor Sunday-schools, nor the four rules of arithmetic, nor Bible societies, can preserve a people from starving ...". [20] Nor has he the slightest patience with religious divisions, his own religion being one of policy rather than of conviction. In contrast, Carleton lays great weight on religion, Sunday schools and Bible societies. He sees Roman Catholicism as a hindrance to the "moral education" and thereby the more responsible social behaviour of the peasantry.

Neither author questions the justice of the social structure, however much they may criticize its abuses. The Tory notion of the union of aristocrat and peasant, in order to preserve the old relationships and values in the face of an advancing bourgeoisie, is found in both Barrington and Carleton, the self-elected spokesmen of their respective classes. Barrington is unusual in his outspoken criticism of the behaviour of his peers, but his basic attitude to the peasantry is the same as theirs. Both authors were Liberal Conservatives, convinced of the innate simplicity and good-will of the peasantry and of the innate generosity and honour of the gentry, although Barrington had his serious doubts about the younger generation. Barrington's conviction that "whatever is, is

---

18. ibid., p. 267.
19. ibid., p. 269.
20. ibid.

right"[21] was strengthened by the French Revolution and the 1798 rebellion in Ireland, and this conviction may be said to have been shared by Carleton. The unfortunate weakness in their position was that they based their conviction on a conception of the Ireland of their younger days, even though thirty-four years separated them. Nostalgia is a sentiment common to the writings of both.

The contrast between the life of gentry and peasantry was of course enormous. They differed in race, religion, culture, sometimes even in language; their only common bond was the land. On the material level peasant life varied from misery to comfortable subsistence: in this regard, as André Boué points out,[22] Carleton's peasants were better off than most peasants of the day. Nevertheless, he was very much aware of the material circumstances of the majority of the peasants, and he evidently wanted his readers to acquire a complete picture of prevailing living conditions. To this end he goes into great detail concerning such matters as homes, dress and food. For example he takes the reader with him into the village of Findramore, which is the scene of "The Hedge School". The village consists of "a range of low thatched houses on each side of the road"; smoke may be observed curling up from the houses, not only through the makeshift chimneys, but also "bursting out of the doors and windows; the panes of the latter being mostly stopped at other times with old hats and rags, were now left entirely open for the purpose of giving it free escape". Before each of these houses or cabins is a dunghill "with its concomitant sink of green, rotten water" in which a pig may perhaps be wallowing luxuriantly. The village is not entirely composed of such cabins: here and there may be seen "a stout, comfortable-looking farm-house, with ornamental thatching and well-glazed windows", which presents every appearance of substance and comfort. Most of the dwellings, however, have the outward characteristics of the cabins.[23]

---

21. Barrington I, p. 270.
22. William Carleton (1973) Part 2, ch. 2.
23. Works II, pp. 822-823.

In "Phelim O'Toole's Courtship"[24] Carleton takes the reader inside a peasant cabin, one of "the humblest description" where "the catalogue of ... furniture may appear to our English readers very miserable". Yet Carleton adds: "if every cabin in Ireland were equally comfortable, the country would be comparatively happy".[25] It can be seen from the following description that Carleton took an interest in the material life of the peasantry, and that his antiquarian eye for detail was fully employed. The floor of the cabin, he says,

> was about sixteen feet by twelve; its furniture rude and scanty. To the right of the fire was a bed, the four posts of which ran up to the low roof; it was curtained with straw mats, with the exception of an opening about a foot and a half wide on the side next the fire, through which those who slept in it passed. A little below the foot of the bed were ranged a few shelves of deal, supported by pins of wood driven into the wall. These constituted the dresser. In the lower end of the house stood a potato-bin, made up of stakes driven into the floor, and wrought with strong wicker-work. Tied to another stake beside this bin stood a cow, whose hinder parts projected so close to the door, that those who entered the cabin were compelled to push her out of the way ... Above the door in the inside, almost touching the roof, was the hen-roost, made also of wicker-work; and opposite the bed, on the other side of the fire, stood a meal-chest, its lid on a level with the little pane of glass which served as a window. An old straw chair, a few stools, a couple of pots, some wooden vessels and crockery, completed the furniture of the house.[26]

24. TS² (1833); reprinted in Works II.
25. Works II, pp. 1055-56.
26. ibid.

The appearance of the people is concomitant with the state of their dwellings. Typical inhabitants of a village like Findramore, which Carleton takes as representative of the villages to be found in Ireland, might be "a stout-looking woman, with watery eyes, and a yellow cap hung loosely upon her matted locks", or "a toil-worn man, without coat or waistcoat; his red, muscular, sunburnt shoulder peering through the remnant of a skirt [read shirt], mending his shoes with a piece of twisted flax ... or, perhaps, sewing two footless stockings ... to his coat, as a substitute for sleeves".[27] The children of the cabin present a still more tattered appearance. Phelim O'Toole's childhood apparel was "in great measure, the national costume of some hundred thousand young Hibernians in his rank of life ...". In his infancy he could be seen running about in "a cast-off pair of his father's nether-garments ... the wrong side foremost", or "in a pair of stockings which covered him from his knee-pans to his haunches, where, in the absence of waistbands, they made a pause — a breach existing from that to the small of his back".[28]

Carleton is careful to emphasize that these are the conditions of life of the "humblest class", the cottiers. Their diet consisted largely of buttermilk and potatoes; the pig was kept to pay the rent. The fast disappearing class of yeoman-farmers lived in a solidly comfortable way, ate a varied diet and dressed decently. Carleton loves to evoke the comfortable cheer in farmers' houses, with bacon hanging round the fire to smoke, bread baking in the oven and the pantry full of good things. Though the majority lived in a humble way, Carleton echoes Barrington in suggesting that they remained cheerful enough as long as they had sufficient to eat.

It was natural that the living conditions of the peasantry should be at least implicitly contrasted with those of the upper classes. Although Carleton never describes the interior of big houses or the daily lives of their inmates, he gives an impression of tables covered

27. "The Hedge School", Works II, p. 823.
28. "Phelim O'Toole's Courtship", Works II, p. 1038.

with crystal and silver, sumptuous apartments, excellent
food and wine and genteel amusements. His gentry are not
the riotous sportsmen of Barrington's memories, but refined and accomplished gentlemen and gentlewomen. True to
the perspective of the stories, Carleton presents them
only as their tenants see them. They do not work the land,
and they travel to faraway places. To the peasant they are
almost another, higher species.

This distance had existed from time immemorial.
As Oscar Handlin remarks, the lord of the manor "was expected to be proud and luxurious, but humane and generous;
just as the peasant was expected to be thrifty and respectful. Even bitterly burdensome privileges were not open to
dispute".[29] Therefore, as Redfield emphasizes, to describe
relations between landlord and tenant as between exploiter
and exploited is not sufficient.[30] This polarized analysis,
while essentially true, merely describes the basis of the
socio-economic system, and adds little to the clarification
either of the peasantry's conception of themselves or of
the role played by the gentry in shaping their lives. Margaret MacCurtain observes that "There is a whole range of
feelings — superiority, contempt, admiration, prestige, in-
adequacy, self-sufficiency — to be experienced by the peasant. There are examples of goodness and excellence to be
emulated, of baseness and wickedness to be avoided, in the
exchanges between peasant and élite".[31] The peasantry are
in part defined by the presence of the gentry, and unless
the landlord abuses his privileges to the extent that the
tenant's livelihood is threatened, the tenant will not
complain.

Carleton, however, restricts his comments on the
gentry-tenant relationship to the respect felt by the tenant for his landlord, and the affection of the tenant for
a good landlord. By living on his estate the landlord
could do much to ease the life of his tenant, and by making
the tenant feel secure he could do much to ease the disturbances of rural society.

29.   The Uprooted (Boston 1951), p. 23.
30.   Peasant Society and Culture, p. 64.
31.   "Pre-Famine Peasantry in Ireland", pp. 189-190.

Oscar Handlin[32] has described what in his opinion
constitute the fundamental characteristics of peasant society the world over. These are a bond with the land from
which their livelihood comes and which has been in their
family for generations; an intense attachment to the local
community by reason of common pursuits, mutual aid and in-
termarital ties; and a conception of marriage as function-
al, and of the family as an economic unit in which each
member possesses a clearly defined role. The peasant lived
within this structure and from it his values naturally
sprang. Land and family were preeminent. In Carleton's
description of peasant life such values are clearly to be
seen and he goes to some lengths to demonstrate peasant
values and the peasant code of honour to his English readers. His peasants are closely attached to the land (although as Boué remarks they are seldom seen working it),
but the almost mystical relationship suggested by John Wilson Foster[33] does not appear in Carleton's pages. It may
very well be that this mystical bond existed, but the characteristics of English peasants in this regard, as reported by Redfield, were very probably shared by Irish peasants
also. Their bond was practical rather than mystical; when
evicted, or in time of blight, they starved.

Carleton's peasants are attached in a remote way to the
idea of national independence; to them it means no great
upheaval in the social structure, but rather the exchange
of Anglo-Irish Protestant landlords for native Irish Catholic landlords. Carleton could not understand these particular loyalties, doubtless because he left the colonial di-
mension out of his analysis. The peasants' loyalty to a
good landlord is undivided, but even more endearing is the
persistent love and loyalty they show their families. Within the peasant family mutual aid and support know no bounds.
Familial loyalty goes beyond the nuclear and into the extended family, and even further into loyalty towards faction and party.

---

32. The Uprooted, pp. 7-14.
33. Forces and Themes in Ulster Fiction, p. 5.

Carleton's peasants usually marry for love, but
the high incidence of elopement in his stories points to
the money basis in marriage contracts. In this the peasantry were of course no different from other classes at
the same time. There are a great number of scenes of marriage "bartering" in Carleton's writings. For example,
Phelim O'Toole and his father give due notice that they
will come "courting" to Peggy Donovan. They bring whiskey
with them, as was the custom, and arrange for a match-maker
to make his appearance. Phelim's mother advises them not
to make a match "except they give that pig they have".[34]
Carleton remarks later:

> These humble courtships very much resemble the
> driving of a bargain between two chapmen; for,
> indeed, the closeness of the demands on the one
> side, and the reluctance of concession on the
> other, are almost incredible. Many a time has a
> match been broken up by a refusal on the one part,
> to give a slip of a pig, or a pair of blankets,
> or a year-old calf. These are small matters in
> themselves, but they are of importance to those
> who, perhaps, have nothing else on earth with
> which to begin the world.[35]

Essentially the same but on a higher economic level is the
hard headed — and hard hearted — bargaining between Ellish
Connell and Father Mulcahy in "The Geography of an Irish
Oath" about a marriage contract between Ellish's son and
the priest's niece. Ellish knows the reason for the great
attention which the priest has paid to her family of late,
and when he broaches the question of what Dan Connell would
expect as a fortune with an accomplished girl of respectable connections, she staggers him by demanding a thousand
pounds and by brushing aside the value of such accomplish-
ments as spoken Irish and playing the bagpipes. She finally agrees to take only four hundred pounds, and when the
much shaken priest departs, she tells her husband that "Four

---

34. "Phelim O'Toole's Courtship", Works II, p. 1054.
35. ibid., p. 1055.

hundhre wid a priest's niece ... is before double the money wid any other. Don't you know, that when they set up for themselves, he can bring the custom of the whole parish to them?"[36]

Carleton in no way admires Ellish Connell's materialism, but he evidently enjoys the sight of her driving a hard bargain with the parish priest. On the other hand, he would hardly have considered her action particularly dishonourable; indeed, the whole tendency of his stories is to show that the peasant code of honour is extremely commendable. The great majority of the peasants are honest. They fight fairly, if brutally. Being generous to a fault, they will beggar themselves to help a neighbour and will expect the same assistance in time of trouble. Respectability, decency and self-sufficiency are highly valued, and they are very ashamed when they cannot support themselves and have to take to begging. Carleton points out all of these virtues with a great deal of pride as being the true nature of the Irish peasant, unknown to the generality of his readers.

The "hinges" between the two distinct rural groups of gentry and peasantry are those individuals who do not live off the land and who know more of the outside world than do the peasantry.[37] It is useful in treating Carleton's description of rural life to regard such figures as the priest and the schoolmaster as "hinge" figures, not least because it may help to explain the esteem in which the peasantry held them. Redfield remarks that "peasants know of and are dependent upon more civilised people" and that the peasant is "not self-sufficient in his moral or intellectual life".[38] He aspired to these "hinge" positions for his sons because in them lay knowledge and power. This is not to suggest that the peasant did not have respect for his own way of life. He was traditional and conservative to the core and could not envisage a society in which gentry and peasantry

---

36. "The Geography of an Irish Oath", Works II, p. 944.
37. Redfield, pp. 43-44.
38. ibid., p. 133.

did not exist. But he was humble, and while setting store by his own mode of life was prepared to admit its limitations and the superiority of the clever and the educated. Furthermore, he took simple pride in seeing one of his own class enter this category. Education and the priesthood, on which Carleton's peasants placed such a high value, may therefore be explained both in terms of a colonized people seeking to redeem their self respect, and in terms of the identifiable characteristics of peasantry the world over. They respected the priest, for example, not only because he had supported them in times past and was the minister of their religion, but also because he was a man of knowledge who linked them to the higher life.

André Boué emphasizes that Carleton writes from his memories of the past, and that although he lived in Dublin for fifty years the city hardly ever enters his work. Clogher and its neighbourhood provide the setting for those stories of peasant life in which realism is dominant. However, since Carleton is concerned to present the Irish peasantry as a whole, the Clogher valley serves him as a symbolic decor which he adapts as the exigencies of his work demand.[39] It is true that Carleton wishes to preserve a picture of the peasantry of former times, but his nostalgic backward look is used to point to the sad contrast between the Ireland of his youth and the Ireland of his maturity. At both these stages the social structure is the same.

It has been said of Ireland in the 1840's that "With O'Connell's moral guidance in the political sphere, with the motivation towards embourgeoisement taking hold of the Irish countryside through the educational system of an indigenous Catholic Church, it only needed the dramatic intervention of the Famine to bring about the decline of the peasantry".[40] Carleton's work is valuable in that it not only preserves the characteristics of this vanished society but reveals — as will be seen from the remaining two

39. William Carleton (1973) Part 2, ch. I.
40. MacCurtain, pp. 197-198.

sections of this chapter — the inevitability of its dissolution through forces at work within its structure.

C. LANDLORDS, AGENTS AND THE LAND SYSTEM

The stories of Carleton reflect a constant preoccupation
with the social and economic relationships prevailing between landlord and tenant in the Ireland of his time. The
power of Irish landlords over their tenantry was, and always had been, very great. In 1780 Arthur Young had observed:

> It must be apparent to every traveller, through
> that country, that the labouring poor are treated
> with harshness, and in all respects so little con-
> sidered, that their want of importance seems a
> perfect contrast to their situation in England
> ... The landlord of an irish estate, inhabited by
> roman catholicks, is a sort of despot who yields
> obedience in whatever concerns the poor, to no law
> but that of his will ... and what is liberty but
> a farce, and a jest if its blessings are received
> as the favour of kindness and humanity, instead of
> being the inheritance of RIGHT?[1]

The situation had not altered radically a half century later when Carleton published his Traits and Stories. By 1830
Roman Catholics had been relieved of most of their disabi-
lities, but the landlord still had considerable power over
his tenants and the legislature made no attempt to curb
this power. Some landlords were humane, others oppressive,
but most seem to have been indifferent to their tenants.
    Catholics had been given the opportunity to vote
in 1793, and the forty shilling freeholders ("forties")
were a potentially powerful voting group. In "An Irish
Election in the Time of the Forties" (1847) Carleton shows
how this group were manipulated by their landlords, being
driven to the polls like sheep to vote en bloc for the

---

1. A Tour in Ireland Part 2, pp. 29-30.

landlord's chosen candidate. He succeeds in conveying the atmosphere of such an election, characterized by "systematic corruption equally gross and ingenious, and ... gregarious and brutal degradation". The lower classes were "seized upon by a spirit of licentiousness and tumult, that was agreeable to their reckless habits, their utter ignorance, the low moral standard by which they were regulated, as well as by the unparalleled political corruption which animated and characterized their superiors". But the morals of the peasantry, however low they may have been at such times, were neither as low nor as objectionable as those of the gentry who grossly manipulated their "ignorant, semi-barbarous, destitute, whipped, and trampled-on serfs ...".[2] While they continued to obey their landlords the "forties" retained their votes, but as soon as their political potential was realized they were disenfranchized. The Emancipation struggle had proved how dangerous the vote was in the hands of Catholic tenants, and accordingly the 1829 bill, although it gave Catholics the right to sit in Parliament, at the same time raised the property qualification and thus effectively prevented the majority from exercising direct political influence.[3]

The type of landlord who figures so largely in "An Irish Election" is not to be found in the earlier stories. Most of Carleton's landlords are absentees and ignorant of their tenants' way of life. They are, however, neither evil nor vicious and their sins are those of omission rather than commission. The real villains of the rural scene are the agents, or middlemen, who treat the tenants harshly and make an unreasonable profit out of them.

Although Carleton rebukes landlords as a class, the landlords who actually appear in the early stories are invariably good and wise. They are model landlords who live on their estates among their tenants; they are God-fearing and thoroughly respectable gentlemen; and they are fair

---

2. DUM XXX (1847), p. 176.
3. Electoral manipulation and mob violence at the scene of an election were of course not peculiar to Ireland. For the situation in mid nineteenth-century England see for example N. Gash, Politics in the Age of Peel (London 1953), ch. 6.

magistrates who know their people and are trusted and respected by them. They mix with their tenants as a landlord should: Captain Wilson comes to the feast at the end
of "The Station" and carries on a lively conversation with
Father Philemy while the humble folk gape. Shane Fadh recalls how the much respected Squire, "landlord both to my
father and father-in-law",[4] had come to his wedding many
years previously to wish the young couple well and to wel-
come them as tenants. Like Squire Dickson of "Larry M'Farland's Wake" and Mr. Eccles who appears in "The Geography
of an Irish Oath", this Squire was "an encouraging and indulgent landlord",[5] who helped his tenants to cultivate
and improve their holdings as long as they were honest and
industrious. Similarly, Mr. Eccles will not accept a sus-
piciously high rent from Peter Connell; if forced to meet
such a high yearly sum Connell would not be able to improve
the land, and Eccles knows that this would be in the interest of neither party to the transaction. Such landlords
are indulgent to those who have fallen on hard times:
Squire Dickson does not evict the M'Farlands when they
cannot pay their rent. The results of such wise behaviour
are seen in the comfortable living standards of the majority of the peasantry, their higher standard of morals, and
the harmonious communities over which these landlords pre-
side.

It is clear that Carleton wrote such stories of
peaceful communities and harmony between the classes in order to encourage the landlords of his day to behave in a
more responsible way. His didactic purpose can be seen
very clearly in the stories of "Tubber Derg or the Red
Well" and "The Poor Scholar" and even more clearly in a
note appended to "The Poor Scholar" in the collected edition of Traits and Stories, where he comments sourly that
"the Irish landlords have disentitled themselves to the
favourable notice taken of them in the text".[6]

---

4. "Shane Fadh's Wedding", Works II, p. 702.
5. ibid.
6. "The Poor Scholar", Works II, p. 1126.

Carleton's didactic method is not to cite specific acts of cruelty by the landlords, but rather to demonstrate the harm done when a landlord neglects his tenants and leaves them to the tender mercies of a middleman. Having made his demonstration he then proceeds to lecture the landowning classes on the best way to treat their tenants. Maria Edgeworth had sketched the unhappy consequences of absenteeism for the landlords in The Absentee (1812), and Jonah Barrington had many bitter words to say on the subject in his Personal Sketches (1827). Both of these authors spoke of the unhappy consequences for the tenants, and it is certain that Carleton was influenced by Edgeworth. But whereas she interested herself primarily in the landlord Carleton deals mainly with the tenant. He expounds the subject later at greater length in his novel Valentine M'Clutchy (1845). All three commentators were conservative by temperament and conviction, and wished to turn the clock back to what they agreed were idyllic pre-Union days. It is interesting to note that while admitting that the negligence of the landlords is the ultimate cause of the obvious misery of tenants and the disturbed state of society, they all lay the greatest blame on the middleman. He was the obvious scapegoat.

"Tubber Derg or the Red Well"[7] is set at the end of the Napoleonic wars when the drop in the prices paid for agricultural produce had caused a general depression in Ireland. It relates the sad case history of Owen M'Carthy, a hard-working, honourable farmer whose family had been on the same land for generations. When the slump comes he is unable to meet his rent and determines to seek justice from his landlord. Because he and his family have been such reliable tenants he is convinced that the landlord will remit his rent until the bad times are over. He walks the hundred miles to Dublin, where he is met with indifference from the landlord and is referred to his agent. The agent lies about M'Carthy's character and his soundness as a tenant and finally evicts him. The M'Carthys are forced to take to the shameful road of the mendicant. This

---

7. Cf. ch. I, section D, note 9.

all too common occurrence causes Carleton to launch an attack on bad landlords, the duties they fail to fulfil and their responsibility for the happiness of the tenant and the maintenance of the public peace. It is bad landlordism in general which is to blame for the state of affairs prevailing in the country.

Carleton not only censures negligent landlords for their absenteeism but also criticizes the failure to provide a poor law,[8] although it is on the first of these points that he places by far the greater emphasis. With regard to the latter he gives vent to an almost Dickensian indignation:

> Is it to be thought of with common patience that a person rolling in wealth shall feed upon his turtle, his venison, and his costly luxuries of every description, for which he will not scruple to pay the highest price — that this heartless and selfish man, whether he reside at home or abroad, shall thus unconscionably pamper himself with viands purchased by the toil of the people, and yet not contribute to assist them, when poverty, sickness, or age, throws them upon the scanty support of casual charity?[9]

On the one hand absentee landlords squander abroad the money wrung from their tenants, whom they use merely as a source of income; on the other hand there are certain resident landlords who neglect their tenants almost as much. One instance of the latter's neglect is their refusal to assist mendicants, many of whom are former tenants who have been evicted for non-payment of rent. Carleton claims that the gentry are aware that it is the classes who can least afford to help beggars who support them with food and money; it is fully in keeping with the gentry's inhuman neglect of the poor not to encourage the introduction of a system which would make poor relief compulsory on the landlords. For this reason the state of the country is wretch-

---

8. A poor law was first enacted for Ireland in 1838.
9. Works I, p. 959.

ed, and the landlords are in reality damaging their own interests. The tenants who help paupers are themselves living on the margin of subsistence, and because of this extra burden they cannot pay their rent. As a consequence they are themselves evicted, and thus the landlord loses loyal and reliable tenants.

As well as the purely human and economic results of neglect by landlords, Carleton mentions two other disturbing consequences — the one religious and the other political. Roman Catholics feel compelled by their religion to support the poor, for they consider this a good work which will count towards the remission of sins. From the Protestant point of view this attitude should not be encouraged. More gravely, perhaps, mendicants exert an immoral influence on the class by whom they are supported. They carry stories of the times to come when "heresy" will be defeated and Roman Catholicism exalted. Their hosts listen enthusiastically to such stories, and Carleton asserts that many mendicants had acted as spies and messengers for the 1798 rebels. These evils would be abolished if the gentry would but recognize the necessity of a poor law, as the poor would then be confined to their own parish. Carleton evidently knew the landlords well enough to realize that only an appeal to their self-interest could move them.

Although Carleton cared for the poor and unjustly treated he entertained neither democratic nor republican sentiments. He abhorred the thought of armed rebellion, which the establishment of a republic would certainly imply, and held that the rights of property were sacred. However, while he emphasized the rights, he also emphasized the duties of property. The landlord has a moral duty to help his tenants. If he neglects this duty he breaks the unwritten tenant-landlord contract and the tenant takes understandable, though not excusable action:

> Is it to be wondered at that he, and such as he,
> should, in the misery of his despair, join the
> nightly meetings, be lured to associate himself
> with the incendiary, or seduced to grasp, in the

stupid apathy of wretchedness, the weapon of the
murderer? By neglecting the people; by draining
them, with merciless rapacity, of the means of
life; by goading them under a cruel system of
rack rents, ye become not their natural benefact-
ors, but curses and scourges, nearly as much in
reality as ye are in their opinion.[10]

The lesson to be learnt from this state of affairs is obvious, and Carleton spells it out as a lesson to be learnt
before it is too late. The eleventh hour has come: "Common policy, common sense, and common justice, should induce the Irish landlords to lower their rents according to
the market for agricultural produce, otherwise poverty,
famine, crime, and vague political speculations, founded
upon idle hopes of a general transfer of property, will
spread over and convulse the kingdom".[11]

But the Irish landlords were never to learn this
elementary lesson. Fifty years earlier Arthur Young had
tendered them comparable advice:

> it is manifest that the gentlemen of Ireland never
> thought of a radical cure from overlooking the
> real cause of the disease [agrarian agitation],
> which in fact lay in themselves, and not in the
> wretches they doomed to the gallows. Let them
> change their own conduct entirely, and the poor
> will not long riot. Treat them like men who ought
> to be as free as yourselves: put an end to that
> system of religious persecution which for seventy
> years has divided the kingdom against itself; in
> these two circumstances lies the cure of insur-
> rection, perform them completely, and you will
> have an affectionate poor, instead of oppressed
> and discontented vassals.[12]

These precepts had also been ignored. Although religious
discrimination was less manifest in 1830 than it had been

---

10. ibid., p. 951.
11. ibid., p. 957.
12. A Tour in Ireland Part 2, p. 30.

in Young's time, Catholic Emancipation had not brought any
immediate benefit to the peasantry, who still had to pay
tithes to the clergymen of the Church of Ireland.[13] This
bitterly resented impost is not, however, dealt with in
Carleton's early stories, although it caused a great deal
of agitation in Ireland in the 1830's. Carleton later
wrote about the tithe controversy in his novel The Tithe
Proctor (1849), but at this stage it was the problem of
landlordism to which he attached the greatest importance,
and the policy of rack-renting especially preoccupied him
in this connection.

The ultimate result of rack-renting was to drive
the poorest into mendicancy, and to deprive the country of
the independent class of yeomanry who deemed it more prudent to emigrate before they too were reduced to begging.
This class was dwindling fast, and now there existed only
"the extreme ends of society — the wealthy and the wretched".[14] Carleton maintains that if the yeoman farmers —
"the only men, who ... were capable of becoming the
strength and pride of the country"[15] — had been encouraged
by wise landlords, the poorer tenants would not so easily
have been incited to revolt, since before them they would
have had the example of the independent farmer who had won
his place by industry and thrift. He also maintains that
the landlord is too socially remote ever to act as a spur
to the tenants' ambition in the way that the farmers can.

The agent was the absentee landlord's representative.
Middlemen or agents leased large tracts of land from the
original owner, to whom they paid a fixed sum of rent.
They then proceeded to lease the land in small lots to the
peasantry, whom they could charge whatever rent they
pleased. It was a job often taken on by the "squireens",
small landowners who hoped to make a large profit with

---

13. Cf. pp. 85-86 above.
14. "Tubber Derg or the Red Well", Works I, p. 971.
15. ibid.

little work.[16] The middleman system became more wide-
spread as absenteeism increased, and the system and its
representatives were detested by the peasantry. Few stories of the period contain an account of good and honest
agents. Arthur Young had characterized the agents as follows:

> Living upon the spot, surrounded by their little
> undertenants, they prove the most oppressive spe-
> cies of tyrant that ever lent assistance to the
> destruction of a country. They relet the land,
> at short tenures, to the occupiers of small
> farms; and often give no leases at all. Not sa-
> tisfied with screwing up the rent to the utter-
> most farthing, they are rapacious and relentless
> in the collection of it.[17]

But he added: "... let not the reader misapprehend me; it
is the situation, not the man, that I condemn".[18]

Carleton not only blamed the situation; he also
blamed the man. He respected the landlord class and was
prepared to forgive them, but he felt no such respect for
the middleman. The landlords are soundly berated for
their inhuman neglect of the peasantry in "Tubber Derg",
but it is the agent who is seen to be evil. The most notorious agent in all of Carleton's stories, however, is
Yellow Sam of "The Poor Scholar", who is certainly the model for Valentine M'Clutchy in the novel of that name. It
is interesting to note that the agent is not spoken of in
general terms: unlike the bad landlord the bad agent is
given an identity.

Yellow Sam is typical of all rapacious agents,
and his criminal actions serve as a catalogue of all the
evils of the middleman system. He is agent for the absentee landlord Colonel B—, an essentially good-hearted and
principled man whom he has been cheating for many years.

---

16. That the middleman's hopes of a large profit were not invariably
    realized can be seen from for example F.S.L. Lyons, "Vicissitudes
    of a Middleman in County Leitrim, 1810-27" Irish Historical Stu-
    dies IX (1954-55), pp. 300-318.
17. A Tour in Ireland Part 2, p. 14.
18. ibid., p. 15.

The Colonel has lost much income through Sam's dealings,
but more tragic for both the Colonel and the tenants is
the loss of good-will caused by the incredible scale of
Sam's rapacity and injustice. Sam has exacted such duty
labour from the tenants that his own farms are run at
little expense to himself. The tenants must neglect their
own farms to work for him: if they refuse they are evicted, or their rents are raised, and they have no legal
means of redress. When their natural guardian is not present they are at the mercy of his representative. They
must pay bribes of from ten to fifty guineas when their
leases come up for renewal.[19] These sums are separate
from the usual renewal fee, and even when the tenant has
paid the bribe Sam may still refuse to renew his lease.[20]
He also withholds receipts, thus forcing the tenant to pay
the same rent twice. That Sam could exact such amounts of
money from the tenants reflects their desperation for land
and the pressure of population on the available land: if
one man would not pay what was asked, another would.
Another aspect of the power of an unscrupulous agent is
revealed in the complaint that Sam's dozen or more illegitimate children are provided for from the estate. The
M'Evoy's had been evicted from good land to make room for
Sam's illegitimate daughter and her husband, whom Sam had
promoted to bailiff. The mothers of these children were
presumably tenants' daughters who were too afraid of the
agent's power over their families to refuse him their fa-
vours. Carleton makes no direct comment on this — he went
only as far as the prudishness of contemporary literary
convention would allow him.

Carleton advises landlords to live on their
estates if they can, but failing that never to appoint
needy men as their agents. While he deems agents necessary to the running of an estate, they should be respectable
men who are never placed in a position of absolute power.
In "The Poor Scholar" he points out to the landlords that
many agents make fortunes by cheating both landlord and
tenant: "A history of their conduct would be a black cata-

19. Works II, p. 1120.
20. ibid., p. 1127.

logue of dishonesty, oppression, and treachery".[21] Agents like Yellow Sam are hated by the tenants, to whom they appear as the devil incarnate. It is said of him that he "was born widout a heart, an' carries the black wool in his ears, to keep out the cries of the widows an' the orphans, that are long rotten in their graves through his dark villany!"[22] Lest the reader think that Carleton is exaggerating, he underlines the authenticity of this characterization by a note to the effect that this was actually said of a particular agent who ran two or three estates. Such men could be rooted out, all landlords respected and all tenants happy, if every absentee landlord learnt the lesson the Colonel is forced to learn.

Encouraged by a responsible Catholic curate who has taken an interest in Jimmy M'Evoy, Colonel B— determines to travel to his northern estates to investigate Jimmy's allegations against Yellow Sam. He travels incognito, like Lord Colambre in The Absentee, and collects incriminating evidence against his agent not only from the tenants but also from the neighbouring gentry who can be relied upon to be impartial. It may be safely claimed that Carleton borrowed this device from Maria Edgeworth, but his story reads much more like a documentary than The Absentee. Colambre is given a personality whereas the Colonel is merely an instrument for the conveying of information.

B— finds the big house in a state of decay. It is a symbol not only of the ruin of his lands, but of the decay of his tenants' living conditions and of the natural landlord-tenant relationship — a symbolism which Carleton underlines when he remarks that "that which blights the industry of the tenant — the curse of absenteeism — had also left the marks of ruin stamped upon every object around him". B— begins to learn that absenteeism "constitutes one, perhaps the greatest, portion of Ireland's misery".[23] He is the good landlord who is willing to learn a lesson, and Carleton is much more gentle and conciliatory towards

---

21. ibid., p. 1112.
22. ibid., p. 1076.
23. ibid., p. 1117.

landlords here than he had been in "Tubber Derg". Having
removed his evil agent and caused justice to be done, the
reformed landlord who is now loved by his tenants sets to
work and discovers that he is actually a shrewd man of
business; he had neglected his property more from "want of
consideration" than from "want of feeling".[24] Most absentees are ignorant of their tenants and are content to receive "their half-yearly remittance in due course, without
ever reflecting for a moment upon the situation of those
from whom it [has been] drawn".[25] But the resident gentry
are equally ignorant of their tenants' life and culture so
that it is not absenteeism alone, but ignorance and neglect on the part of landowners generally, which is responsible for the hopeless condition of large sections of
the peasantry and the violent state of society. In other
words Carleton believes not only that landlords have a duty to ensure the proper running of their estates, but that
they should actively promote the welfare and "moral education" of their tenants. He concludes that the peasantry
are not oppressed, and causes the responsible, enlightened
priest to proclaim to Colonel B—:

> There is, to be sure, an outcry about their op-
> pression; but that is wrong. Their indigence and
> ignorance are rather the result of neglect ...
> from the government of the country — from the
> earl to the squireen. They have been taught
> little that is suitable to their stations and du-
> ties in life, either as tenants who cultivate our
> lands, or as members of moral or Christian socie-
> ty.[26]

This identification of priest and landlord as members of
the landowning establishment, with a common interest in
the good behaviour of the peasantry, seems more likely to
be deliberate than to be a mere "slip of the pen".[27] By

---

24. ibid., p. 1125.
25. ibid., p. 1126.
26. ibid., p. 1114 (my underlining).
27. Carleton had revised the story without removing the expression
    and he often removed what he considered would cause offence; cf.
    ch. I, pp. 31-32.

causing the priest to talk to the Colonel as his equal, and to be frank with him about the duties of landlords and the criminal behaviour of some tenants, Carleton may be trying to assure his landowning readership of the good intentions of the Catholic clergy. The story was published in the period of the tithe war, when many Catholic priests were urging tenants not to pay tithe and when the clergy were suspected of wanting to take over the wealth of the country. Carleton, here, and also in "The Funeral and Party Fight", shows the reader responsible priests who are interested in the orderly running of the country and the humane treatment of the ordinary people. They realize the weaknesses of the Irish peasant — his propensity to drunkenness and fighting, his low moral standards — and they join with other established figures of authority in combating these evils. But as men of religion they can adopt the role of the conscience of the establishment, and remind both landlord and tenant of the duties of their stations without wishing to change the structure of society in any way.

Carleton's solution to the miserable state of the country is that the propertied classes should take an interest in their tenants and legislation be passed to aid the destitute: "A rich country and poor inhabitants is an anomaly ... The great secret ... of the dissensions that prevail among us is the poverty of the people ... Let their condition be improved, and the most fertile source of popular tumult and crime is closed".[28] The landlords are the most suitable class to undertake this responsibility. They are the natural protectors of the poor, who expect them to act as their guardians. Apart from fulfilling this natural role and thus protecting the people from abuse and from famine, a landlord who followed the example of Colonel B— would find "that in promoting [the tenants'] welfare, and instructing them in their duties, he was more his own benefactor than theirs".[29]

From the tone of "Tubber Derg" and "The Poor Scholar" it is obvious that in 1833 Carleton believed that

28. "The Poor Scholar", Works II, p. 1127.
29. ibid., p. 1126.

if the landlords were handled properly they would respond to encouragement and improve their habits. He had always disapproved of violence, and was of the opinion that moderation and proper respect for property on the part of tenants, and humanity and a proper appreciation of their own interests on the part of landlords, could be combined into a force that would work for the benefit of the country as a whole. In this he underestimated both the rapacity and short-sightedness of the landlords, and the cumulated effect of centuries of oppression on the tenants. He was out of tune with his times in that the gathering forces of nineteenth century nationalism were not apparent to him. It is true that the great national leader Daniel O'Connell did not take up the cause of oppressed tenants: he exploited the tenant vote in order to gain Emancipation but thereafter directed all his energies towards the repeal of the Union. O'Connell was himself a landlord, and oppressed his tenants just as much as any Anglo-Irish Protestant,[30] but he did show the mass of the people that by uniting they could gain what they wanted. They continued to press for what they wanted for the remainder of the century.

Carleton also over-estimated his own influence, or rather the power of reasoned argument. He thought that what seemed so logical to him, and what was so clearly in the best interests of the landlords themselves, if pointed out with sufficient force — as in "Tubber Derg" and "The Poor Scholar" — must have the desired effect. It can be argued that he made the same type of mistake here as he had made in the religious question. By "understanding" the position of the proprietors he lost his bearings and natural loyalty, and in so doing failed to see the central point: Ireland was a colonized country and the landlords represented the colonial power. No matter how much the peasantry might love and respect a kind landlord, they

---

30. For an account of Daniel O'Connell's estate and the treatment he meted out to his tenants see Campbell Foster, Letters on the Condition of the People of Ireland[2], pp. 394-398.

never forgot this basic fact. In neglecting and oppressing their tenants the landlords were merely adding wrong to wrong.

The same fundamental criticism of Carleton may be differently expressed by saying that his very reformism blinded him to the realities of the situation that he was describing. The peasantry were conservative by nature and in good times did not demand any radical changes. The most they envisaged, as expressed by Jemmy Murray in "Tubger Derg or the Red Well", was the "good time comin', when we'll pay our money to thim that won't be too proud to hear our complaints wid their own ears, an' who won't turn us over to a divil's limb of an agent".[31] These "good times" would be when Catholic Irish landlords replaced Protestant Anglo-Irish or English landlords. Robert Redfield has remarked that when there was resentment against a landlord, it was in cases where "someone had failed to preserve the traditional and approved roles and statuses of gentry and peasantry".[32] The peasantry as a whole did not regard their relations with the gentry as those of oppressed with oppressor; they simply believed that the gentry, being knowledgeable and powerful, should be correspondingly generous and just. Carleton indeed adopts this peasant attitude by making the majority of his resident landlords humane and respected for their position and their behaviour. By holding up the example of Colonel B— he also tries to encourage the landlords to see themselves in the same light and to live up to society's expectations of them. But he had set himself a hopeless task, as the subsequent history of the country was to show.

Carleton's writings on Irish rural society, and especially on the landlord-tenant relationship, do not merely preserve a picture of a lost way of life as he had intended. They also display the colonial structure at work. The land system was such that the peasantry were in a powerless position, unable to change anything by their own efforts, unable to understand the complex economic forces to

---

31. Works I, p. 949.
32. Peasant Society and Culture, p. 135.

which they were subject. The agricultural situation in
England had shown the same pattern of events, population
explosion, consolidation of large holdings, agrarian unrest; but there the development of industry had at least
provided work for many of the farm labourers who migrated
to the cities, although this is not to deny that there
were violent reactions to change in the rural England of
the 1830's.

In Ireland there was no industry to absorb even a
portion of the peasantry and the issue was further complicated by the destructive mechanism of colonialism. Though
the colony was an old one and there was no manifest racial
difference between colonizer and colonized, the similari-
ties between the two groups were only superficial: cultu-
rally and in religion there were huge differences, and it
is these differences that Carleton clearly reveals. On
one level animosity is displayed in the peasants' contempt
for the law and religion of the colonists. On another level, the ignorance of both groups about the culture of the
other appears to create an unbridgeable gap between them.
In Ireland another tier was thus added to the usual pattern of class differences.

D. VIOLENCE

After the rebellion of 1798 severe repressive measures
were passed to ensure the peace of Ireland, and for the
first thirty years of the new century the country was governed by one Insurrection act after the other. Coercion,
sporadic famine, the attempted consolidation of large
estates after the close of the Napoleonic wars, the fight
for Catholic Emancipation until 1829, and agitation
against tithes after 1830 combined to keep the country in
a perpetual state of disturbance, and this disturbance is
duly reflected in Carleton's work.

Crime and violence are met with in Carleton's
stories on the interpersonal and communal planes. Horse

stealing in "The Donagh", fratricide in "Lha Dhu",[1] murder
in "The Miller of Mohill"[2] and "The Midnight Mass", to
name but a few instances, are the types of violent crime
that may occur in any community. Of lesser offences
against the laws of the land, not necessarily accompanied
by violence, the most frequent in Carleton's society is
illicit distilling. Carleton does not really regard this
practice as a crime, and neither does the peasant community. It is a harmless means of adding to slender incomes
and poteen drinking constitutes an integral part of peasant enjoyment. There are numerous references in the stories to a keg of poteen being fetched for use at christe-
nings, weddings and wakes, and to ease marriage negotia-
tions. Similarly, unlicensed public houses (shebeen houses) flourished in the countryside on the sale of illegal
whiskey and smuggled tobacco. In a few stories poteen distilling or poteen drinking is connected with tragedy —
Larry M'Farland falls into a stream and drowns when making
his drunken way home after a distilling session; the gauger is murdered while tracking down a still in "The Illicit Distiller or the Force of Conscience";[3] a mother and
her infant son die as a result of rough treatment by the
gauger and a party of soldiers who are trying to find a
store of poteen in "The Broken Oath". But for the most
part illicit distilling is looked on humorously. The
struggle between distillers and gauger is treated as a
game which the most quick-witted wins, and Carleton takes
whimsical pride in showing how the gauger is confounded by
peasant ingenuity.

Communal violence is peculiar to societies in which a deep
malaise is present. In Carleton's society this type of
violence is shown to occur on two levels; firstly among
the peasants themselves, one faction or party breaking the
heads of another faction or party in a kind of ritual,
traditional warfare. Secondly there is warfare between
two classes, the owners and the occupiers of land, and it

1. "Lha Dhu or the Dark Day", DUM IV (1834); reprinted in Works II.
2. The Illustrated Dublin Journal I (1861); never reprinted.
3. CE X (1830).

is here that secret societies enter the picture and where the most bitter resentments and the cruellest crime and punishment are concentrated.

Carleton often declares that the Irish are belligerent by nature and that one of the greatest joys in an Irishman's, or indeed an Irishwoman's, life is to take part in a good fight. A wedding or fair would be incomplete without a free-for-all. It is the greatest sorrow in the diminutive tailor Neal Malone's life that no matter how hard he tries he cannot provoke anybody into fighting with him.[4] The lack of battlescars calls his manhood seriously into question.

Fighting is represented as a ritual, cathartic element in Irish society, but Carleton is very careful to distinguish between faction fighting, which occurs among Roman Catholics, and party fighting where Protestants and Catholics are engaged. Factions group themselves around two warring families, or two rival townlands or parishes, or spring up spontaneously at places of pilgrimage or fairs. Very often the original cause of enmity lies buried in the far distant past: the O'Callaghans and the O'Hallaghans of "The Battle of the Factions" fight about a law suit which had happened a century before their time, and likewise the Dorans and the Flanagans disrupt Shane Fadh's wedding by fighting about some undefined law suit. The enmity between the warring factions in "The Station" is never motivated, and the Findramore and Scanlon "boys" in "The Hedge School" seem to fight each other from a sense of duty and a love of battle rather than for any specific reason.

"The Battle of the Factions" is narrated with great relish by Pat Frayne, the schoolmaster, who has the mark of many an engagement upon his body. The battle that he describes — one might almost say relives — to a delighted audience is of almost epic proportions: it is bloody and ends tragically, but despite the tragic element the

---

4. "Neal Malone", The [Dublin] University Review and Quarterly Magazine I (1833); reprinted in Works I.

tone of the narrative is humorous. Pat sets this tone
when he philosophizes on the Irishman's legendary love of
a good fight. The latter is

> the <u>acumen</u> of his enjoyment; and woe be to him
> who will venture to go between him and his amuse-
> ments. To be sure, skulls and bones are broken,
> and lives lost; but they are lost in pleasant
> fighting — they are the consequences of the sport,
> the beauty of which consists in breaking as many
> heads and necks as you can ...[5]

Fists, cudgels scientifically and lovingly prepared,
spades, shovels, stones — any weapon that comes to hand is
used to beat the enemy. The humour of the piece is gro-
tesque, even macabre. At one point the O'Hallaghans are
driven back to the graveyard, and being short of weapons
they furnish themselves in their desparation with "the
skull, leg, thigh and arm bones, which they found lying
about the grave-yard". These are the perfect weapons.
"Out they sallied in a body — some with these, others with
stones, and making a fierce assault upon their enemies,
absolutely <u>druv</u> them back — not so much by the damage they
were doing, as by the alarm and terror which these unex-
pected species of missiles excited".[6] The spirit of the
fight is almost surrealistic: even killing is done with
good cheer. To illustrate this vital point Pat gives an
example of the kind of exchange that can be heard between
the combatants:

> "... for the sake of my wife and childher, Ned
> Hallaghan, spare my life".
> "So we will, but take this, any how" — (whack,
> crack, whack, crack).
> "Oh! for the love of God, don't kill — (whack,
> crack, whack). Oh!" — (crack, crack, whack —
> <u>dies</u>.)
> "Huzza! huzza! huzza!" from the O'Hallaghans.
> "Bravo, boys! there's one of them done for ...".[7]

5. <u>Works</u> II, p. 734. This story was first printed in <u>TS</u>[1] (1830).
6. <u>Works</u> II, p. 738.
7. <u>ibid</u>., p. 736.

Unfortunately, one combatant is killed with the blade of a scythe. Pat Frayne's grandfather, aged hero of many battles, has been watching the fight with the critical eye of the perfectionist, and remarks to Pat that he has never seen "purtier fighting, within his own memory ... But, to do him justice, he condemns the scythe and every other weapon except the cudgels; because, he says, that if they continue to be resorted to, nate fighting will be altogether forgotten in the country".[8] All in all, despite the tragic death of one of the O'Callaghans, and the subsequent life-long derangement of beautiful Rose O'Hallaghan — not to mention the demise of many an unnamed hero — this battle is judged to have been one of the greatest ever fought, deserving of record in the annals of the race.

Pat Frayne pronounces on the essential qualitative difference between a faction and a party fight. In the latter the enmity is deeper because it is not half-forgotten law suits but clearly defined political and religious differences that separate the two sides. Pat observes wryly that this "is a mighty great advantage; for when this is adjuncted to an intense personal hatred, and a sense of wrong ... it is apt to produce very purty fighting and much respectable retribution".[9] He drops his light, racy tone when describing the ominous air hanging over a town before a party fight, but adds pragmatically that while party fighting is bad for trade, faction fighting makes business go briskly. People want to stay in town to witness the fun of the faction fight and to shout encouragement at their own side, but all those not involved stay out of the way when a party fight is about to begin.

"The Funeral and Party Fight" is a story devoted to party fighting; and in keeping with this more serious and divisive form of battle the narrator is a local gentleman, who can be expected to take an inclusive and impartial view of the events.[10] Pat Frayne is allowed to narrate "The Battle of the Factions" because as a schoolmaster his language can be made "sesquipedalian" and amusing, and be-

---

8. ibid., p. 740.
9. ibid., p. 734.
10. For the narrative structure of this story see ch. III, pp. 145-146.

cause he can be relied upon, as one who himself has taken part in the battle, unwittingly to transmit its bloodthirsty and essentially native Irish nature. Naturally he is in no way impartial. Party fights, however, were not a manifestation of such innocent Celtic amusement but of a deep and bitter division between those who made up the population of the north of Ireland. The battle lines were drawn up along economic, political, religious and cultural divides; the issues were clear, the parties were in deadly earnest, and each death was registered as a victory or a defeat for land and religion. When the Doran and Flanagan factions have been separated, Shane Fadh's uncle concludes that after all "we're all Irishmen, relations, and Catholics ... and we oughtn't to be this way".[11] These bonds of nationality, family and religion are precisely what is missing between the parties, and the fighting is correspondingly more bitter and destructive.

Faction fighting is good training for party fighting and Carleton claims that it is "an integral part of an Irish peasant's education".[12] Denis Kelly, who has been trained first as a faction and later as a party fighter, is the champion of his party and despite his wife's protests trains their son to follow in his footsteps:

> "Lanty, ma bouchal, what'll you do when you grow a man?" ...
> "Ho! ho! the Casey's! I'll bate the blackguards wid your blackthorn, daddy!" ...
> "Well, Lanty, who more will you leather, ahagur?"
> "All the Orangemen; I'll kill all the Orangemen!"[13]

When Denis Kelly dies as a result of injuries sustained in the party fight this same son, now aged fourteen, swears vengeance:

> "Oh! the murdherers ... that killed my father;
> for only for them, he would be still wid us: but,
> by the God that's over me, if I live, night or day

11. "Shane Fadh's Wedding", Works II, p. 695.
12. "The Funeral and Party Fight" (retitled "The Party Fight and Funeral"), Works II, p. 765.
13. ibid., p. 771.

I will not rest, till I have blood for blood; nor
do I care who hears it, nor if I was hanged the
next minute".[14]

Thus the party spirit is handed down from one generation
to the next. One may imagine the same oath being sworn in
an Orange home, although Carleton never suggests as much.

The immediate cause of the party fight described
in this story is the land. An Orangeman has taken the
farm of an evicted Catholic tenant named Grogan. The narrator adds that Grogan had not paid his rent for over three
years and that the landlord had been if anything over-in-
dulgent. The eviction was therefore justified but the local Ribbon society nevertheless threatened reprisals on
anyone who dared rent the land. At last Vesey "Vengeance"
Johnston, a bluff thorough-going Orangeman, takes it and
successfully repulses a Ribbon attack. Some of the Ribbonmen are killed, others are caught and transported. Both
Orangemen and Ribbonmen prepare to do battle royal on the
day of the next fair.

When the day comes, the atmosphere hanging over
the town is compared to "the calm, gloomy silence that pre-
cedes a thunder-storm ...". The people transact their
business hurriedly; after four o'clock "the busy stir and
hum of the mass [settles] down into a deep, brooding, por-
tentous silence, that [is] absolutely fearful". The main
street is deserted and "free for action". Before the
battle the antagonists gravitate to their respective public
houses. In this warming-up period they glare at one another whenever they meet on the street: "the eye [is] set
in deadly animosity, and the face marked with an ireful
paleness, occasioned at once by revenge and apprehension".[15]
Then the storm breaks and the battle commences with single
combat between the champions of the respective sides, Kelly
and Grimes. When the Orangeman has been felled a general
struggle ensues. The narrator remarks on the different
physical characteristics of the parties. "In the Orange
line the men were taller, and of more powerful frames; but

14. ibid., pp. 788-789.
15. ibid., p. 781.

the Ribbonmen were more hardy, active, and courageous".
This is because the Catholics live in the mountains, to
which they "had been driven at the point of the bayonet"
in times gone by, and because the Protestants and Presbyterians "who came in upon their possessions" occupy the
more fertile land. Therefore the Catholic is "like his
soil, hardy, thin, and capable of bearing all weathers",
while the Protestant is "larger, softer, and more inact-
ive".[16] The Orangemen have the unfair advantage of being
allowed to bear firearms which they do not scruple to use.
The town is a veritable battlefield, with dead and wounded
lying on the ground in pools of gore. The contrast with a
faction fight is intense. There are no "friendly" exchanges, the air is charged with hatred and desire for vengeance, and the parties are unevenly matched because of the
Orangemen's firearms. There is little sense of a fair
fight and no joy in the science of wielding a cudgel.

Carleton tries to find some reason for "many of
the atrocities and outrages which take place in Ireland".[17]
One is the depth of family feeling; but another fundamental
cause of outrage is the kind of education Catholic Irishmen receive in their hedge-schools, where they are encouraged to become members of factions and are not given any
moral training. A "more enlightened system of education"
might break the vicious circle of hereditary conflict.
"But, unhappily, there is a strong suspicion of the object
proposed by such a system; so that the advantages likely
to result from it to the lower orders of the people will be
slow and distant".[18] This is the opinion of the narrator's
brother, a Protestant gentleman presented as liberal in his
views, and the school system to which he refers was that
set up by the proselytizing societies.[19] It may be concluded that Carleton regards faction fighting as in part a
form of training for party fighting, and open party fights
as a reflection of socio-economic, religious and cultural
divisions. Such party fighting took place mostly in the

---

16. ibid., p. 784.
17. ibid., p. 787.
18. ibid., p. 770.
19. Cf. ch. I, pp. 63-64.

north of Ireland; and behind the warring parties lay the
secret societies.

Carleton's attitude in "The Funeral and Party
Fight" is that of the liberal who abhors violence. He condemns both sides and indicates some of the underlying causes of the conflict. His tone is one of saddened liberalism, appropriate to a man who himself had risen from the
ranks of the morally unenlightened "lower orders". As a
child he had taken part in these fights and he knew the
spirit which animated them. As a sometime schoolmaster
and a self-educated man he saw the solution to the problem
in terms of "moral education". The only problem here is
that he confines his analysis to the Roman Catholic peasantry. He never defines "moral education", and never addresses himself to the question of why the Protestant
Orangemen are as bloodthirsty and vengeful as their Catholic neighbours.

Faction and party fighting on the one hand, and the activities of the secret societies and the attempts of the government to suppress them on the other hand, are but two
sides of the same phenomenon. The frustrations of a colonized and oppressed people will always express themselves
in violence. In the early nineteenth century the peasants
bore the brunt of Ireland's economic decay. Their standard
of living, miserable to begin with, declined even further
and they lived in constant fear of eviction. Their bond
with the land was not only economic: for many of them the
small holding had been in the family for generations, and
the family was partly identified by its land. Farming was
the only way of life known to them and they fought desperately to maintain what little they had.

The secret societies — essentially conservative
in nature — played a large part in the agrarian disturbances which ravaged the country. They were a prominent
feature of Irish life and Carleton has much to say of their
role in rural affairs. When studying these societies one
should strictly speaking distinguish "between those of
purely local origin and those derived to some extent from
overseas ideologies. The United Irishmen and Young Ireland

fit into the second category. The Whiteboys ... belong to the first".[20] Now to Carleton, Ribbonmen and Whiteboys are synonymous and the terms are interchangeable. Moreover, he attributes the political aspirations of the United Irishmen to what he terms the Ribbon society, as is apparent from "Rickard the Rake" (1838), Rody the Rover (1845) and even "Phelim O'Toole's Courtship" (1833). When reading Carleton's accounts of the secret societies one must therefore be aware that to him their aspirations were twofold: to secure the tenure of the land and to bring about political and constitutional change. Carleton concentrates on the local Whiteboy/Ribbon societies, but he places them within the framework of a larger "conspiracy" with republican aspirations. As a firm supporter of the Union Carleton could have no sympathy with republicanism; as an opponent of violence he abhorred the methods employed by the societies even though he might sympathize with their demands for a better land system. He was an advocate of gradualism, and of a system where each party to the social contract accepted the responsibilities of which he tried to make them aware.

Both "Phelim O'Toole's Courtship" and "Confessions of a Reformed Ribbonman" (later entitled "Wildgoose Lodge") deal with the workings of the local Ribbon society, and present a very unflattering, unheroic image of its membership, leadership and activities. "Confessions of a Reformed Ribbonman" describes the revenge taken on a farmer who had prosecuted some Ribbonmen for stealing weapons from him and maltreating him when he tried to resist. The malefactors were arrested and transported, and to the Ribbon society the farmer was guilty of informing. The fate of all traitors is exemplified in the hideous reprisals executed upon him and his family. Over 130 men set fire to his house, Wildgoose Lodge, and all its inmates, men, women and children, perished in the flames. The story is based on a genuine incident which had occurred in Co. Louth.

---

20. T. Desmond Williams, ed., Secret Societies in Ireland (Dublin etc. 1973), pp. 6-7.

126

What interests Carleton is the question of what kind of men would perform such a "hellish murder".[21] Can the Irish peasantry possess such evil and cruel natures? The narrator of "Confessions" is a former member of the Ribbon society who had been present at the burning; he can therefore speak with authority on these questions. He relates how he is called to a "select meeting" of the local branch of the society, a meeting which is to take place "at the solemn hour of midnight"[22] in the parish chapel: the secrecy of the society is underlined by the anonymity of the summons which he receives. When he arrives he finds six or seven men standing on the altar and about forty men sitting on the altar steps. Among the latter are "some of the most malignant and reckless spirits in the parish".[23] He greets the Captain and gives the secret Ribbon handshake. Members continue to flock into the chapel and as each approaches the altar he receives two or three glasses of whiskey; to the sacrilege of meeting in the chapel in order to plan an act of vengeance is added the profanity of drinking.

The interest of the story centres not on the ordinary Ribbonmen but on the Captain and his inner circle. It is made plain that the majority are neither particularly evil nor particularly bloodthirsty. Once they have become members, however, they are forced on pain of execution to attend the meetings of the society and to participate in its actions. The Captain reminds them of the oath they have taken to obey him, and he makes them all swear an additional oath of secrecy. They go to Wildgoose Lodge unwillingly, and some even attempt to intercede for the lives of the family. Their reaction to the burning is described as follows: "some of them fainted, and others were in such agitation that they were compelled to lean on their comrades. They became actually powerless with horror: yet to such a scene were they brought by the pernicious influence of Ribbonism".[24] As they leave the scene of the crime the

21. Works I, p. 944.
22. ibid., p. 936.
23. ibid., p. 937.
24. ibid., p. 943.

Captain finds it necessary again to warn them to keep silent. If they inform "there is them livin' that will take
care the lase of your own lives will be but short".[25]

We are thus clearly given to understand that it
is the Captain and his intimates who bear the chief burden
of guilt for the atrocity. The Captain, who is the local
schoolmaster, appears outwardly calm at first. But as he
prepares to address the assembly, the narrator watches him
closely and perceives his true nature; he then proceeds to
describe the Captain in appropriately melodramatic terms:

> I could observe ... a dark shade come over his
> countenance, that contracted his brow into a deep
> furrow, and it was then, for the first time, that
> I saw the satanic expression of which his face,
> by a very slight motion of its muscles, was cap-
> able. His hands, during this silence, closed and
> opened convulsively; his eyes shot out two or
> three baleful glances ... his teeth ground against
> each other, like those of a man whose revenge
> burns to reach a distant enemy ...[26]

His closest confederates are more open in their desire for
revenge; their faces and actions plainly indicate the depth
of their passion. But the Captain remains for the most
part cool and collected, and only occasionally — as when he
sets fire to the house — does he reveal himself in all his
satanic fury: "His eyes blazed from beneath his knit eye-
brows with a fire that seemed to be lighted up in the in-
fernal pit itself". He issues the order "No quarter — no
mercy ...";[27] he refuses to allow his victims to die "by
the weapons of their enemies"[28] — instead they must burn to
death; and it is he who mercilessly thrusts a woman and her
child back into the flames. Such is the diabolical nature
of a Ribbon leader and the merciless nature of Ribbon
crime.

---

25. ibid., p. 944.
26. ibid., p. 938.
27. ibid., p. 942.
28. ibid., p. 943.

"Confessions of a Reformed Ribbonman" is a piece
of literary sensationalism, surely calculated to strike
terror into the heart of the reader and to confirm his
worst suspicions. The ringleaders of the Ribbon society
are represented as common criminals or even worse. They
incite young men to crime, and even as they show no mercy
to their victims, no mercy should be shown to them. Carleton goes no further than to reproduce what is ostensibly
an eye-witness account of the scene, and from the point of
view of technique the story is certainly a remarkable
piece of work. It seems likely, however, that it is as
much an example of propaganda as "A Pilgrimage to Patrick's
Purgatory" or "The Broken Oath". "Confessions of a Reformed Ribbonman" was originally published in 1830 in The Dublin Literary Gazette. This periodical circulated chiefly
among the upper classes, where Carleton's sentiments could
be sure to win unmitigated approval.

In "Phelim O'Toole's Courtship" Carleton treats
Ribbonism in its more everyday aspects, trying through the
character of Phelim and his activities to give some impression of the type of men who joined the Ribbon society
and their reasons for doing so. Phelim is not fundamentally evil. He is the darling of his parents and a favourite
with the girls, in great demand at weddings and wakes and
"the hero of the parish".[29] His political awareness as a
member of the Ribbon society is treated with heavy irony:
"Phelim was ... a great Ribbonman; and from the time he
became initiated into the system, his eyes were wonderful-
ly opened to the oppressions of the country".[30] He can
invent an alibi for a friend on the spur of the moment,
and on many occasions succeeds in having his fellow Ribbonmen acquitted, "leaving the Attorney-General, with all his
legal knowledge, out-witted and foiled".[31] But for all
his cleverness he is finally arrested, and his angry re-
flections in his prison cell expose the motivation and the
nature of such a Ribbonman:

---

29. Works II, p. 1044.
30. ibid., p. 1045.
31. ibid., p. 1046.

> His patriotism rose to a high pitch; he deplored
> the wrongs of his country bitterly, and was clear-
> ly convinced that until jails, judges, and assiz-
> es, together with a long train of similar griev-
> ances, were utterly abolished, Ireland would never
> be right, nor persecuted "boys", like himself, at
> full liberty to burn or murder the enemies of
> their country with impunity.[32]

Along with these ironically reported sentiments, Phelim
also curses the Ribbon system and those who had inveigled
him into it. What he is chiefly embittered about is having been caught. However, the Ribbon society looks after
its own and "The expenses of his defence were drawn from
the Ribbon fund".[33] Carleton adds in a customarily didactic postscript:

> We have attempted to draw Phelim O'Toole as close-
> ly as possible to the character of that class,
> whose ignorance, want of education and absence of
> all moral principle, constitute them the shame
> and reproach of the country. By such men the
> peace of Ireland is destroyed, illegal combina-
> tions formed, blood shed, and nightly outrages
> committed.[34]

Secret societies were evil and vengeful, their
leaders depraved and their members dupes. Some of the
latter were indeed captured and punished for their offences. Yet the kind of barbarous retribution against the
Ribbonmen which Carleton describes at the end of "Confessions of a Reformed Ribbonman", and which he writes about in
his autobiography as having witnessed in Louth in 1817,[35]
was hardly calculated to make the peasantry believe in the
just supremacy of the law. To censure landlords and government for neglecting the material well-being of the peasantry was a position which Carleton could rationally and
immediately adopt, whereas the contemplation of physical

32. ibid., p. 1073.
33. ibid., p. 1074.
34. ibid., p. 1075.
35. The Autobiography of William Carleton (1968), p. 114.

violence and inhumanity would seem, on the evidence of
these early stories, to have bereft him of the ability to
associate cause and effect. It must be recognized that in
this respect he was no different from the legislators responsible for the country's plight. It is therefore all
the more interesting to note that in later years he depart-
ed from the facile theory of deficient moral instruction
as an explanation of peasant violence, and began instead
to suggest what might be called more overtly political causes. In Rody the Rover, an improving novelette published
in 1845 in Duffy's "Library of Ireland" series, he presents
the wandering Ribbonman as an agent provocateur who incites
the people to commit outrages and collects a handsome re-
ward for uncovering the "plot" to the authorities at Dublin
Castle. And in Valentine M'Clutchy, published in the same
year, he advances the opinion that the great majority of
agrarian crimes are the fault of landlords and their a-
gents, a self-destructive response by the peasants to an
alien legal system which serves only to punish the weak
and never to protect them. The thesis advanced in Rody
the Rover — already adumbrated in "Rickard the Rake", a
story published seven years previously[36] — proved highly
irritating to some sections of the public, as may be gathered from the text of a letter which Carleton felt ob-
liged to send to The Nation newspaper shortly after the
appearance of the novelette:

> Sir — Although I have been always reluctant to
> obtrude myself upon public notice, except through
> the medium of our national literature, yet I beg
> upon the present occasion to make an observation
> or two, with your permission, in connexion with
> that literature and myself.
>
> I have heard from many sources that a very ge-
> neral impression exists that in my last volume,
> but one, to wit, "Rody the Rover", I have deliber-
> ately connected the vile Ribbon system, against
> which that work was written, and to which I am

---

36. "Rickard the Rake. In Three Snatches" DUM XI (1838).

told it has already done such serious damage, with the government of the country. Now, I most unhesitatingly contradict and deny this, and say that no honest person who has ever read the book could arrive at any such conclusion; in fact there is no assertion of the kind in it. That I spoke harshly of government for encouraging the spy and detective system I admit; but in doing this I only exercised a legitimate right — a right which every honest man and sincere lover of true liberty should exercise so long as government shall continue to keep such an odious and unconstitutional body in its employment.

I have only to conclude by saying that it is more in compliance with the solicitations of my friends, than from any wish to stand either well or ill with government that I take the trouble to disclaim motives which I never entertained, and which were imputed to me by my enemies.

I beg, sir, to subscribe myself, with much respect, your faithful servant,

W. Carleton.

Clontarf Crescent, Nov. 5 1845.[37]

From this half-hearted though elegant disclaimer we may deduce that the accusation implicit in Rody the Rover was not altogether without foundation. Characteristically enough, there seems to be no evidence that the far more significant political thesis of Valentine M'Clutchy commanded equal public attention at the time; and Carleton failed to exploit this simple yet fundamental insight in his later works on Irish peasant life.

In almost all of his work Carleton presents the Irish peasantry as simple, kindly but excitable people. The paradoxical Celtic temperament allows good and evil to coexist, and the people can be led into either exemplary or violent behaviour. They have neither the moral fibre nor

---

37. The Nation (Dublin), 15 November 1845, p. 74.

the independence of mind necessary to find their own salvation. In his final analysis of this disturbing and
puzzling situation Carleton admits that the peasantry have
real grievances, and that they are forced into violent
measures — or rather into supporting the advocates of such
measures — because they have nowhere else to turn. He accordingly suggests the only remedy that a Liberal Conservative could find: if authority ensured that the people
were instructed in true religion, treated generously with
regard to the land and ruled firmly but justly, they would
willingly respond by repudiating the Ribbon system, em-
bracing sound moral principles and living happily ever after as grateful, contented tenants. In adopting this attitude Carleton may have been influenced by his wish to
secure a government pension, and consequently by the need
to satisfy a particular public, but in spite of these
pragmatic considerations a note of sincerity runs through
his work. Although he does not question the basis of the
social structure he strongly criticizes its abuses: those
in authority bear the chief responsibility for the smooth
running of society, and they are accused of failing to discharge it.

Since the Celtic temperament alone cannot explain
why the people are sometimes lazy, brutal and degraded,
Carleton tries to find scapegoats upon whom he can lay part
of the blame — these range from the Catholic church to
landlords and agents, republican agitators, and others who
simply exploit the people for their own ends without having their true interests at heart. However, Carleton's dilemma here is that while he is unable with honesty to claim
that the authorities in the form of landlords or government
are working for the benefit of the common people, his belief in the Union and the established social hierarchy prevents him from formulating a comprehensive solution to the
problem.

Frantz Fanon's thesis concerning the psychological
degradation of colonized nations provides one answer to the
question which thus perplexed Carleton and his Liberal contemporaries. Fanon argues with uncompromising force that
an oppressed people, the colonized, are regarded by their

oppressors, the colonizers, as passive, emotional, superstitious, powerless and stupid, and that the colonized
also see themselves in this light.[38] The resultant frustrations find their only possible expression in spontaneous, sporadic violence on the part of those oppressed.
Such violence is very often turned upon the perpetrators'
fellow-countrymen, and in nineteenth century Ireland it
was seen not only in faction and party fighting but also in
the actions of the agrarian secret societies. Among the
uneducated peasantry violence took the place of words, and
the peasant threw himself headlong into unorganized rebellion in a desperate effort to assert his own identity.

As a peasant who had risen dramatically in the
world Carleton had a clearer overall picture of the state
of Ireland than had the subjects of his stories, but his
insight did not extend to the formation of a coherent political analysis. His fear of violence led him to reject
armed revolution; his awe of authority and respect for
rank, while less exaggerated than it might have been, led
him to regard benevolent despotism on the part of the colonial power as the only possible source of reform. To
him, as to most peasants and landlords, the possession or
non-possession of property divided mankind into two separate categories of being. He saw beauty, romance, depth of
feeling and much else in Irish peasant culture, although
he was not unaware of the material deprivation which was
also involved. But at the same time he saw respectability,
law, order and majesty in English or Anglo-Irish culture:
here were the authority, the power and all those other attributes which he had learned to admire as the only basis
for right living. A synthesis of the two cultures did not
appear to be possible, and Carleton's writings therefore
had the restricted aim of making peasant culture better
known to the gentry, who might discharge their responsibilities more successfully if they understood their tenants
as well as Carleton did.

---

38. Cf. Frantz Fanon, Peau Noir, Masques Blancs (Paris 1952) and Les
    Damnés de la Terre (Paris 1961).

In the dilemma of Carleton's love of the peasantry and admiration for the gentry may be found an explanation of his lack of a consistent attitude. Certainly it would be unjust to judge him with the hindsight of the latter half of the twentieth century. It would have been simpler for him and perhaps beneficial to his reputation had he adopted and maintained a single point of view. Maria Edgeworth, Samuel Lover and Charles Lever, even Griffin and the Banims spoke out of a fundamental security in their various positions and a conviction that their understanding of the situation was correct. It might be said that Carleton, however unconsciously he may have done so, reflected the national state of mind more accurately than any of these authors. The proud Protestant nation had disintegrated after the act of Union, and the economic decay which manifested itself after 1815 continued until far into the nineteenth century. In this context, Carleton displays colonialism and its evils at work in the land system and the legal system and in the relationships between owners and occupiers of land — relationships which were further complicated by racial and religious distinctions, and which carried with them the embryo of violent social unrest.

CHAPTER III.
NARRATIVE STRUCTURE AND CHARACTERIZATION

A. INTRODUCTORY

The previous chapters have examined Carleton's portrayal
of peasant religion and society and the main emphasis has
been laid on Carleton as a social commentator. The present chapter will examine the more specifically literary
side of his work, analyzing the structure of his stories
and his characterization of the people both as individuals
and as a race. Representative stories have been selected
for this analysis as Carleton quite often repeats his basic characterization and plot structure.

Carleton cannot be placed in any one literary category.
He wrote stories, novels, poetry and even a play which is
now lost. His writings were published in a variety of magazines and journals and by a variety of publishers from
1828 until his death.[1] He regarded himself, and was regarded by many of his contemporaries, as one of the greatest figures in Irish literature. He wrote almost exclusively about the peasantry and drew his subject-matter
from their lives, but his writings were by no means disinterested: he did his best to promote religious and later
social reform, and he wrote for many parties and shades of
opinion. It would be a mistake, however, to suppose that
he had no consistent view of his own, for underlying his
varying analyses of the roots of distress in Ireland and
his varying remedies for its relief is a strong conviction

---

1. Cf. Appendix II below and the bibliography in André Boué, William
    Carleton (1973), pp. 520-538.

that mutual respect and good will and moral behaviour on the part of all classes would cure the ills of the country.

Carleton's works belong to the regional tradition in European fiction. The regional novelists of early nineteenth century Europe were in advance of historians in their interest in ordinary people and they too have their antecedents in other genres: the travel books of such authors as Arthur Young and the regional poems of such poets as Robert Burns. The regional setting and the depiction of ordinary people is in its turn rooted in the Romantic movement.

It may also be mentioned that Carleton belongs to that branch of Romanticism which includes Walter Scott and Robert Burns. Burns' "The Cotter's Saturday Night", written in 1785, praises the innocence and purity of the Scottish peasantry and idealizes the simple as opposed to the sophisticated. While Carleton finds fault with the peasantry, he nevertheless believes them to be fundamentally good. Permeating his work is the feeling that the city is evil and the countryside pure.[2] He sometimes employs nature in a rather Wordsworthian manner; this may be seen in "Ned M'Keown", where the narrator recalls his childhood in the valley of the Black Pig and his awakening to the joys of nature:

> Many a day, both of sunshine and storm, have I, in the strength and pride of happy youth, bounded, fleet as the mountain roe, over these blue hills! Many an evening, as the yellow beams of the setting sun shot slantingly, like rafters of gold, across the depth of this blessed and peaceful valley, have I followed, in solitude, the impulses of a wild and wayward fancy, and sought the quiet dell, or viewed the setting sun, as he scattered his glorious and shining beams through the glowing foliage of the trees, in the vista, where I stood; or wandered along the river, whose

2. This attitude is particularly marked in "Lha Dhu or the Dark Day" (1834) and "The Misfortunes of Barney Branagan" (1841), but it is to be found everywhere in Carleton's work.

banks were fringed with the hanging willow,
whilst I listened to the thrush singing among
the hazels that crowned the sloping green above
me ...[3]

This kind of joy in the powers of nature is to be observed
even more clearly in "The Midnight Mass", where the narrator remarks on the sight of the river that it "filled the
mind with those undefinable sensations of pleasure insepa-
rable from a contemplation of the sublimities of nature".
He reminisces on his experiences of mountain climbing:

> Well do we remember, though then ignorant of our
> own motives, when we have, in the turmoil of the
> elements, climbed its steep, shaggy sides, disap-
> pearing like a speck, or something not of earth,
> among the dark clouds that rolled over its sum-
> mit, for no other purpose than to stand upon its
> brow, and look down on the red torrent, dashing
> with impetuosity from crag to crag, whilst the
> winds roared, and the dark clouds flew in columns
> around us, giving to the natural wildness of the
> place an air of wilder desolation.[4]

However, Carleton more often employs natural sce-
nery to set the atmosphere for his stories, as may be observed in "Confessions of a Reformed Ribbonman" where the
horror of the events depicted is reinforced by the dark
night and the storm.[5] In his early stories especially,
Carleton frequently employs nature when reflecting on the
insignificance of man and the power of God. Having described the appearance of the aurora borealis, the narrator of "The Priest's Funeral" comments:

> There is, I think, no phenomenon equal to this in
> beauty and sublimity; the firmest mind cannot
> look upon it without awe approaching almost to
> fear; and as the gorgeous spectacle disports it-
> self in splendour over the heavens, this very

3. Works II, p. 655.
4. ibid., p. 853.
5. This can also be observed in "The Funeral and Party Fight" (1830).

dread, joined with the inimitable beauty of the
vision, fills the soul, heart, and imagination,
with the full sense of divine power.[6]

As well as being a social realist and a polemicist, Carleton could at times display an extraordinary degree of mawkish sentimentality. This sentimentality is
also to be found in the works of other regional writers
like Burns, Scott, Edgeworth and (less often) Galt. The
most notable example of sentimentality in Carleton is present in "Jane Sinclair or the Fawn of Springvale": it is
indicative of the change in taste that while "Jane Sinclair" is now almost unreadable, it was very popular in
Carleton's own time.[7]

Carleton was not alone among nineteenth century
Irish writers in his preoccupation with social and moral
issues:

> The English novelist was concerned with social
> choice and personal morality, which are the great
> issues of European fiction. But to the Irish no-
> velist these were subordinated to questions of
> race, creed, and nationality — questions which
> tend of their nature to limit the range and power
> of fiction. Yet for the Irishman these were the
> crucial points by which he was given social iden-
> tity.[8]

Carleton's work cannot be analyzed or evaluated without
taking his treatment of "race, creed, and nationality" into account.

Carleton's few stories of fantasy[9] are his only work with
no other immediate aim than that of entertainment. His

6. Tales of Ireland, pp. 50-51. Cf. also "The Funeral and Party
   Fight", Works II, p. 766.
7. DUM VII (1836); reprinted 1841, 1843, 1850, 1852 and in Works II.
8. Flanagan, The Irish Novelists, p. 35.
9. "The Three Tasks or the Little House under the Hill" The Dublin
   Literary Gazette (1830), reprinted in Works II; "Neal Malone" The
   [Dublin] University Review and Quarterly Magazine (1833), reprinted in Works I; "The Three Wishes. An Irish Legend" DUM XIV
   (1839); "A Legend of Knockmany" Chambers' Edinburgh Journal
   (1841); and "The King's Thief" Commercial Journal and Family He-
   rald (1855).

deep social commitment sometimes resulted in artistic considerations — especially that of composite unity — being
sacrificed to the exigencies of the particular thesis being expounded. Many of his stories are openly didactic,
and as well as intruding in his own person to point a moral Carleton very often inserts long digressions which
break the flow of events. But his didacticism does not
merely manifest itself in digressive passages or moral
comments: it lies in the very spirit of his work. Characterization, plot, setting and atmosphere are all directed
towards exemplifying the spirit and form of life of the
Irish people. Though the entertainment value of his work
should not be ignored, to Carleton the short story and the
novel were vehicles for the discussion of social and moral
issues; he was not at all preoccupied with fiction as
"art" and it is quite evident that content interested him
more than form. Indeed, his purpose had so decisive an
influence upon the form and content of his fiction that
the critic cannot use purely artistic criteria of evaluation. Carleton must be read primarily as an exponent of
a vanished culture and way of life, and although he in many ways may be viewed as a "flawed genius" questions of
literary or artistic quality are largely irrelevant.

B. DIDACTIC NARRATIVE STRUCTURE

The early stories have as their organizing principle
Carleton's ever-developing thesis of the evils of Roman
Catholicism. They do not purport to be fictional; on the
contrary they claim to offer documentary evidence in support of the thesis. They are therefore structured with
the aim in view of assembling a body of damnatory "facts"
(a recurring word) which will tell against the Roman Catholic Church.

On the other hand, the Traits and Stories which
followed are organized around the idea of illustrating
Irish peasant character and society. The focus has now
shifted from the Church and religion to the common people
whom Carleton wishes to present in all their complexity.

Accordingly the structure of these stories varies greatly
and in the vast majority artistic perfection is again subordinated to the over-riding purpose. This is not to deny
that many of the stories in the collection are amusing:
here, however, I am concerned to analyze the underlying
didacticism present in the vast majority of them. Carleton understood the art of teaching by pleasing, and even
"Denis O'Shaughnessy going to Maynooth" and, to a lesser
extent, "Phelim O'Toole's Courtship" have a didactic purpose: "Denis O'Shaughnessy" to illustrate the reasons for
young men entering the priesthood and what to Carleton
were the undesirable consequences of the veneration of
young priests by the community, while "Phelim O'Toole's
Courtship" questions the idealism of the young men who
joined secret societies.

Didacticism is indeed the characteristic feature of Carleton's stories and in terms of overall structure they may
be divided broadly speaking into those stories which aim
directly at teaching peasant or landlord in Ireland how to
attain the good life spiritually and socially, and those
which teach the reading public more about the Irish peasantry.[1] In the spirit of all didactic tales the narrator
is omniscient. This didacticism is in no way surprising
given the role Carleton had chosen to play, first as an
apologist of the élite and later as a member of the establishment intelligentsia. He was of course not alone in his
didacticism, as any examination of contemporary literature
in Britain or Ireland will reveal, but while didacticism in
English authors was directed towards improving social conditions and uplifting the moral tone of the people, Carleton and other Irish writers were also concerned with estab-
lishing their own national identity — a specifically colonial preoccupation.

In the early stories aimed directly at gentry or
peasantry an interesting mechanism is discernible. These

---

1. This division, though arbitrary, roughly corresponds to the division between the CE stories and the stories from TS onwards; cf.
   chs. I and II respectively.

tales are built aroung the usual structure of introduction,
exposition and resolution, but what sets them apart is the
nature of the change which leads to the resolution and the
agent of that change.   It is clear that Carleton operated
with the set of oppositions present in the community and
it may be noted that the irreconcilable oppositions present
in Carleton's own mind emerge very clearly from the stories.
These oppositions are primarily based on religion and class,
and the Catholic-Protestant opposition cuts across class
boundaries to appear on the twin levels of tenant-tenant
and tenant-landlord relationships.   There is thus tension
between the owners and the occupiers of the soil, but tension also appears between the occupiers independently of
religious considerations and is expressed in battles of an
only superficially religious character, or in inter-tenant
violence over evictions and subsequent relettings.   A further underlying opposition in the larger context is the
racial, Irish-English opposition; this does not find direct
expression in the stories, but it gave rise to racial feeling which, together with a complex of social and political
oppositions, produced a sense of inferiority and superiority respectively.   These feelings had far-reaching consequences for Carleton's presentation of Irish character.[2]

In the first group of stories under consideration the narrator, who is one of the protagonists, is an outside agent
in contrast to the narrators of the later stories, who purport to come from the community.   These stories present the
reader with the phenomenon of a narrator entering the community from the outside, analyzing it and bearing witness
to the event which changes it in some way.   It can be observed that the community does not possess within itself
the means of change, and to Carleton change is imperative
if the peasantry (and Irish society as a whole) are to improve.   The change advocated (implicitly or explicitly) is
not necessarily progress; indeed, as has already been pointed out,[3]   Carleton would prefer a return to the social and

----
2.   Cf. section D below.
3.   Ch. II, p. 94.

moral order of the Ireland of his youth rather than a march forward into democracy.

In the Christian Examiner stories, especially in the overtly propagandistic stories of "The Broken Oath", "Father Butler", "The Death of a Devotee" and "The Priest's Funeral", change comes about through adversity and the agent of change is the Bible; the nature of the change is therefore a moral and/or spiritual one, and the narrator is a Protestant gentleman far enough removed from the other protagonists to be able to judge them "objectively". Each story bears witness to the conversion of an individual from Roman Catholicism to the Protestant religion, and in each story a tragic event is the catalyst. In "The Broken Oath" Henry Lacy is sobered by the sentence of death which is passed on him; James Butler of "Father Butler" comes to his senses when he realizes that both he and Ellen Upton will die with their love unfulfilled because Father A— has tricked them; and Father Moyle of "The Death of a Devotee" comes to entertain "Scriptural views of religion"[4] as a result of some mysterious crime committed in his youth. All three are on the brink of death at the time of the stories. Like Henry Lacy, James Butler comes to the knowledge of true religion too late to find peace on earth, but both Lacy and Butler find their mortal confusion and doubts resolved by the light of the Bible. They pass this knowledge on to their next of kin and their stories end on a triumphant if tragic note. All three protagonists are changed through the agency of the Scriptures where they find the path to self-knowledge in the word of God. An interesting sub-plot in "Father Butler" is the gradual conversion of the labourer Lanty Nolan, who is motivated by curiosity to enquire into the nature of Protestantism; through the agency of the Bible and with the encouragement of his landlord he is gradually converted, not only becoming morally a better man but also achieving greater independence of mind. From a didactic point of view this demonstrates that the transition to "true religion" does not always require the catalyst of tragic personal experience to bring it about,

---

4. Tales of Ireland, p. 2.

and it also points to the benevolent influence which a good and conscientious landlord can have over his tenants.

The narrators of these stories play a passive part in the events and make no direct attempt to convert the main protagonists. In "The Broken Oath" the narrator relates Lacy's life history and sits with him in the condemned cell. In "Father Butler" the narrator talks to the protagonists and merely helps his tenant Nolan along the path the latter has already discovered for himself. He does not proselytize; on his death bed James Butler refutes the accusations of those who have claimed that the narrator has converted him. Again, in "The Death of a Devotee" and its sequel "The Priest's Funeral", the narrator takes part in the events he describes as if to underline the truth of his story, but his part is not an active one. In all these stories the narrator is on the side of the saved, observing their difficulties and final salvation as a kindly friend. Through this structure the Christian Examiner stories inexorably build up a damning body of evidence against the Church of Rome and, through the qualitative difference apparent between the saved and the lost, demonstrate the beneficial effects of Protestantism on the individual and on society at large.

The confessional stories of "A Pilgrimage to Patrick's Purgatory" and "Confessions of a Reformed Ribbonman" are also structured around more or less cathartic events which cause a basic change in the protagonists' way of life and thought. In both stories the protagonist makes a journey to the place where he is to have a horrific experience. He is by no means passive: in "A Pilgrimage to Patrick's Purgatory" he goes through the forms of the devotions and in "Confessions of a Reformed Ribbonman" he participates by his very presence in the burning of Wildgoose Lodge. The narrators of these stories, who come from the ranks of the peasantry, can be seen by their language and attitudes to have risen to the rank of gentleman, and they both look back at the turning point in their lives. The didactic structure of these stories is similar: the reader is conducted step by step through the motions of what Carleton claims to be the two great evils of the coun-

try, superstitious Roman Catholic practices and violent
agitation. It is shown how the people act in such circumstances and how the priests and popular leaders play on the
gullibility of the peasantry for their own ends. Both protagonists recoil from the actions in which they participate, thereby proving themselves to be more enlightened
than the majority and dissociating themselves from what
they have seen and done.

In all the stories so far referred to it can be
observed that the change which comes about in the protagonists is a moral one, and while it leads to a better way of
life it also sets them apart from the community at large
— they become different but better men. The moral implication here is that the pathway to salvation is lonely but
rewarding.

"The Battle of the Factions" and "The Funeral and
Party Fight" are interesting exceptions from a structural
point of view to the group of stories which are openly didactic. Violent action takes place but the characteristic
linear progression is lacking inasmuch as no change can be
seen in the community before and after the battles. This
society is incapable of healing itself; thus the structure
of the stories reflects the structure of the communities.
It may be added that the narrative technique of "The Funeral and Party Fight" also departs from Carleton's norms,
reflecting an unusual degree of preoccupation with the
problem of first-hand reporting. The "I" of the story, who
has been absent at the time of the main action, is responsible only for the introduction and the account of the concluding funeral; the party fight is described to him by his
brother, who had actually witnessed it, the attack on Vesey
"Vengeance" is related in the words of a participant, and
the attitudes of the people are explored by the Roman Catholic parish priest. The intransigence of the parties is
stressed not only by the narrator but also by his brother
and the parish priest, and the latter is represented as a
lone voice crying in the wilderness of bigotry and mindless
hatred. In a rather different manner, the intransigence of
the factions in "The Battle of the Factions" is underlined
by Pat Frayne's rollicking, devil-may-care mode of narra-

tion, his indifference to killing and his obvious admiration for the faction fighters.

In the stories directly concerned with social issues, notably "Tubber Derg or the Red Well" and "The Poor Scholar", the didactic element is uppermost. The narrator of these stories breaks continually into the flow of events with long, digressive interpolations; he addresses the reader directly, providing factual evidence to support his thesis and discoursing at length on the true nature of the Irish peasantry. Both stories are structured around journeys of discovery and both are circular in form in the sense that after a long struggle the families concerned regain their previous happiness; but there is a contrast with the stories of violence in that a positive conclusion is reached. Owen M'Carthy makes a fruitless journey to Dublin to plead with his landlord and then travels home to Tubber Derg. His family is evicted and goes through seventeen years of hardship before eventually returning. Both of Owen's journeys have a didactic effect: by identifying with him and his family the reader learns of the heartlessness of landlords, the malignity of agents and the virtues of hard work. In "The Poor Scholar" Jemmy M'Evoy's journey to Munster instructs the reader as to the good nature of the peasantry and the nature of the hedge school, and Colonel B—'s journey of discovery to his estate teaches both the good Colonel and the reader about the cupidity of agents, the suffering of helpless tenants and the benevolent effects of good landlordism. In both stories the nature of the change is a rise to prosperity, but it is significant that the effort which brings this change about is an individual one. The virtues of self-help are therefore another aspect of the underlying didacticism, while the necessity of perseverance and of patience in adversity is underlined at the same time.[5] It must nevertheless be emphasized that while Carleton saw the possibility of change for the better coming about through the personal efforts of individual peasants he despaired of the capacity of the peasant community as a whole for moral, civil or spiritual self-re-

---

5.   Cf. the characterization of Owen M'Carthy, pp. 166-168 below.

newal. He did, however, realize that all these elements were interrelated and chose the element of morals as the most important of all.[6] Education was not something the peasantry could provide for itself: it had to come from outside. Good example and good landlordism were necessary to eradicate evils present in the society.

The second didactic group of tales, those aimed primarily at teaching the wider reading public more about the people, differ significantly in narrative structure from the stories of religion, social evils and violence. No significant change occurs in the course of the narrative and no outside agent enters either to precipitate a change or to observe the protagonists. These are stories which characterize the Irish peasantry by describing their life and customs. They may be subdivided into stories which are more or less openly didactic and stories of fantasy or near fantasy which are didactic only in terms of Carleton's overall aims.

"Ned M'Keown", "The Three Tasks", "Shane Fadh's Wedding", "Larry M'Farland's Wake" and "The Battle of the Factions"[7] form a separate unit within Traits and Stories, in which most of the tales belonging to this group appeared. "Ned M'Keown" acts as a prologue: the narrative framework is provided by members of the village community sitting round the fire drinking in Ned's public house and telling stories to one another. The atmosphere is one of comfort, nostalgia and satisfaction. The reader "overhears" the storytellers of the community and "participates" in peasant entertainment. The nature of the peasantry's amusements, values, code of honour and attitudes is revealed both in the stories related and in the reactions of the listeners present. There is little or no authorial intrusion — the community speaks for itself.

That this was originally to have been the structure of Traits and Stories as a whole is clear from Carle-

6. On moral education cf. ch. II, p. 125.
7. Four of these five stories were printed for the first time in TS[1] (1830); the fifth story, "The Three Tasks", had been published earlier the same year in The Dublin Literary Gazette by way of preliminary publicity for the forthcoming collection.

ton's parenthetic comments at the end of "The Battle of the Factions", the last story of the unit: "It was the original intention of the author to have made every man in the humble group about Ned M'Keown's hearth narrate a story illustrating Irish life, feeling, and manners ..." However, by the time he came to "The Battle of the Factions" he had found his self-imposed structure too limiting. Such a plan, he considered,

> would ultimately narrow the sphere of his work, and perhaps fatigue the reader by a superfluity of Irish dialogue and its peculiarities of phraseology. He resolved therefore, at the close of The Battle of the Factions, to abandon his original design, and leave himself more room for description and observation.[8]

Authorial description and observation certainly result from the abandonment of Carleton's original design: the stories which follow "The Battle of the Factions" are also wider in scope, ranging outside of the village community to deal with current Irish problems, and the point of view shifts from that of the peasants themselves to that of the middle and upper classes.

Elements which differentiate the stories told around Ned's fireside from the rest of Traits and Stories are: the absence of an omniscient narrator and the consequent absence of "improving" digressions; the cosy atmosphere where the reader is aware of the cold night outside, the fire and drink, the feeling of "community"; and the story being told to other people, a convention which is reinforced by the comments made by the hearers on what they are told. The stories are therefore both the tale which is told and the environment in which it is told. These stories illustrate, as intended by Carleton, "Irish life, feeling, and manners" in an immediate way not achieved by the more openly "directed" stories of this group. Within this structure Carleton could not have exposed the evils of landlords as in "Tubber Derg" and "The Poor Scholar": a peasant narrator would not have been felt

8. Works II, p. 740.

as reliable when he described instances of injustice. Similarly, a peasant narrator could not have adopted the "objective" tone of the narrator of "The Party Fight and Funeral", as he would have been ideologically involved with either the one side or the other. Nor could such a narrator take an objective view of the secret societies, religion or superstition. Carleton wished to write about these subjects but at the same time to convince his readers of the inherent goodness of the Irish people. It was for this reason more than from a fear of tiring the reader "by a superfluity of Irish dialogue" (which is generously employed in the later stories in any case) that he abandoned his original plan.

The guiding hand of the author is, however, not entirely absent from the first group of stories, and the feelings of nostalgia and fellowship are shared by author and community alike. This is apparent in the introductory "Ned M'Keown", where the author speaks nostalgically (in the first person singular) of his youth spent in the part of the country where Ned lives; in the nature of the stories told — a wedding, a wake, a faction fight and a fairytale; and very clearly in the only direct comment which the author allows himself, concerning Andy Morrow, the sole Protestant of the group. Carleton reflects

> that although there was a due admixture of opposite creeds and conflicting principles, yet even then, and the time is not so far back, such was their cordiality of heart and simplicity of manners when contrasted with the bitter and rancorous spirit of the present day, that the very remembrance of the harmony in which they lived is at once pleasing and melancholy.[9]

"Ned M'Keown" not only creates the atmosphere for the stories which follow; it also introduces the narrators and outlines the structure of the community in which they live. The stories told are in character with their tellers. "Honest, blustering, good-humoured Ned", "the inde-

---

9. "Shane Fadh's Wedding", Works II, p. 683.

fatigable merchant of the village",[10] who is always trying
and failing to make his fortune by some wild form of spe-
culation, relates the tale of fantasy "The Three Tasks" in
which the hero becomes very wealthy by a combination of
sheer luck and magic. "Shane Fadh, who handed down traditions and fairy tales",[11] relates the story of his own
wedding, one of the most memorable events in the history
of the community. "Tom M'Roarkin, the little asthmatic
anecdotarian of half the country, remarkable for chuckling
at his own stories",[12] relates "Larry M'Farland's Wake",
and Pat Frayne the schoolmaster relates "The Battle of the
Factions" in a tone and language entirely appropriate to
the character of a schoolmaster. Had the original plan not
been abandoned, Andy Morrow, Bob Gott, "old M'Kinny" and
Alick M'Kinley would also have told stories. Of these potential storytellers and audience only Andy Morrow and
Alick M'Kinley reappear to comment briefly on the stories
told. One of the most lively personages in the group,
though not a storyteller, is Ned's wife Nancy. Her function in the household is to keep the M'Keown business on
its feet, and her function in the stories is to act as a
link between the various members of the group. Another
linking device in the first two stories is the legend related in "Ned M'Keown" by the repository of tradition,
Shane Fadh, of how old Squire Grames used to come back
from the dead, riding a horse with a loose shoe, to haunt
a man who had cheated him. When Shane has finished this
anecdote the company is made rigid with terror by hearing
a horse with a loose shoe approach the house. The mysterious stranger who enters is discovered at the end of the
next story, "The Three Tasks", to have cheated the
M'Keowns out of money.

Within this framework, with its prevailing atmosphere of comfort and mutual trust, a picture of peasant
values is allowed to emerge. It is significant that only
"The Three Tasks" is a legend with fairytale elements. It
too has its direct point of contact with the peasant com-

---

10. "Ned M'Keown", Works II, p. 655.
11. ibid., p. 659.
12. ibid.

munity; for Ned stresses that the home of the Magennis'
was in a place that they all know[13] and explains the story
as the origin of the popular song "The Little House under
the Hill".[14] Ned himself is a living instance of the way
in which such stories are handed down: he heard it, he
says, from "ould Terry M'Phaudeen".[15] Taken together the
five stories of the group give a composite picture of
Irish life: the legend and fantasy of "The Three Tasks"
illustrate Irish imagination at work, the tales of a wedding, a wake and a faction fight illustrate three areas of
peasant life and custom, and the description of the group
and their comments illustrate Irish attitudes to such matters.

Two sentiments shared by the community are voiced
by Shane Fadh: one is the belief in the superiority of the
landlords of former times and the other is the belief that
all Protestants are damned.[16] Another characteristic attitude is the community's totally unsentimental reaction
to Larry M'Farland's fate. The moral point of this story,
voiced by M'Roarkin, is that "living or dead, them that
won't respect themselves, or take care of their families,
won't be respected ...".[17] Larry was a wastrel and both
he and his family came to tragic ends. This example is
used by Nancy as a stick with which to beat Ned for his
wasteful practices, and the exchanges between Nancy and
Ned link the story of Larry with the description of the
games played at his wake. The wake games are all about
"kissing and marrying, and the like of that", says Andy
Morrow, to whom they are being explained;[18] and many remarks are made about the superior qualities of Irishmen as
lovers, remarks which reflect the community's self-image.
The comments of the audience are missing from "The Battle
of the Factions", where agreement and delight in the
events on the part of the company must be assumed. In the

13. ibid., p. 667.
14. ibid., p. 681.
15. ibid., p. 667.
16. ibid., p. 702.
17. "Larry M'Farland's Wake", Works II, p. 715.
18. ibid., p. 719.

last story, then, apart from some introductory exchanges, the original framework of Traits and Stories has already broken down.

The remainder of the second group of didactic tales are differentiated by the role of the narrator. He is a "digressive narrator ... concerned with dialogue, that is, dialogue with himself, with his characters, with his subject-matter ... and not least with his readers".[19] By intruding to point to a moral or to expand a particular theme Carleton is returning to his practice in the Christian Examiner stories. However, the narrator is now sympathetic to the people, their character and living conditions, and he very often emphasizes that he himself comes from a peasant environment and can therefore pronounce authoritatively upon it. And in contrast to the five stories at the beginning of Traits and Stories, which are nostalgic vignettes of communal life, these remaining stories deal more specifically with peasant character and with current conditions.[20]

In Carleton's few tales of fantasy or near fantasy the didacticism lies more in the purpose of the stories than in their content or structure. For example, "Moll Roe's Marriage or the Pudding Bewitched"[21] is a story told by a senachie at a wake. It begins with a preface on the extravagant nature of Irish humour and the seemingly incongruous custom of providing amusement in a house of mourning. The lesson of the preface is then illustrated by the story. Carleton himself sometimes seems to adopt the narrative posture of such a senachie: one can imagine, for example, "Neal Malone", a story of pure entertainment which shades off into pure fantasy, or "Alley Sheridan. An Irish story" being related around a fireside or at a wake. Indeed it is evident that Carleton was influenced by the story-telling tradition which he describes himself both in his Autobiography and in his introduction to the collected edition of Traits and Stories as having wit-

19. Anne R. Clauss, "Digression as Narrative Technique in Contemporary Fiction", diss. Wisconsin (1970), p. 78.
20. The complex question of character in TS is dealt with in sections C and D below.
21. Published in The Citizen or Dublin Monthly Magazine no. 17 (1841).

nessed in his childhood. His mother was a repository of
"the old sacred songs and airs of Ireland" and his father
was a senachie:

> As a teller of old tales, legends, and historical
> anecdotes he was unrivalled, and his stock of
> them was inexhaustible. He spoke the Irish and
> English languages with nearly equal fluency.
> With all kinds of charms, old ranns, or poems,
> old prophecies, religious superstitions, tales of
> pilgrims, miracles, and pilgrimages, anecdotes of
> blessed priests and friars, revelations from
> ghosts and fairies, was he thoroughly acquainted.
> And so strongly were all these impressed upon my
> mind, by frequent repetition on his part, and the
> indescribable delight they gave me on mine, that
> I have hardly ever since heard, during a tolerab-
> ly enlarged intercourse with Irish society, both
> educated and uneducated — with the antiquary, the
> scholar, or the humble senachie — any single tra-
> dition, usage, or legend, that, as far as I can
> at present recollect, was perfectly new to me or
> unheard before, in some similar or cognate
> dress.[22]

The oral tradition of story-telling would clearly be important in a general consideration of Carleton as a narrator.[23]

In conclusion it may be said that most of Carleton's stories are openly didactic in form and content, but whereas
The Christian Examiner stories are propagandist and unsympathetic to the Irish people the stories in Traits and
Stories try to analyze their character and living conditions in a more constructive manner. This difference can
be seen in characterization, in the role played by the
narrator and also in the nature of the digressions. An

22. Works II, pp. 645-646.
23. In this study I have chiefly concerned myself with the content
    and social context of Carleton's works. The problem of Carle-
    ton's relationship to the oral tradition is a fascinating and im-
    portant one which would repay separate investigation.

exception to this didactic structure is found in the first
five stories of Traits and Stories where the narrator re-
tires into the background and the people speak for themselves. Carleton found this narrative structure too limiting: he wished to take up current issues in his stories
in order to influence the opinion of his readers with regard to the nature of the peasantry and the best measures
for ensuring peace and justice in the country. He reverted therefore to open direction of events and to moral
lectures both on the characters and on the incidents depicted.

C. CHARACTERIZATION I: TYPICAL CHARACTERS

As portrayed by Carleton the Irish peasantry are by no
means a totally homogeneous group. As has been demonstrated, the term "peasantry" covers a variety of people in
different material circumstances;[1] they are unified by
their economic and social position as tenants who work the
land primarily for their own subsistence. Carleton wishes
to stress the variety of character and attitudes belonging
to the peasantry of his day and to characterize them as a
whole class. Despite individual variety of circumstances,
temperament and attitudes, Carleton claims that there are
certain character traits shared by the peasantry and
unique to them, and for the most part his stories are concerned with illustrating these national characteristics.
This is particularly the case with the stories from
Traits and Stories on, and from these may be deduced
Carleton's characterization of the people as a class and
as a race.

As has already been indicated in Chapter I,
Carleton's Christian Examiner stories exhibit not only anti-Catholic but also anti-Irish prejudice. This is clear
both from the overtly propagandist content of the stories
and from the characterization of Catholics and Protestants,[2] where the greatest emphasis is laid on the reli-

---

1. Cf. ch. II, pp. 88-90.
2. Cf. ch. I, p. 68.

gion of the protagonists and they are characterized accordingly. A consistent modification of this standpoint can be discerned in the stories which follow "Denis O'Shaughnessy going to Maynooth"; from blaming Rome for what he regards as the superstitious, indolent and violent character of the people, Carleton begins to broaden his field of enquiry about the miserable state of the country into areas other than the purely religious. He finds that the land system is responsible for many of the more unattractive traits of the Irish peasantry, and he consequently develops new criteria for describing and evaluating them.

Carleton works with a firm, unquestioning belief in the concept of national character. In "The Poor Scholar" he declares that "Of all the national characters on this habitable globe, I verily believe that that of the Irish is the most profound and unfathomable; and the most difficult on which to form a system, either social, moral, or religious".[3] However, before any system can be "founded" the peasantry must be understood. Carleton causes Father O'Brien to remark to Colonel B— that

> it is the landlords of Ireland who know least
> about the great mass of its inhabitants; and I
> might also add, about its history, its litera-
> ture, the manners of the people, their customs,
> and their prejudices. The peasantry know this
> and too often practise upon their ignorance.
> There is a landlord's Vade mecum sadly wanted in
> Ireland ...[4]

Carleton takes upon himself the role of providing "a landlord's Vade mecum", and in the course of his work he tries to draw the landlord and tenant classes closer together by making them understand one another.

Carleton had pandered to Anglo-Saxonist ethnocentrism in the Christian Examiner stories, and although he later tries to balance the picture some traces of his former attitude inevitably remain. Although he moves away from propaganda, operating as he does in terms of a natio-

3. Works II, p. 1077.
4. ibid., p. 1112.

nal character, and remaining in spirit close to the colonist élite while gradually ceasing to be one of its apologists, questions of race and class remain in his arsenal. But before moving on to an analysis of the peasantry as a class it will be in order here to examine some of the typical characters in Carleton's peasant world.

True to his declared aim of portraying the Irish peasantry in all their complexity Carleton operates with a limited number of types acting in typical situations.[5] In his efforts to be objective he presents both the good and the bad qualities of the group, and the priests young and old, the hedge schoolmaster, the ne'er-do-well, the yeoman farmer and the active and passive woman types may be said to provide a representative cross-section of the peasantry.[6]

The "young priest" Denis O'Shaughnessy closely resembles the picture drawn in "A Pilgrimage to Patrick's Purgatory" and "The Station"; and all three characters foreshadow Carleton's description of himself in his Autobiography[7] where he refers to his candidacy for Maynooth. Denis is represented as "a first-rate specimen" of the young priests who are "the most interesting and comical class, perhaps, to be found in the kingdom".[8] The author is careful to underline the realism and typicality of his characterization by frequent reference to the "category" of young priests and by such explanatory remarks as: "Many of my readers may be inclined to exclaim that the character of Denny is not to be found in real life; but they are mistaken who think so". To stress his point, and perhaps also to distract attention from the exaggeration of which

5. For this typology in its baldest form see the sketches reprinted from IPJ in Carleton's Tales and Sketches, illustrating the Character, Usages, Traditions, Sports, and Pastimes of the Irish Peasantry (Dublin 1845).
6. It may be observed here that in his stories Carleton seems to be unable to create individual characters. This is not, however, always true of his novels: see for example Valentine M'Clutchy, the Irish Agent; or, Chronicles of the Castle Cumber Property (1845) and The Black Prophet. A Tale of Irish Famine (1846).
7. 1968 edition, p. 33 and passim.
8. "Denis O'Shaughnessy going to Maynooth", Works II, p. 977.

he is actually guilty, he adds later in the same passage: "In fact were I to detail some of the scenes of his exhibitions as they were actually displayed, <u>then</u> I have no doubt I might be charged with coloring too highly".[9]

As well as being an entertaining story, "Denis O'Shaughnessy" demonstrates the character of the typical young priest and describes his social status. To fulfil this purpose the character of the young priest in question must be credible, and for this reason Carleton does not confine his account merely to describing and illustrating the typical characteristics of such a personage. Denis' character is traced from the time when he was the young son chosen for the priesthood until the eve of his departure for Maynooth. The story thus treats of character development rather than static, "typical" character alone, and Carleton exhibits in the course of the story both the distinctive young priestly characteristics and the social reasons for their development.

Denis is highly pedantic, pompous and pseudo-learned. As one destined for the priesthood he is "cherished, humored in all his caprices, indulged in his boyish predilections, and raised over the heads of his brothers, independently of all personal or relative merit in himself".[10] He grows from a boy who delights in the magic of words and the flaunting of irrelevant learning into a young man who has become tremendously self-assured, vain, haughty, insensitive and ambitious, but although he is insufferable he can also be simple, humble and affectionate. This development is represented by Carleton as being both typical and unavoidable in the case of the young priest.

Denis' father delights in showing off his son's cleverness: "This was usually done by commencing a mock controversy, for the gratification of some neighbor to whom the father was anxious to prove the great talents of his son". His delight and the delight of the neighbours is unbounded: "There's the boy that can rattle off the

---

9. <u>ibid</u>., p. 992.
10. <u>ibid</u>., p. 977.

high English, and the larned Latin, jist as if he was born wid an English Dictionary in one cheek, a Latin Neksuggawn [Lexicon] in the other, an' Doctor Gallagher's Irish Sarmons nately on the top of his tongue between the two".[11] Young Denis can prove Phadrick Murray to be an ass and also proves to the great satisfaction of his listeners that the Protestant Church was invented by Luther and the Devil.[12] He fulfils his social role very competently, speaking and acting as a future priest of the Church, and his glory brings increased self-esteem not only to his family but to the whole community. Carleton allows Denis to speak for himself: he is unhampered by shyness and indulged by his elders, whom he almost hypnotizes with the exuberance of his language. He knows how to turn this to good account: in the true character of the young priest his learning "blazed with peculiar lustre whenever he felt himself out at elbows; for the logic with which he was able to prove the connection between his erudition and a woollen-draper's shop, was, like the ignorance of those who are to be saved, invincible".[13] Carleton illustrates the privileged position of the young priest in the family: in the course of the controversies he has with his father Denis refers to him as "an ungrammatical man"[14] for whose ignorance he blushes. Old Denis is not in the least offended and Carleton adds that such expressions, far from displaying a lack of affection, are "only the licenses and embellishments of discussion, tolerated and encouraged by him to whom they were applied".[15] Denis is merely acting and speaking in the manner approved of for a young priest.

As he grows older Denis becomes increasingly more haughty and withdrawn and he adds to his consequence and authority by dressing in black, appearing only on horseback, eating beef and mutton with a knife and fork and taking his meals apart from the rest of the family. He in-

---

11. ibid., p. 978.
12. The latter passage is not included in Works but is reproduced inter alia in D.J. O'Donoghue's edition of TS (1896), vol. IV, pp. 78-86.
13. Works II, p. 982.
14. ibid., p. 978.
15. ibid., p. 982.

sists on being called "Dionysious" by his parents and on
being addressed as "Sir" by his brothers and sisters, but
his offended family excuse his behaviour, by reasoning, in
the words of his mother, that "The ways o' them that have
great larnin' as he has, isn't like other people's ways —
they must be humored, and have their own will, otherwise
what 'ud they be betther than their neighbors?"[16] Denis is
fawned on and indulged by all and sundry for his supposed
learning and for the exalted position he is one day to occupy. This treatment "absolutely turned his brain, and
made him probably as finished a specimen of pride, self-
conceit, and domineering arrogance"[17] as it was possible
to find. Arrogance and self-importance are, however, but
one side of his or any young priest's character; he is also shrewd and clever. He refuses to allow Father Finnerty
to have his father's colt until he has definitely received
permission to enter Maynooth, and he proves his ability to
extricate himself from a very tricky situation when Owen
Connor finds him making love to his daughter Susan.

   Denis, the young priest, is characterized as much
by his flights of imagination and dreams of future glory as
he is by his language and actions. He delights his adoring
family by imagining himself as a parish priest at some time
in the rosy future, proceeding on his way to a Station followed respectfully by his curates, "gazing with odiferous
admiration upon the prospect about us, and expatiating in
the purest of Latin upon the beauties of unsophisticated
nature". He is saluted with due respect by the peasantry,
and as they approach the house of the Station "No sooner do
we parsave ourselves noticed, then out comes the Breviary,
and in a moment we are at our morning devotions". He is
treated with awe and reverence, and in order to show that
he can "conciliate by love as readily as [he] can impress
them with fear" he relaxes and chats with the family.[18]
The author's rather inept satirical hand is in evidence in
this passage, which is reminiscent of the kind of self-reve-

---

16. ibid., p. 989.
17. ibid., p. 998.
18. ibid., p. 1002.

lation sometimes to be found in the eighteenth century essay.

For Denis entering the priesthood has little to do with the love of God. This is seen clearly when he finally realizes that he loves Susy Connor and love and ambition struggle within him for mastery. Whereas Denis' falling in love is perhaps not typical of the behaviour of the young priest his explanation of his dilemma is totally plausible. He tells Susy that "the disgrace of refusing to enter the Church would lie upon me as if I had committed a crime". He would disappoint and humiliate his whole family. But there are other considerations which weigh more heavily with him. The Catholic Church

> is likely to rise from her ruins. I believe that
> if a priest did his duty he might possess miracu-
> lous power. There is great pomp and splendor in
> her ceremonies, a sense of high and boundless
> authority in her pastors; there is rank in her
> orders sufficient even for ambition. Then the
> deference, the awe, and the humility with which
> they are approached by the people -- ah! Susan,
> there is much still in the character of a priest
> for the human heart to covet. The power of say-
> ing mass, of forgiving sin, of relieving the de-
> parted spirits of the faithful in another world,
> and of mingling in our holy sacrifices, with the
> glorious worship of the cherubims, or angels, in
> heaven — all this is the privilege of a priest,
> and what earthly rank can be compared to it?[19]

He is hypnotized, intoxicated with the power of the Church: such dreams of spiritual power and social position are as much a part of his character as his extravagant language and obnoxious behaviour, and they are in accord with the Irish peasant's view of the position and power — spiritual and temporal — of the priest. There is a certain incompatibility between the two Denises — the pompous prig and the lover — and in artistic terms the characterization is not

---

19. ibid., p. 1025.

entirely successful. However pompous Denis may be, and however hurtful to his family, Carleton nevertheless succeeds in making him sympathetic. He is seen to have a capacity for generosity, and his haughtiness is displayed both as the inevitable result of the exaggerated respect shown to him and as something slightly ridiculous.

Thomas Flanagan considers that "Denis O'Shaughnessy" should have ended when Denis and his father return home triumphantly bearing the bishop's letter of admission to Maynooth, and that when Carleton causes Denis to reflect on his true motives for entering the priesthood he "has come to a belated sense of his duty, and spoils his effect by a long account of Denis' change of heart".[20] Flanagan therefore evaluates the story without the ending that Carleton gave it. This somewhat dubious method can only be adopted if one ignores Carleton's purpose in writing the story. It was certainly composed to entertain but also to illustrate the character of the young priest and the reasons for young men entering the Church. Carleton's ending to the story in fact rounds it off very well. The long scene with Susan is saved from melodrama by Owen Connor who, enraged at finding the "makin's of a priest" making love to his daughter, thumps him smartly on the head with his stout cudgel exclaiming: "Your sowl to the divil, you larned vagabone ... is this the way you're preparin' yourself for the church?" Denis immediately drops his former pose of sorrowful lover who speaks plain English and retorts in his old style: "Why, you miserable vulgarian ... I scorn you from the head to the heel ... desist, I say, and don't approximate, or I will entangle the ribs of you!"[21]

As a typical young priest, Denis' character is represented as ludicrous by Carleton's standard, the standard which he expects his readers to share. Denis is bumptious and amusing, but his motivation for becoming a priest is hardly pure and disinterested. The final section of the story, ending with Denis' departure from Maynooth to marry

---

20. The Irish Novelists, p. 289.
21. Works II, p. 1029.

Susan, is integral to its very nature, and the vein of
rich, high comedy which runs through it serves to counterbalance its more serious aims.

The hedge schoolmaster is a vital part of the rural community and many such schoolmasters appear in Carleton's stories. Mat Kavanagh of "The Hedge School" is perhaps the
most fully treated in terms of characterization but even
he is not as fully rounded as Denis O'Shaughnessy, the
young priest. With the exception of Mr. O'Connor, the
schoolmaster in "Neal Malone" who is present in the story
to act as a warning to Neal of the dangers of married life,
all of Carleton's schoolmasters share similar characteristics. This lack of individual characterization is interesting in itself and underlines Carleton's presentation of
typical rather than individual character in his stories of
Irish life. The hedge schoolmaster had largely disappeared
from the rural scene by 1830; Carleton was aware of this
fact and wrote to preserve the characteristics of a vanished group for posterity.

The schoolmaster was second only to the priest in
learning and in the respect he commanded from the peasantry
on this account. If a peasant's first wish was that his
son should become a priest, his second wish was for him to
become a schoolmaster. Carleton often remarks on the love
of learning apparent amongst the Irish peasantry: this love
of learning was carried over into respect for those who
possessed it and ambition for young men to scale its dizzy
and magical heights.[22] Accordingly a son who had ambitions
in that direction was, like the young priest, greatly indulged by his parents, excused from work, allowed to remain
at school and furnished with the books and clothes necessary to his station, often at great expense to his family.
The typical master in Carleton's stories is very
learned in the classics and mathematics and Carleton adds
that "young men educated in Irish hedge schools, as they
were called, have proved themselves better classical scholars and mathematicians, generally speaking, than any pro-

22. Cf. ch. II, pp. 100-101.

portionate number of those educated in our first-rate academies".[23] One of the striking characteristics of these schoolmasters, or "philomaths" as they call themselves, is their pedantry demonstrated in the collection of curious problems, pure intellectual exercises like that posed to the visiting Cambridge graduate by Mat Kavanagh: "An' how would you find the solid contents of a load of thorns?"; or the mathematical poser put to Mat himself by a travelling schoolmaster while they watch a young pupil dancing: "... what angle does Dick's heel form in the second step of the treble, from the kibe on the left foot to the corner of the door forninst him?"[24]

Characteristic of all schoolmasters is what Carleton terms their "immorality", for which they are, if anything, admired by the peasantry:

> Hedge Schoolmasters were a class of men from whom morality was not expected by the peasantry; for, strange to say, one of their strongest recommendations to the good opinion of the people, as far as their literary talents and qualifications were concerned, was an inordinate love of whiskey, and if to this could be added a slight touch of derangement, the character was complete.

A master shows most learning and teaches ten times better when he is drunk; opinion has it that "... 'tis always the cleverest that you'll find fond of the drink".[25] Mat Kavanagh lives up to this exciting standard.

The schoolmaster resembles the young priest in his delight in extravagant language and his ability to entertain. The cruel master who has received a richly deserved thrashing at the hands of his pupils in "The Poor Scholar" appears at school next day "with one of his eyes literally closed, and his nose considerably improved in size and richness of color".[26] He pacifies his pupils by addressing

---

23. "The Hedge School", Works II, p. 821. P.J. Dowling, The Hedge Schools of Ireland (1935; revised edition Cork 1968), pp. 55 ff. concurs with this judgement.
24. Works II, pp. 844, 846.
25. ibid., p. 819.
26. ibid., pp. 1099-1100.

them with mock gravity, amusing and flattering them and thus salvaging what remains of his authority.

This particular master is famous for his learning and notorious for his cruelty: Carleton remarks in "The Hedge School" that "in truth most of the hedge masters were unfeeling tyrants",[27] and indeed a man who is himself one of the tribe warns Jemmy M'Evoy of the cruelty he is likely to meet with, "for there are larned Neros in Munster, who'd flog if the province was in flames".[28] The "knavish tyrant" of "The Poor Scholar" is a "mercenary pedagogue" who adjusts his indulgence to the children according to the wealth of their parents. Foiled in his attempts to secure Jemmy's savings, he retaliates by turning him out of doors when he is seriously ill, and when Jemmy recovers and returns to the school the master beats him senseless. In "The Hedge School" Carleton gives further examples of the brutal and sadistic practices of some hedge masters:

> Instances have come to our own knowledge, of masters, who, for their mere amusement, would go out to the next hedge, cut a large branch of furze or thorn, and having first carefully arranged the children on a row round the walls of the school, their naked legs stretched out before them, would sweep round the branch, bristling with spikes and prickles, with all his force against their limbs, until, in a few minutes, a circle of blood was visible on the ground where they sat, their legs appearing as if they had been scarified. This the master did, whenever he happened to be drunk, or in a remarkably good humor.

It is not surprising to hear that "Sometimes the brothers and other relatives of the mutilated child would come in a body to the school, and flog the pedagogue with his own taws ..." or "beat him until few symptoms of life remained".[29] In view of the evidence of Carleton's stories it is rather surprising to read in Dowling that "Carleton gives

---

27. ibid., p. 840.
28. "The Poor Scholar", Works II, p. 1094.
29. Works II, pp. 841-842.

the impression that discipline in the Hedge Schools was not, as a rule, severe; rather the opposite ...".[30]

The schoolmasters perform important functions other than teaching. Pat Frayne, "who read and explained the newspaper for 'old Square Colwell'",[31] is "premier" to the company that meets in the evenings in Ned M'Keown's house; and both Mat Kavanagh and Cornelius O'Flaherty of "The Geography of an Irish Oath" perform the office of scribe to their communities, writing letters to sons who are abroad, petitions to the landlord or agent, and drawing up oaths. The schoolmaster is usually the leader or "Captain" of the local branch of the Ribbon society,[32] and indeed when the Findramore men meet to discuss the question of procuring a schoolmaster they agree that they might as well kill two birds with one stone: acquire a schoolmaster for the children, and for themselves "a masther that would carry 'Articles' [Whiteboy or Ribbon oaths and regulations], an' swear in the boys ... an' between ourselves, if there's any danger of the hemp, we may as well lay it upon strange shoulders".[33] Mat Kavanagh is saved at the last moment from execution for a Whiteboy crime, but the master of "Confessions of a Reformed Ribbonman", like so many other masters, is executed.

The hedge schoolmaster is then a learned pedant who enjoys a great deal of respect on account of his position and performs extra-scholarly functions necessary to the community. He is usually fond of whiskey, often extremely cruel, but always gregarious and greedy. By keeping an ironic distance from his schoolmasters Carleton is able to detail all the facets of their characters without condemning them outright.

Having examined Carleton's characterization of the young priest and the hedge schoolmaster, those links with the "higher life",[34] we must now turn to the peasantry them-

---

30. The Hedge Schools of Ireland, p. 45.
31. Works II, p. 659.
32. Cf. ch. II, p. 128.
33. "The Hedge School", Works II, p. 826.
34. Cf. ch. II, p. 101.

selves. Owen M'Carthy and Larry M'Farland are representative of two very different types of men to be found among the peasantry, while Ellish Connell and Rose O'Hallaghan represent two contrasting types of women.

Owen M'Carthy is a perfect example of the group of small independent farmers, "the only men, who, if properly encouraged, were capable of becoming the strength and pride of the country".[35] Carleton assures the reader, as ever, of the authenticity of the portrait: "The following story owes nothing to any coloring or invention of mine ...". He knew the man and relates his tale of woe not so much as an exercise in characterization but as "a moral lesson to Irish landlords".[36]

Owen M'Carthy comes of "a long line of honest ancestors, whose names had never, within the memory of man, been tarnished by the commission of a mean or disreputable action". His family believe that they have the blood of kings flowing in their veins and that they are "a branch of the MacCarthy More stock". They are of high integrity, extremely proud and stern, but unfailingly kind-hearted and generous to those less fortunate than themselves. The family have "a hereditary feeling of just principle" as well as "a correct knowledge of their moral duties" and "a strong feeling of family pride". They are a byword for honesty, integrity and generosity in the district and Owen lives up to the family reputation. He is "an industrious, inoffensive small farmer, beloved, respected, and honored". He aids the people around him with a kind of taciturn kindness, a "quiet benevolence"[37] which is not forgotten by his neighbours when he and his family fall on hard times.

The house at Tubber Derg is made to symbolize Owen's state. While he is still in comfortable circumstances, the white painted house situated in beautiful natural surroundings gives an air of "contentment, industry,

---

35. "Tubber Derg or the Red Well", Works I, p. 971.
36. ibid., p. 945.
37. ibid., p. 946.

and innocence".[38]   But a combination of a national depression, a bad landlord and a villainous agent places Owen in financial difficulties: the house "ceased to be annually ornamented by a new coat of white-wash; it soon assumed a faded and yellowish hue, and sparkled not in the setting sun as in the days of Owen's prosperity. It had, in fact, a wasted, unthriving look, like its master".[39] The family is driven out of Tubber Derg, and seventeen years later, when they are again able to take a farm, Owen makes the house resemble Tubber Derg as closely as possible. The story is circular in structure: it opens with Owen sitting on a bench before his door in the evening sun, contentedly singing, with his family about him and his wife Kathleen and the maids milking. The same scene and the same atmosphere of rural contentment recur at the end.

The burden of Carleton's characterization of Owen M'Carthy is that he is first and foremost a good Christian subjected to unjust treatment. He is tender to his wife and children and generous to the poor. He is pious and trusts in the goodness of God even in the midst of his greatest affliction. When the family is evicted and forced to beg Owen has no words of reproach for those responsible for their shameful fate: "We are ... a poor an' a sufferin' family; but it's the will of God that we should be so, an' sure we can't complain widout committin' sin. All we ax now, is, that it may be plasin' to him that brought us low, to enable us to bear up undher our trials".[40] When his favourite daughter dies of hunger and disease, Owen is broken hearted, but instead of railing at the cruelty of the agent and the neglect of the landlord he falls on his knees and exclaims: "I thank you, O my God! I thank you, an' I put myself and my weeny ones ... into your hands. I thank you, O God, for what has happened! ... You loved the weeny one, and you took her ... an' we can't be angry wid you for so doin'".[41]

---

38. ibid., p. 945.
39. ibid., p. 950.
40. ibid., p. 962.
41. ibid., p. 956.

Carleton holds it up as a Christian virtue that Owen M'Carthy bears no grudge against those who have treated him unjustly. The fate of M'Carthy mirrors that of too many small farmers who are driven to ruin or emigration by the neglect of the landlords in a time of depression. With his characterization of Owen M'Carthy, presented in his ususal didactic manner and exploiting the full range of literary sentiment, Carleton wishes to demonstrate that such men are honest and industrious and entirely undeserving of their bitter fate.[42] It is not these farmers who enter secret societies to take revenge on landlords, agents, or those foolish enough to take farms from which others have been evicted. Like Owen, these men accept their fate as being the will of God. Their utter helplessness and lack of resistance in this matter, which reflects not only their religion (also shared by the Ribbonman) but also the essentially conservative nature of the small farmer,[43] is applauded by Carleton. Owen is in fact Carleton's image of the ideal Irish peasant, noble in sentiment, generous, honest and God-fearing, and he writes of him in a reverential tone bordering at times on nostalgic sentimentality.

Very different is the attitude adopted to Phelim O'Toole[44] or Larry M'Farland, both of whom are characterized as harum-scarum ne'er-do-wells, talented and clever but without the moral fibre necessary to succeed in adversity. Despite personal tragedy and great injustice Owen finally regains his former position through determination and industry. Like the M'Evoy's of "The Poor Scholar", who are originally of the same social class, the M'Carthy family are law-abiding and decent. In their code of honour elements such as independence, respectability and sobriety play a large part. Like Phelim O'Toole, Larry M'Farland comes from a lower social class, and despite the fact that examples of industry are also to be found among such people Carleton never adopts the same attitude of re-

---

42. For another treatment of the same problem see Carleton's novel
   The Emigrants of Ahadarra (1848).
43. Cf. ch. II, p. 116.
44. Cf. ch. II, pp. 129-130.

verence to them as he adopts to the independent farmers. Phaddy Sheemus Phaddy and his wife have worked themselves up into a comfortable position, as have Ellish and Peter Connell, but while he respects their efforts Carleton allows himself to be ironic at their expense.[45] They can get drunk, be shrewd and cunning and find themselves in ludicrous situations, whereas these elements of behaviour never appear in connection with the M'Carthy's or the M'Evoy's, whose sterling qualities and simple character are eulogized and idealized and serve to heighten the pathos and injustice of their fate.

"Phelim O'Toole's Courtship" is in the tradition of the tall story with a picaresque protagonist who is amusing and reprehensible at the same time. Phelim and Larry M'Farland have many characteristics in common, but Larry is a figure more typical of the tenant farmer and may therefore be analyzed here. His history is that of a man who goes down in the world through his own negligence and lack of the correct attitudes, and Carleton's didactic method is to contrast Larry and his wife Sally with his brother Tom and his wife, who begin with exactly similar opportunities but succeed where Larry and Sally fail. Larry is an excellent farm labourer who never has any trouble in finding work, but he is "a light, airy young man", proud of his abilities, who likes to dance and drink and dress "above his station". There is none of Owen M'Carthy's steadfastness and constancy about Larry: he never stays with any one farmer for more than a year at a time and is always to be found at fairs and wakes, drinking, dancing and enjoying himself in the company of Sally Lowry, who has exactly the same character as himself. Tom is not by any means as gifted as his brother but has the advantage of being "a sober, industrious boy". While Larry marries the feckless, penniless Sally, Tom marries "Val Slevin's daughter, that had a fortune of twenty guineas, a cow and a heifer, with two good chaff beds and bed-

---

45. These characters appear in "The Station" and "The Geography of an Irish Oath" respectively.

ding".[46]   The two young couples take a farm together, sharing a double house and fourteen acres, and the character contrast is immediately apparent from their ambitions: Larry swears that he will make the land yield such good crops that he will become wealthy, whereas Tom more soberly hopes that if they work hard they should be able to live decently and comfortably. Tom is "up early and down late",[47] improving the farm and asking every man's advice about farming methods. Larry does very well in his first fit of enthusiasm, but then boredom causes him to go back to his old habits of drinking and attending fairs. Sally equally neglects her duties, and where Tom and Biddy (Nelly on p. 713) steadily work themselves up into comfort and respectability, Larry and Sally just as steadily slide down into utter poverty.

A major factor in this downward slide is Larry's need to impress others. He could never save money or even keep enough for necessities like rent and clothing for the family, because when he went to fairs he took money with him in case anyone treated him and he would have to treat back.[48] Likewise, he would offer to stack the Squire's corn or cut his hay while his own crops rotted in the ground: "he'd then get some one to cut it down for him — he had to go to the big house, to build the master's corn; he was then all bustle — a great man entirely — there was non such".[49] On the other hand both Sally and Larry are very generous, all too generous for their own good, helping anyone who asks and neglecting their own business in the process. They have no sense of proportion and are afraid "of being thought unneighbourly". The narrator sums up their lack of success:

> you see both himself and his wife neglected their
> business in the beginning, so that everything
> went at sixes and sevens. They then found them-
> selves uncomfortable at their own hearth, and had

---

46.   "Larry M'Farland's Wake", Works II, p. 704. Cf. the remarks on peasant values in ch. II, pp. 98-100.
47.   Works II, p. 705.
48.   ibid.
49.   ibid., p. 706.

no heart to labor: so that what would make a
careful person work their fingers to the stumps
to get out of poverty, only prevented them from
working at all, or druv them to work for those
that had more comfort, and could give them a better male's mate [meal's meat] than they had themselves.[50]

The rather schematized portrait of Larry's character has
psychological probability: a clever man, he aimed at the
wealth and happiness he saw in the Squire's family but
achieved neither because, as the narrator would have it,
he did not realize that success demands a capacity for
hard work and stamina of a kind he did not have. Carleton
pounds his message home. The miserable fate of the M'Farland's was by no means inevitable; they were "two that
might have done well in the world, had they taken care of
themselves — avoided fairs and markets — except when they
had business there — not given themselves idle fashions by
drinking, or going to dances, and wrought as well for
themselves as they did for others".[51]

The moral in the story is very reminiscent of Mary Leadbeater's Cottage Dialogues among the Irish Peasantry,[52] which carries the same message but is even more
openly didactic and "improving". Leadbeater employs a similar contrastive method: in the first volume of Cottage
Dialogues her Nancy and Tim and Rose and Jem resemble Sally and Larry and Biddy and Tom respectively. Nancy and
Rose are traced from adolescence to maturity, and while
careful, hard-working, constant Rose thrives, Nancy's
faults bring her ultimately "to sorrow, shame, poverty,
and death".[53]

---

50. ibid., p. 707.
51. ibid., p. 714.
52. 2v., London 1811-13. There is an interesting Scottish parallel
    to Cottage Dialogues in Elizabeth Hamilton, The Cottagers of
    Glenburnie (Edinburgh 1808).
53. p. 268. In the second volume, which came out in response to the
    favourable reception of the first, Leadbeater endeavours to "per-
    form the same service to the Men of the Cottage, that was in the
    first Part designed for their Consorts" (p. iii).

Carleton presents the reader with two types of peasant women, the shrewd, hard-working farmer's wife and the beautiful, innocent young girl. There are of course shades in
between, but generally speaking peasant women in Traits
and Stories approximate either to the active Ellish
Connell or the passive Rose O'Hallaghan type of "The Geography of an Irish Oath" and "The Battle of the Factions"
respectively. Women rarely occupy such a prominent place
as men in the stories and in this respect Ellish Connell
is unique. Her history is traced from the time she marries Peter Connell through her growing prosperity to her
death. She is by no means a tender little flower — she is
plain and homely — but what she lacks in beauty she com-
pensates for in energy, and she makes the fortunes of the
family. Peter is naturally lazy and fun-loving, and had
he "been married to a woman of a disposition resembling
his own, it is probable that he would have sunk into indolence, filth, and poverty". Ellish is much more intelligent than Peter and therefore never tells him what to do:
"Her mode of operation was judiciously suited to his tem-
per. Playfulness and kindness were the instruments by
which she managed him".[54] She wheedles him into hard work
and prevents him from making fatal mistakes. Meanwhile
she herself is a model of industry and initiative: Peter
develops into a big farmer and she into a successful shop-
keeper. Carleton characterizes her as a large, bustling,
cheerful woman with whom the people love to deal. She
flatters, competes and plans, is cautious, thrifty, acute
and energetic, always pleasant, never imperious. Ellish
subordinates every action of her life to the business of
making money: it is to this end that she has her children
educated. However, she never makes an ostentatious display of her wealth and considers it bad for business to
involve herself in politics. Her sure knowledge of the
behaviour and the business ethics necessary for acquiring
wealth, which she passes on to her son-in-law, serve to
characterize her in all essentials: "tell truth; be sober;
be punctual; rise early; persavere; avoid extravagance;

---

54. "The Geography of an Irish Oath", Works II, p. 931; cf. the characterization of Larry M'Farland.

keep your word; an' watch your health. Next: don't be proud; give no offince; talk sweetly; be ready to oblage, when you can do it widout inconvanience, but don't put yourself or your business out o' your ways to sarve anybody".[55] In all her busy life of money-making Ellish has no time for religion, and she dies before she can attend to her soul. This circumstance, in addition to her extremely materialistic nature, makes her less than an ideal woman for Carleton albeit she is a pattern of industry. He admires her energy and good sense but censures her neglect of God, which is not a pleasing thing in a woman. Other industrious, vigorous women appear in Carleton's pages: Nancy M'Keown, Katty, wife of Phaddy Sheemus Phaddy, the women of "Barney Brady's Goose", Mrs. Sheridan of "Alley Sheridan" are all clever and enterprising women who can manage their husbands and their homes. They are all to be admired but not adored. It is significant that Carleton allows himself to portray them with humour, kindly and ironic, while never a whiff of laughter enters his depiction of such women as Rose O'Hallaghan.

This other predominant type of woman in Carleton's stories has much in common with Dickens' more nauseating heroines. Like Dickens and unlike Thackeray, Carleton could not be ironic about the archetypal "good little woman". In keeping with her character, she never takes a prominent part in any of the stories but modestly and shyly occupies her place in the background. It may be remarked that few such women could genuinely have existed among the peasantry, and it is significant that most women of this sort appear as young unmarried girls. After marriage, one presumes, they would metamorphose into the first type. Carleton's adoration of his mother,[56] his weakness for female company,[57] and his respect for literary and social convention all contributed to his concept of

55. ibid., p. 945.
56. This adoration is evident both from Carleton's Autobiography and from the passage on his mother in the introduction to the collected edition of TS.
57. That Carleton was fond of women can be deduced from his Autobiography and from some of the letters printed in André Boué, William Carleton (1973); e.g. his letter to Lady Wilde, Boué pp. 505-507.

the ideal woman. He admires Ellish Connell for her cleverness but never waxes lyrical about her. It is indicative that she is plain — the ideal woman cannot be both
pretty and clever.

At the time of the story of "The Battle of the
Factions" Rose O'Hallaghan is about nineteen years old.
She is so well beloved by both factions that "there wasn't
a man, woman, or child, on either side that wouldn't lay
their hands under her feet".[58] She and John O'Callaghan,
who belongs to the opposite faction, are in love with one
another; but true to her modest nature she merely indicates her "taciturn approval" of John's love, glancing at
him shyly and blushing. John saves her from drowning when
she faints in alarm while crossing an improvised bridge
over a swollen river. She had at first been afraid even
to step on the bridge: "her courage as often refused to
be forthcoming".[59] When John has revived her with a kiss
and she learns that it is he who has saved her, "a faint
smile played about her mouth, and a slight blush lit up
her fair cheek, like the evening sunbeams on the virgin
snow ...". The families make up their quarrel and John
and Rose are engaged to be married. It is a perfect
match: "John was as fine a young man as you would meet in
a day's travelling; and as for Rose, her name went far and
near for beauty: and with justice, for the sun never shone
on a fairer, meeker, or modester virgin than Rose Galh
O'Hallaghan".[60] Unfortunately the epic "Battle of the
Factions" takes place a week before their wedding day:
John is killed by Rose's brother, whom she instantly
strikes down, dropping her passivity for one fatal moment.
When she recovers from her horror "her senses [are] found
to be gone for ever ... She is, indeed, a fair ruin, but
silent, melancholy, and beautiful as the moon in the sum-
mer heaven".[61]

Rose O'Hallaghan's beauty, meekness, modesty and
virginity are all attributes of Carleton's ideal woman.

58. Works II, p. 726.
59. ibid., p. 730.
60. ibid., pp. 732-733.
61. ibid., p. 740. Cf. the somewhat similar fate of Jane Sinclair in
    "Jane Sinclair or the Fawn of Springvale".

To take some other examples: Peggy Gartland of "The Midnight Mass" is a "fair, artless girl" whose "love and sympathy were pure as the dew on the grassblade".[62] Susan
Connor is "slender, and not above the middle size; but
certainly, in point of form and feature, such as might be
called beautiful ...". She is "a sweet picture of innocence and candor".[63] And again: "Her great charm consisted in a spirit of youthful innocence, so guileless that
the very light of purity and truth seemed to break in ra-
diance from her countenance".[64] All of these women unque-
stioningly accept the decisions of their menfolk and live
for them alone. Though there are great differences between active and passive women — of whom it is evident
that the latter are regarded as being the more "feminine"
— none of them attempt to stray outside the confines of
the home.

The pictures considered here are genre pictures drawn from
Carleton's memories and intended primarily for "foreign"
consumption. Either because of his lack of artistic sense
or because of his eagerness to instruct, Carleton never
permits the reader to draw his own conclusions about the
characters in question. He tells, shows and tells again
in the manner of a sympathetic journalist or social historian rather than a writer of fiction. Denis O'Shaughnessy
is his most successful portrait; but even there the didactic intention appears to outweigh literary considerations.

D. CHARACTERIZATION II: THE IRISH PEOPLE

The introduction to the collected edition of Traits and
Stories concludes with the following sentence:

> I have endeavoured ... to give a panorama of Irish
> life among the people — comprising at one view
> all the strong points of their general character
> — their loves, sorrows, superstitions, piety,

---

62. Works II, pp. 883-884.
63. "Denis O'Shaughnessy going to Maynooth", Works II, p. 994.
64. ibid., p. 1023.

amusements, crimes, and virtues; and in doing this, I can say with solemn truth that I painted them honestly, and without reference to the existence of any particular creed or party.[1]

In the course of the introduction Carleton sketches his view of Irish character: "the character of an Irishman has been hitherto uniformly associated with the idea of something unusually ridiculous ...". He adds that he "rejoices" in the opportunity to remove "many absurd prejudices which have existed for [sic] time immemorial against his countrymen".[2]

However, it is clear that Carleton while lovingly painting a composite picture of the life and character of the people nevertheless took as his model the prevalent English stereotype of the Irish Celt.[3] For this he cannot be censured — indeed he could scarcely have avoided doing so — and it is interesting to perceive which elements of the stereotype he supported, which elements he tried to counterbalance and what he attempted to add to the general picture of Irish character. A note of paradox runs through his characterization of the people: he finds cleverness and duplicity, exuberance which sometimes has disastrous consequences, a love of learning side by side with superstition, honesty and pride in family co-existing with indolence and improvidence. Thus, though he accepts that much of what is said about Irish people is justified, he protests that they have hitherto undescribed good qualities.

Carleton maintains and sets out to prove that the Irish are an extraordinarily clever people. This quality manifests itself in "readiness of wit", "fertility of invention"[4] and a "natural quickness of penetration and shrewdness...".[5] Carleton nevertheless sees two sides to the cleverness of the people: they are humorous and love stimulating talk and

---

1. _Works_ II, p. 653.
2. _ibid._, p. 641.
3. On anti-Irish prejudice cf. ch. I, pp. 66 ff.
4. "Condy Cullen; or, the Exciseman Defeated" _Tales and Sketches_ (1845), p. 276.
5. "The Station", _Works_ II, p. 751.

fun, but their quickness of wit sometimes leads them into
minor crimes and perjury in courts of law. One of the favourite means employed by the peasantry to outwit their
superiors is to act as simpletons. They are clever enough
to realize that the suspicions of the gentry, who regard
their tenants as an inferior species, will not be aroused
by this play. In accordance with his new policy of showing Catholic clergymen in a favourable light and exemplifying that they too are to be counted among the upholders
of law and order, Carleton causes no less a personage than
a Catholic bishop to address a group of peasants on their
besetting sin:

> I warn you both against falsehood and fraud; two
> charges which might frequently be brought against
> you in your intercourse with the gentry of the
> country, whom you seldom scruple to deceive and
> mislead, by gliding into a character, when speak-
> ing to them, that is often the reverse of your
> real one; whilst at the same time you are both
> honest and sincere to persons of your own class.[6]

Part of the ambivalence of Carleton's position can be seen
in his attitude to this phenomenon: he denounces it and is
amused by it at the same time.

The gentry may not be able to penetrate the mask
of the simpleton, but the "gauger" or exciseman knows a
little more about what he has to deal with; and while it
may be easy to fool the landlord the gauger is a more worthy foe. The battle between these traditional enemies is
"the struggle between mind and mind — between wit and wit
— between roguery and knavery".[7] In "Condy Cullen; or, the
Exciseman Defeated" the struggle between Condy Cullen the
illicit distiller and Stinton the gauger — a battle of
giants — is won by the distiller: the sharp and experienced
Stinton proved to be no match for Condy Cullen, who was
"descended from a long line of private distillers, and, of
course, exhibited in his own person all the practical wit,

6. "The Poor Scholar", Works II, p. 1109.
7. "Condy Cullen; or, the Exciseman Defeated", Tales and Sketches
   p. 276.

sagacity, cunning, and fertility of invention, which the
natural genius of his family, sharpened by long experience, had created from generation to generation, as a
standing capital to be handed down from father to son".[8]

Phil Purcel is a character taken from the same
mould as Condy Cullen, but "Phil Purcel the Pig-Driver"[9]
goes further than "Condy Cullen" in displaying Carleton's
view of anti-Irish prejudice among the English. Although
Phil Purcel is "a knave of the first water" his duplicity
is not immediately apparent: "The assumed simplicity of
his manners was astonishing, and the ignorance which he
feigned, so apparently natural, that it was scarcely possible for the most keen-sighted searcher into human motives to detect him".[10] As a "Professor of Pig-driving"
he undertakes "a professional trip to England"[11] which
proves very lucrative. He sells his pigs to a Yorkshireman and retaining only one sets off across the country.
He has trained the animal to escape from its sty and follow him, and by "selling" it again and again he proceeds
towards his destination very economically. We witness
Phil's encounter with a gentleman whom he forces to buy
the pig. The gentleman invites his wife and some other
ladies to come and look at Phil, "for he is the greatest
simpleton of an Irishman I have ever met with", and they
come "in order to hear the Irishman's brogue, and to amuse
themselves at his expense".[12] They hold to the letter of
the Irish stereotype — while Phil is assumed to be violent, stupid, ill-spoken, wild and primitive, he also appears quite attractive. Having a low opinion of him they
do not expect him to be in the least sensitive, and they
discuss him within his hearing. The gentleman feels
called upon to reflect solemnly: "Good heavens! what barbarous habits these Irish have in all their modes of life,
and how far they are removed from anything like civilisation! ... What an amazing progress civilisation must make

---

8. ibid., p. 275.
9. First published in TS[2] (1833); reprinted in Works II.
10. Works II, p. 905.
11. ibid., p. 909.
12. ibid., p. 912.

before these Irish can be brought at all near the commonest standard of humanity".[13] The lady has noticed on Phil's face "a lurking kind of expression, which is a sign of their humor, I suppose".[14] Phil is of course enjoying himself hugely at the expense of the gentry, whiling away an hour in flirting with the ladies, making a nice profit by the transaction and securing bed and breakfast for himself and his pig. At their parting the Englishman has nothing but "contempt for the sense and intellect of Phil: nothing could surpass it but the contempt which Phil entertained for him".[15]

This story is in itself very amusing but has a double edge. In English magazines and newspapers cartoonists often used the symbol of the pig when depicting Irish conditions. "It was a shorthand method of conveying just those brutish, primitive, and dirty qualities which were associated with the vast majority of Irishmen".[16] The pigs which Phil has sold to the Yorkshireman leap to freedom over the walls of their sty and gallop wildly around the countryside, wreaking havoc and ingeniously evading capture by the country people. Carleton rather snidely comments that "the conflict was conducted on the part of the Irish pigs with a fertility of expediencey [sic] that did credit to their country, and established for those who displayed it, the possession of intellect far superior to that of their opponents".[17] Irish pigs who are cleverer than Englishmen, even though the Englishmen in question are Yorkshire peasants, and an Irish peasant who outwits and laughs at an English gentleman — these elements are hardly to be found in the contemporary stereotype of the Irishman. Carleton has turned the pig image on its head and has used it to poke gentle fun at those who employ it, just as he has demonstrated the nature of the mind behind the simple face and ragged appearance of men like Phil Purcel. André Boué has pointed out that Carleton sometimes mocks at the false idea which

13. ibid., p. 914.
14. ibid., p. 912.
15. ibid., p. 915.
16. Curtis, Anglo-Saxons and Celts, p. 58.
17. Works II, p. 910.

Englishmen had of the Irish. "Bien avant Shaw, Carleton s'est attaqué au mythe du Stage Irishman en le ridiculisant".[18] Phil Purcel is indeed the stage Irishman with a difference. He is full of blarney, he is amusing, and his linguistic blunders or "bulls", while equal to anything to be found in the Edgeworth Essay on Irish Bulls,[19] are deliberately committed. It serves his purpose admirably to conform to the stereotype in speech, action and dress.

In the introduction to the collected edition of Traits and Stories Carleton has more to say on the consequences of the traditional image of the Irishman:

> The habit of looking upon him in a ludicrous
> light has been so strongly impressed upon the
> English mind, that no opportunity has ever been
> omitted of throwing him into an attitude of gross
> and overcharged caricature, from which you might
> as correctly estimate his intellectual strength
> and moral proportions, as you would the size of a
> man from his evening shadow.

Concerning the view of Irishmen in English drama he remarks: "There the Irishman was drawn in every instance as the object of ridicule, and consequently of contempt; for it is incontrovertibly true, that the man whom you laugh at you will soon despise".[20] In "Phil Purcel the Pig-Driver" the tables are turned and the Englishman is made the object of ridicule. However, although he has no name other than "the Englishman", he is not ridiculed specifically because of his nationality; he appears in a ridiculous light because his contempt for the "barbarous" Irishman is so profound that he cannot credit him with any intelligence and so is cheated.[21] Stinton the gauger does not at first make the comparable mistake of assuming that distillers are simpletons, and his struggle with Condy Cullen is an ongoing battle of equals: Condy wins in this

18. William Carleton (1973), p. 320.
19. By Richard Lovell Edgeworth and Maria Edgeworth (London 1802);
     see also Florence C. Scott, "Teg — the Stage Irishman" Modern
     Language Review XLII (1947), pp. 314-320.
20. Works II, pp. 641-642.
21. In contrast, "The Misfortunes of Barney Branagan" (1841) has many
     passages emphasizing the villainy of Englishmen in Ireland.

particular round, but one is left with the impression that Stinton may very well win in the next. Carleton has here progressed a long way from his representation of the Irish peasant as a half-wit, the representation apparent in the early stories where the predominant traits are ignorance, cunning and superstion.

Cleverness with a more serious intent is displayed in the courts of law, where the "simpleton" technique is favoured by those who come to swear alibis for friends charged with crimes of a political (agrarian) nature. Phelim O'Toole is a past master in the art of swearing alibis; he confounds the best legal brains and in turn exasperates and amuses the prosecuting counsel. Phelim, in his turn, is outwitted by Fool Art — another master — and in the end is caught and imprisoned.

With the air of a connoisseur, Carleton compares the Irish, English and Scottish people as to their abilities in the noble art of swearing oaths: "The Englishman ... will depose to the truth of this or that fact, but there the line is drawn ... The Scotchman, on the other hand, who is the metaphysician in swearing, sometimes borders on equivocation. He decidedly goes farther than the Englishman, not because he has less honesty, but more prudence". Carleton glories in the superior abilities of his countrymen in this area:

> But Paddy! Put _him_ forward to prove an _alibi_ for
> his fourteenth or fifteenth cousin, and you will
> be gratified by the pomp, pride, and circumstance
> of true swearing. Every oath with him _is_ an epic
> — pure poetry, abounding with humor, pathos, and
> the highest order of invention and talent. He is
> not at ease, it is true, under _facts_; there is
> something too commonplace in dealing with them,
> which his genius scorns. But his flights — his
> flights are beautiful; and his episodes admirable
> and happy. In fact, he is an _improvisatore_ at
> oath-taking; with this difference, that his _ex-_

> _tempore_ oaths possess all the ease and correctness of labor and design.[22]

So far Carleton works within the terms of reference of the stereotype, but he adds a rather Swiftian sting. "Paddy" may distort the facts to suit his own convenience or that of his friends, but

> Let epic swearing be treated with the same courtesy shown to epic poetry, that is, if both are the production of a rare genius. I maintain, that when Paddy commits a blemish he is too harshly admonished for it. When he soars out of sight here, as occasionally happens, does he not frequently alight somewhere about Sydney Bay, much against his own inclination? And if he puts forth a hasty production, is he not compelled, for the space of seven or fourteen years, to revise his oath?[23]

Carleton celebrates the ability of the peasantry to outwit their superiors and reprimands them for doing so, but this very ability manifests itself in his work as a kind of guile, which by definition is the attribute of an inferior proving the necessity of firm rule. Undermining the legal system in this manner and refusing to take the oath seriously is a perfect demonstration of the age-old contempt and distrust of the peasantry for what they regard as an alien and repressive legal system. At the same time as praising the quickness of wit of his countrymen and refuting their supposed stupidity, Carleton places himself at a distance from them when he warns their superiors of the tricks they can get up to.

Already in his fourth story published in The Christian Examiner Carleton had begun to celebrate the liveliness of the Irish peasant community, their high spirits, their delight in feasting and dancing, their love of companionship

---

22. "An Essay on Irish Swearing" (incorporated into "The Geography of an Irish Oath"), Works II, p. 918. The two stories here combined were first printed separately in TS[2] (1833).
23. ibid., pp. 918-919.

and fun. In "The Station", those who go to Father Philemy for confession are characterized as "honest, good-hu-
mored, thoughtless, jovial, swearing, drinking, fighting
Hibernians ...",[24] a perfect analogy to "Paddy" of the
stereotype — the "feckless, devil-may-care, rollicking,
hard-drinking, and hard-fighting peasant ...".[25] Carleton
takes great delight in depicting this side of Irish life
and character. As at Shane Fadh's wedding, food and drink
are abundant at the Station:

> There was plenty of bacon, and abundance of cab-
> bages — eggs, ad infinitum — oaten and wheaten
> bread in piles — turkeys, geese, pullets, as fat
> as aldermen — cream as rich as Croesus — and
> three gallons of poteen, one sparkle of which, as
> Father Philemy said in the course of the evening,
> would lay the hairs on St. Francis himself in his
> most self-negative mood ...[26]

Having confessed their sins, attended Mass and taken Communion, the company proceeds to the serious business of
eating and drinking and all, including the priest, stagger
home gloriously drunk. Up to this point Carleton has
thrown himself wholeheartedly into the merrymaking, but
remembering his duty to The Christian Examiner he reprodu-
ces some of the dinner-table conversation. The latter is
highly amusing, but Carleton primly states that his purpose is to display "the spirit in which a religious cere-
mony such as it is, is too frequently closed".[27] At such
moments one cannot help feeling that his moral concern is
only skin deep, or rather that he tries to be true both to
the world from which he has come and the world which employs him. More than that, perhaps, he enjoys such scenes
but feels that they are in some way symptomatic of the low
moral standard of the Irish. A similar difficulty is to
be seen in his treatment of the great dance in "The Midnight Mass", where "The din produced by the thumping of
vigorous feet upon the floor, the noise of the fiddle, the

24. ibid., p. 754.
25. Curtis, Anglo-Saxons and Celts, p. 52.
26. "The Station", Works II, p. 747.
27. ibid., p. 758.

chat between Barny [the blind fiddler] and the little sober knot about him, together with the brisk murmur of the
general conversation, and the expression of delight which
sat on every countenance"[28] removes the dance far from the
fashionable ball into the area of broad enjoyment. However, Carleton feels constrained to reflect that the
sight "cannot fail to impress an observing mind with the
obvious truth, that a nation of people so thoughtless and
easily directed from the serious and useful pursuits of
life to such scenes, can seldom be industrious and wealthy, nor, despite their mirth and humor, a happy
people".[29]

The author was caught here between two cultures
and two opposing sets of values. On the one hand he delighted in the liveliness of the Irish people, on the
other hand he wished them to live by the code of Samuel
Smiles for their own good. Enjoyment of the kind seen at
"Shane Fadh's Wedding" or "Larry M'Farland's Wake" can
lead to drunkenness and fighting, both moral aberrations of
which Carleton took a serious view. The Irish were infamous for these vices, and that they were wide-spread among
the peasantry of the time may be gathered from the character given to old Frank M'Kenna in "The Midnight Mass": he
is "a snug farmer, frugal and industrious in his habits,
and, what is rare amongst most men of his class, addicted
to neither drink nor quarrelling".[30] Dick Magrath is unlike many of "the lower orders" in that he "is not a quar-
relsome man, nor a drunkard ...".[31] More typical is Ned
M'Keown: when the opportunity presents itself he drinks
away all his money and fastens "a quarrel on some friend
or acquaintance ...".[32] On the communal plane, the scene
at the Station in "Phelim O'Toole's Courtship" may be taken as typical. When the religious rites have been performed, the pilgrims rush off to the drinking booths and

28. ibid., p. 863.
29. ibid., p. 862.
30. ibid., p. 853.
31. "Dick Magrath. A Sketch of Living Character" The Dublin Family
     Magazine; or, Literary and Religious Miscellany no. 5 (1829),
     p. 343.
32. "Ned M'Keown", Works II, p. 656.

the ensuing scene is chaotic: "Tipsy men were staggering in every direction: fiddlers were playing, pipes were squeaking, men were rushing in detached bodies to some fight, women were doctoring the heads of such as had been beaten, and factions were collecting their friends for a fresh battle".[33]

Carleton maintains that a love of fighting belongs to the Irish nature: it is an "innate ... principle in their disposition ...".[34] They are indeed, he says, a curious race: "It has been long laid down as a universal principle, that self-preservation is the first law of nature. An Irishman, however, has nothing to do with this; he disposes of it as he does with the other laws, and washes his hands out of it altogether".[35] Bound up with his love of fighting is the Irishman's view of himself as a man of honour, particularly in affairs of the heart, a view shared by aristocracy and peasantry alike. Phil Purcel tells the English ladies that "the gintlemen from Ireland" are "the boys that fwoight [fight] for yees, and 'ud rather be bringing an Englishman to the sad [sod] fwor your sakes, nor atin' bread an' butther";[36] and Pat Frayne describes the faction fight as the "acumen" of an Irishman's enjoyment. This is all very entertaining and predictable: it is merely "Paddy", the figure who "posed a more serious threat to himself and those with whom he lived than to Irish landlords and English officials".[37] However, when the fighting engaged in is political, the "national trait" no longer appears so amusing. The party fight[38] is one example: to Carleton it is not the fighting, maiming and killing which matter so much as the spirit in which they are carried out. Killing in revenge would seem to him to be inherent in the Irish character. The many instances of informers being executed, and the warnings issued to the Ribbonmen (in "Confessions of a Reformed Ribbonman") both by the example made of an informer

33. Works II, p. 1037.
34. "The Midnight Mass", Works II, p. 854.
35. "The Party Fight and Funeral", Works II, p. 762.
36. "Phil Purcel the Pig-Driver", Works II, p. 913.
37. Curtis, p. 52.
38. Cf. ch. II, pp. 121 ff.

and by the Captain's dark threats, exemplify the prevailing spirit of revenge. There are of course some striking exceptions: Owen M'Carthy, for example, passively accepts the unjust treatment meted out to him and Carleton remarks: "The reader perceives that he was a meek man; that his passions were not dark nor violent; he bore no revenge to those who neglected or injured him, and in this he differed from too many of his countrymen".[39]

Curtis draws attention to the fact that among the pejorative adjectives used about the Irish by Anglo-Saxonists the most damaging

> were those which had to do with their alleged unreliability, emotional instability, mental disequilibrium, or dualistic temperament. The stereotypical Irishman was a kind of Celtic Jekyll and Hyde; he oscillated between two extremes of behavior and mood; he was liable to rush from mirth to despair, tenderness to violence, and loyalty to treachery. The Irish were therefore often treated as an untrustworthy and dishonest people.[40]

The political implications of this judgement were obvious with regard to Irish self-government; and it must be remembered that Carleton unreservedly supports the Union with England. He admits the emotional instability of the Irish peasantry and not only illustrates but also discourses upon it.

The people show their feelings openly, in contrast to 'the more reserved Anglo-Saxons, and their grief is deep and lasting. Carleton finds such grief for the death of a member of the family honourable and a sign of the fine character of the people he is describing. But they can swing quickly from one emotion to the other, and wild mirth and wild grief are by no means incompatible: in "The Poor Scholar" Carleton makes reference to "That inextinguishable vein of humor, which in Ireland mingles even

---

39. "Tubber Derg or the Red Well", Works I, p. 957.
40. Curtis, p. 51.

with death and calamity ..."[41] and in "The Midnight Mass"
he states more specifically that

> The Irish are a people whose affections are as
> strong as their imaginations are vivid; and, in
> illustration of this, we may add, that many a
> time have we seen them raised to mirth and melted
> into tears almost at the same time, by a song of
> the most comic character. The mirth, however,
> was for the song, and the sorrow for the memory
> of some beloved relation who had been remarkable
> for singing it, or with whom it had been a favo-
> rite.[42]

Imagination and a display of emotion are positive qualities, at least to Carleton, but neither is an unmixed
blessing, for if the people were less imaginative they
would be happier and more prosperous. Moreover, it is
imagination combined with "superstition, which also de-
pends much upon imagination, that makes them so easily influenced by those extravagant dreams that are held out to
them by persons who understand their character".[43] Thus
Carleton claims that unscrupulous priests, politicians and
Ribbon agitators pervert the inherent imaginativeness of
the people into a destructive force. However, he counter-
balances the negative connotations of emotionalism and
fantasy by bringing to the attention of his readers the
lesser known qualities of the Irish; significantly, these
better characteristics do not appear in the stereotype
which as Curtis represents it is uniformly negative and
patronizing.

Carleton emphasizes that the people as a whole are remar-
kably hospitable and generous — they are very much attached to their families and are animated by a strong spirit of family pride. Thus, Father Philemy works on Phaddy
Sheemus Phaddy's feelings and shrewdly manages to secure
for himself both mutton and wine in addition to the food

---

41. Works II, p. 1104.
42. ibid., pp. 854-855; Carleton exemplifies this point in "The Geo-
    graphy of an Irish Oath".
43. "Tubber Derg or the Red Well", Works I, p. 952.

already provided by telling him of the delicacies offered
the previous evening at the home of his rival; but apart
from this "there is a generous hospitality in an Irish peasant which would urge him to any strategem, were it even
the disposal of his only cow, sooner than incur the impu-
tation of a narrow, or, as he himself terms it, 'undacent'
or 'nagerly' [niggardly] spirit".[44]

The people are not only hospitable but also generous and grateful for kind deeds. When Owen M'Carthy is
brought low, "to the credit of our peasantry, much as is
said about their barbarity, he was treated, when helpless,
with gratitude, pity, and kindness".[45] Similarly, in his
capacity as a young scholar, Jemmy M'Evoy is treated with
every mark of respect and hospitality while he is on his
way to Munster. When he contracts famine fever it is the
most humble and wretched who take care of him, providing
him with shelter and food although they themselves are
starving. Carleton draws the obvious moral: "to contem-
plate a number of men, considered rude and semi-barbarous,
devoting themselves, in the midst of privations the most
cutting and oppressive, to the care and preservation of a
strange lad, merely because they knew him to be without
friends and protection, is to witness a display of virtue
truly magnanimous".[46] The many scenes of parting testify
to the love the members of a family bear for one another,
and apart from family affection the sense of family dignity
is extremely strong. The M'Carthy family leave their own
district when they are reduced to mendicancy as it would be
shameful for them to be seen begging. Again, the M'Evoy
family is too poor to provide their son with funds for his
venture and the priest organizes a collection for him; Jemmy and his father attend the Mass at which the collection
is to be made "whilst the other members of the family, with
that sense of honest pride which is more strongly inherent
in Irish character than is generally supposed, [remain] at
home, from a reluctance to witness what they could not but

44. "The Station", Works II, p. 756.
45. "Tubber Derg or the Red Well", Works I, p. 950.
46. "The Poor Scholar", Works II, p. 1106.

consider a degradation". But the priest and his congregation have anticipated this and do their best to make the M'Evoy's feel at ease. Carleton draws an enthusiastic moral conclusion: "So keen and delicate are the perceptions of the Irish, and so acutely alive are they to those nice distinctions of kindness and courtesy, which have in their hearts a spontaneous and sturdy growth, that mocks at the stunted virtues of artificial life".[47]

The image of the dirty, lazy, improvident Irish was an ancient one, and in the nineteenth century it was argued that

> Ireland's greatest need was industry, not in the sense of industrialization such as had transformed Great Britain, but habits of industriousness ... Ireland, it was argued, did not need factories and machines so much as a working class willing to live by the code of Samuel Smiles and ready to break the habit of leaning perpetually on spades ...[48]

Larry M'Farland is an object lesson in the want and squalor which follows a lack of industry; and in "The Poor Scholar", while he praises the eagerness with which the labourers, "ragged, half-starved creatures", neglect their work to build a shelter for Jemmy, Carleton adds reprovingly: "An Irishman never works for wages with half the zeal which he displays when working for love".[49] On the other hand Carleton by no means maintains that all Irishmen are lazy, however much he may imply that they generally prefer pleasure to business; what he might have added, but did not, is that the tenant farmers indeed had little incentive to do more than subsist.[50]

To counterbalance the image of the Irish as feckless and improvident Carleton stresses their little known characteristic of perseverance. He digresses at length on this quality in "The Poor Scholar" where the protagonist

---

47. ibid., pp. 1083-84.
48. Curtis, p. 57.
49. Works II, pp. 1103-04.
50. Cf. ch. II, p. 109.

displays great determination in his efforts to raise his
family from poverty:

> It is usual to attribute to the English and Scotch
> character, exclusively, a cool and persevering
> energy in the pursuit of such objects as inclina-
> tion or interest may propose for attainment;
> whilst Irishmen are considered too much the crea-
> tures of impulse to reach a point that requires
> coolness, condensation of thought, and efforts
> successively repeated. This is a mistake. It is
> the opinion of Englishmen and Scotchmen who know
> not the Irish character thoroughly.

These nations mistake the "far-sightedness" of the Irish
because they do not understand the peculiarly Irish method
of pursuing ambition:

> It would be difficult, for example, to produce a
> more signal instance of energy, system, and per-
> severance than that exhibited in Ireland during
> the struggle for Emancipation. Was there not
> flattery to the dust? blarney to the eyes? heads
> broken? throats cut? houses burned? and cattle
> houghed? And why? Was it for the mere pleasure of
> blarney — of breaking heads (I won't dispute the
> last point, though, because I scorn to give up
> the glory of the national character), — of cutting
> throats — burning houses — or houghing cattle? No;
> but to secure Emancipation. In attaining that ob-
> ject was exemplified the Irish method of gaining
> a point.[51]

Concrete instances of ordinary, non-political perseverance
in attaining an objective are given in the portraits of
such hard-working peasants as Owen M'Carthy, Phaddy Sheemus
Phaddy, Ellish and Peter Connell and Tom M'Farland.

The Irish peasantry "were supposed to share the educational and intellectual deficiencies of almost all peasants or

---

51. Works II, p. 1077.

agricultural laborers in Roman Catholic societies".[52]   Carleton most emphatically denies this estimation of the people.   His depiction of their cleverness has already been
discussed; he also underlines the degree in which education
and the educated are respected.   "There is no country on
the earth in which either education, or the desire to procure it, is so much reverenced as in Ireland".[53]   In "The
Hedge School" he indignantly asserts that

> There never was a more unfounded calumny, than
> that which would impute to the Irish peasantry an
> indifference to education.   I may, on the contra-
> ry, fearlessly assert that the lower orders of no
> country ever manifested such a positive inclina-
> tion for literary acquirements, and that, too, un-
> der circumstances strongly calculated to produce
> carelessness and apathy on this particular sub-
> ject.[54]

In spite of their reverence of learning the people may nevertheless be dubbed superstitious, and the education they
receive in the hedge schools is not calculated to make them
moral and independent: indeed it is shameful that their
eagerness for education should be thwarted, or rather betrayed by the moral instruction offered them in these
schools.   Carleton can therefore exclaim, in a statement
which sums up not only his characterization of the people
but also his belief in human perfectibility and his trust
in the presence of absolute criteria by which to evaluate
a "national character": "Alas! what noble materials for composing a national character, of which humanity might be
justly proud, do the lower orders of the Irish possess, if
raised and cultivated by an enlightened education!"[55]

Those Anglo-Saxons who accepted the stereotype had
a very different view of things:

> Where the Celt was child-like, the Anglo-Saxon was
> mature; instead of emotional instability, he could

52. Curtis, p. 56.
53. "The Poor Scholar", Works II, p. 1086.
54. Works II, p. 819.
55. ibid., p. 833.

boast of self-control; he was energetic not lazy,
rational not superstitious, civilized not primitive, clean not dirty, ready to forgive, not vengeful, and prepared to live under the rule of law.
This temperamental antithesis was all-embracing:
it left no loophole for the Irish to share much in
common with their English rulers.[56]

What is most significant here is that the Anglo-Saxons believed that the Celt was as he was by nature, for which
reason no system of government could change him. He had
to be treated firmly like the wayward and sometimes barbarous child he obviously was.

It was noted in Chapter I that Carleton had imbibed a large dose of Anglo-Saxonism[57] which shows itself
clearly in the <u>Christian Examiner</u> stories. This made him
identify with the Anglo-Saxon "in-group", though it must
be stressed that the stereotype which he there employed had
more to do with class and religion than it had to do with
race. The Irishmen in <u>Traits and Stories</u> present a far
more nuanced picture: generally speaking they are shrewd or
even clever, they enjoy the good things of life, they are
kind and unfailingly generous, they love their families and
have a strong sense of pride. Some of them may live in
squalor but these exceptions merely serve to prove the
rule. It is true that they may tend to drink and quarrel,
but it is only when they are violent for political ends
that they incur censure. Carleton found much that was
beautiful in Irish customs -- music, song, the wild beauty
of the traditional keen, imagination and familial affection.
But the dualism of the Irish temperament continued to
puzzle him. He was determined not to follow what he term-
ed the "fashionable" practice of drawing the Irish character "as the model of all that is generous, hospitable, and
magnanimous", and he refused to "extenuate their weak and
indefensible points" while admiring their more praiseworthy
characteristics. He adopted an evolutionary view of the
national character, both when he declared that they "poss-

---

56. Curtis, p. 53.
57. Cf. ch. I, pp. 67-68.

ess the elements of a noble and exalted national character"[58] and when he advocated moral education as the great
cure-all for national deficiencies.

It may be concluded that when Carleton wrote
Traits and Stories it was with the didactic aim of present-
ing the Irish peasantry as he saw them, and that whereas
he no longer subscribed to his earlier thesis he still accepted the premises upon which the stereotypical Irishman
was built. The stereotype provided him with his frame of
reference, and in proof of his objectivity he did not attempt to conceal unfavourable Irish characteristics. In
his depiction of "Irish character" he dealt in terms of an
implicit and sometimes explicit contrast between Irish and
English people. This may be understood in relation to his
declared purpose of delineating the people as they really
were for his English and Scottish readers and for the Anglo-Irish ruling class. Its wider implications are however
interesting, for he evidently felt it incumbent upon him
to act as apologist for his countrymen: there is no arrogance in his portrayal, and positive elements are eagerly
pointed out. This, in addition to Carleton's pride in being treated as Ireland's Walter Scott, is something which
reflects the feeling of racial and cultural inferiority
typical of colonial writers.[59] The characterization in
Carleton's stories is highly schematized and from an artistic point of view very much flawed, and their force consists
primarily in the creation of lively scenes and background
rather than in the deep and consistent analysis of character. Carleton was not content to let his portraits speak
for themselves; instead he used his fictional characters
as illustrative material for his social lecture.

---

58. "The Hedge School", Works II, p. 842.
59. It is this latter point which Donald Davie has failed to under-
    stand in his eagerness to establish Scott's influence on all who
    wrote about the peasantry (cf. The Heyday of Sir Walter Scott,
    ch. VII).

APPENDIX I.

THE INTRODUCTION TO "A PILGRIMAGE TO PATRICK'S PURGATORY"
Reproduced from The Christian Examiner VI
(1828), pp. 268-271.

Superstition, that blind devotion, which draws the individual under its influence to the performance of external works, and un-
necessary ceremonies, without being actuated by the spirit of pure religion, is as natural to the mind not enlightened by true knowledge,
as weeds are to a field that has ceased to be well cultivated; for as
the richest grounds produce the most vigorous thistles, so those remarkable for superstition might have been as eminent for piety, had
the blessed knowledge of truth been communicated to them in due season.
The extent to which this kind of superstition prevails in Ireland, is
inconceivable. I have been acquainted with a young man, a Roman Catholic, of good capacity, educated in the Dublin University, who was in
an uncommon degree a slave to its controul [sic]. In conversation no man
could draw a better distinction between it and true piety, or expose
its absurdities in stronger terms; yet, in reality, he was so much under its influence, that he ascribed, in a great measure, certain calamities which befel him to his habit of eating meat on a Friday! He
has, to my knowledge, taken solemn oaths on the most trifling occasions, even by kissing the Bible, and afterwards broken them when it
suited his convenience so to do -- I have also known him to blaspheme
the name of God in the most fearful manner, — yet, these crimes left
but a slight remorse on his mind, whilst the eating of meat on a Friday kept him always unhappy.

A man must be brought up among the Irish peasantry, and under the influence of superstition, before he can understand its form
and character correctly. Even to live amongst them upon their own level, is not sufficient to enable a man to observe, through every stage
of life, and in the private recesses of every family, the incredible

dominion which this absurd principle exercises over them. No one of a different persuasion from a Romanist, can ever know what happens religiously in the family of a Roman Catholic peasant, because the appearance of any such person, at the hour of prayer, would immediately put a stop to their devotions, and to such forms and ceremonies as might be connected with them; but even if he were permitted to be present, he could understand neither their ceremonies nor their prayers, [sic] I once witnessed the death of a Roman Catholic woman; a scene which left on my mind an indelible impression. There were nearly thirty persons of her own faith present, and but one Protestant, a female, who had been for many years in habits of the kindest intimacy with the dying woman. During her sickness the attention and acts of friendship on the part of this Protestant neighbour had been unremitting, and frequent; and at the moment alluded to, her attachment was evinced by tears of the severest sorrow. Would you believe me, Mr. Editor, when I assure you, that I saw this excellent and pious female compelled to leave this house of death, by the son of that woman who had experienced during her illness, such Christian love and liberality at her hands; — absolutely thrust out, lest the presence of a heretic might communicate a taint of sin to the departing spirit — lest her soul should sustain a spiritual injury from the physical proximity of one who was not a CATHOLIC! This circumstance is strictly true, and I could lay my finger on the head of the man who thus expelled, so rudely and unfeelingly, the friend of his mother. And here I desire to observe, that this is no extreme case; for the Roman Catholic family in question was no way remarkable as being either bigoted or superstitious: but it was only the exercise of an admitted and fundamental principle in the creed of a Popish peasant, written on his heart by every feeling and opinion which he saw in operation around him.

But there is no specimen of Irish superstition equal to that which is to be seen at St. Patrick's Purgatory, in Lough Dearg. A devout Romanist who has not made a pilgrimage to this place, can scarcely urge a bold claim to the character of piety. As soon as a man who is notorious for a villainous and immoral hardihood of character, and has kept aloof from "his duties", thinks proper to give himself up to the spiritual guidance of his priest, he is sent here to wipe out the long arrear of outstanding guilt, for which he is accountable, — to neutralize the evil example of a bad life by this redeeming act of concentrated devotion. It is melancholy to perceive the fatal success to which the Church of Rome has attained, in making void the atonement of Christ by her traditions; and how every part of her complicated, but perfect, system, even to the minutest points, seizes upon some corresponding weakness of the human heart, thereby to bind it to her agreeable and strong delusions. Every spiritual arrangement in her is calculated to turn the steps of the sinner from the cross of Christ. Has he committed a crime? — he is not taught to look with unfeigned repentance to Him, who taketh away the sin of the world; to acknowledge his own vileness, as a sinful and corrupt creature; and to cast his burden upon Christ. Oh no! he must cast it upon some rotten prop — upon St. Francis, upon St. Anthony — upon the blessed Virgin — upon the power of the priest, or upon his own works: all of which rise up in impious competition with the blood of Jesus, rivalling, in the arrogance of human pride, the benefits of his redemption. — When he commits a sin, he must confess it to a fellow sinner; perhaps, to a greater one, too, than himself; he must fast — he must confess — he must pray — he must shed tears, because he thinks that tears make his contrition perfect; and whilst the mind is distracted or puffed up by the performance of these, that have not even the merit of being voluntary, the faith perishes — the heart becomes habituated to self-deception, and the blood of Christ is forgotten in a mechanical routine of deceitful and unprofitable works. Is he sick? — he is not taught to approach, with a trembling hope in the divine mercy through Christ, that awful throne, before which he is shortly to appear — no — he must be anointed by the clergyman — he must confess and receive, and then all anxiety as to the danger of his situation is over — he rests then contented; and, ignorant that there can be no way to happiness but through Jesus, he reposes himself upon the intercession of his priest; who, indeed, says his masses for him, and is neither ashamed nor afraid when he attempts to sell the blood of Christ for money; or to extort from the awakened terrors of a guilty conscience, that pittance which charity would apply to procure him those comforts which the bed of sickness necessarily requires. Sir, I have seen a man who had led an outragiously [sic] wicked life, seized by an illness which was likely to prove fatal; he became alarmed, — for the horrors of eternity, and the wrathful countenance of an angry God, seemed kindling before him. It was appalling to hear the groans and shrieks of the miserable man, as he called upon his priest: I never witnessed any thing so solemn. He did not address himself to God; he did not appear to know that there was mercy for him through the Saviour; neither did he call upon Christ; but he expected it through his priest, and he accordingly called upon _him_. The priest came, the sick man confessed to him, received absolution, and in less than an hour I saw that very man quietly reposing on his bed apparently happy. Here was no change of heart, no spiritual views of the character of God, — of his detestation of sin — of the plan of Redemption furnished by his Son — nor of the simple terms on which the benefits of that redemption are communicated to sinners. No; but because he had confessed his sins to the priest — because the priest had read a form of prayer over him, in which neither his heart nor his tongue could join, inasmuch as he did not understand them; and lastly, because he rubbed a little oil on those parts of his body which had been most instrumental in committing sin. — Upon these forms did the spirit of that man rest for its hopes of eternal salvation. Through these, and not through the blood of atonement, did he expect to be reconciled to God, after an ill-spent life: yet how many thousands die like this man, ignorant of the only means of salvation, in the bosom of a Church calling herself Christian, and claiming holiness as one of the marks peculiar to herself.

It is agreeable to the pride of man to be saved by his own merit; the doctrine recommends itself to the depravity of his nature, for an individual may give himself very large scope in the commission of crime, who believes, that if he fasts, prays, and confesses for it, he can, by these means, exonerate himself from the consequences of guilt. A person who has neglected religion until advanced in years, need not then feel very deep remorse for his dissolute life, nor very serious apprehensions at the hour of death, if he has performed a station to Lough Dearg, thus lulling his old age into a false and treacherous security.

It is a fact, Mr. Editor, that many an unfortunate sinner runs a career of vice and iniquity, on the strength of Lough Dearg; particularly those who reside in that part of the kingdom, where, in consequence of their contiguity to it, a belief in its efficacy is most habitually present in the mind.

But as I commenced this paper with an intention of giving you an account of a pilgrimage which I made, when a Roman Catholic, to this celebrated place, I think I had better not tantalize you, or your respectable readers any longer, but give you at once the narrative. I was, at the time of performing this station (...).

A CHECK-LIST OF THE FIRST EDITIONS OF
CARLETON'S PROSE FICTION

INTRODUCTORY NOTE

This check-list provides a survey of the first editions of
Carleton's sketches, short stories and novels. It is based
on the catalogues of the National Library of Ireland, the
British Library and the Library of Congress, verified by
my own examination of the editions and collated with the
references in Richard J. Hayes, ed. ‚ Sources for the History of Irish Civilisation: Articles in Irish Periodicals
(9v., Boston 1970), and the bibliography in André Boué's
dissertation from 1973, which came into my hands after the
first draft of my check-list was completed and which I here
supplement on minor points.

        Of the bibliographies of Carleton available prior
to the appearance of Boué's dissertation, only two are of
any value to scholars. These are the "Bibliography of Carleton's Writings" in O'Donoghue's Life and the relevant en-
tries in Michael Sadleir, XIX Century Fiction (2v., London
and Los Angeles 1951). O'Donoghue's bibliography is partly
reconstructed from memory and as such is lacking in both
accuracy and detail, while Sadleir's work, which also appears to form the basis of the section on Carleton in the
New Cambridge Bibliography of English Literature, is com-
piled mainly from the point of view of the bibliophile.
Like Boué's bibliography, my check-list helps to establish
a literary chronology and is thus oriented towards the more
specific requirements of the literary historian.

1828   "A Pilgrimage to Patrick's Purgatory" <u>CE</u> VI (1828),
pp. 268-286, 343-362.
— Title in later editions: "The Lough Derg [Dearg] Pilgrim".

"The Broken Oath" <u>CE</u> VI (1828), pp. 425-439 and
VII (1828), pp. 27-39.

"Father Butler" <u>CE</u> VII (1828), pp. 109-119,
192-202, 271-290, 355-365, 423-443.
— Title in later edition: "Father Butler, or Sketches of
Irish Manners".

1829   "The Station" <u>CE</u> VIII (1829), pp. 45-60, 259-269,
422-438.
(= "Sketches of the Irish Peasantry" nos. 1, 2
and 3)
— Title in later edition: "Father Philemy, or the Holding
of the Station".

"Dick Magrath. A Sketch of Living Character" <u>The
Dublin Family Magazine; or, Literary and Religious
Miscellany</u> no. 5 (1829), pp. 336-343.

"The Death of a Devotee" <u>CE</u> IX (1829), pp. 267-283.

1830   "Confessions of a Reformed Ribbonman (An Owre True
Tale)" <u>The Dublin Literary Gazette</u> I, 4-5 (1830),
pp. 49-51, 66-68.
— Title in later editions: "Wildgoose Lodge".

"The Priest's Funeral" <u>CE</u> X (1830), pp. 41-51,
128-142.

"The Three Tasks or the Little House under the
Hill" <u>The Dublin Literary Gazette</u> I, 9-10 (1830),
pp. 129-132, 152-154.
— First complete text in <u>TS</u>[1] (1830), vol. I, pp. 44-92.

"The Brothers" <u>CE</u> X (1830), pp. 205-213, 287-296, 365-377, 440-452.

(= "Sketches of the Irish Peasantry" nos. 4, 5, 6 and 7)

"Lachlin Murray and the Blessed Candle" <u>CE</u> X (1830), pp. 590-610.

(= "Popular Romish Legends" no. 1)

"The Lianhan Shee" <u>CE</u> X (1830), pp. 845-861.

"Alley Sheridan. An Irish Story" <u>NM</u> I, 5 (1830), pp. 544-570.

— Titles in later editions: "Alley Sheridan or the Irish Runaway Marriage", "The Abduction or an Irish Runaway Marriage".

"The Illicit Distiller, or the Force of Conscience" <u>CE</u> X (1830), pp. 928-939.

"The Donagh, or the Horse-Stealers" <u>NM</u> I, 6 (1830), pp. 637-654.

— Title in later edition: "The Horse Stealers".

In <u>TS</u>[1] (1830):

1) "Ned M'Keown", vol. I, pp. 1-43.

2) "An Irish Wedding (Shane Fadh's Wedding)", <u>ibid.</u>, pp. 93-156.

3) "Larry M'Farland's Wake", <u>ibid.</u>, pp. 157-216.

4) "The Battle of the Factions. By a Hedge Schoolmaster", <u>ibid.</u>, pp. 217-275.

5) "The Funeral and Party Fight", vol. II, pp. 1-108.

6) "The Hedge School", <u>ibid.</u>, pp. 109-210.

— Titles in later editions: 1) "Around Ned's Fireside, or the Story of the Squire"; 3) "An Irish Wake"; 5) "A Party Fight" [extract], "The Party Fight and Funeral", "The Curse" [extract]; 6) "The Hedge School and the Abduction of Mat Kavanagh", "Mat Kavanagh, the Hedge Schoolmaster" [abridgement].

1831   "Laying a Ghost" <u>NM</u> II, 7 (1831), pp. 41-48.

— Title in later editions: "Squire Warnock".

"History of a Chimney Sweep" <u>CE</u> XI (1831), pp.
276-291.

"The Landlord and Tenant, an Authentic Story" <u>NM</u>
II, 10 (1831), pp. 383-401.
— Titles in later editions: "Tubber Derg, or the Red Well",
"Owen M'Carthy; an Authentic Story", "Owen M'Carthy, or,
the Landlord and Tenant". First complete text in <u>TS</u>^{2} (1833),
vol. III, pp. 337-475.

"The Materialist" <u>CE</u> XI (1831), pp. 512-532.

"Denis O'Shaughnessy going to Maynooth" <u>CE</u> XI
(1831), pp. 686-696, 765-779, 842-854, 930-945.
— Titles in later editions: "Going to Maynooth", "The Irish
Student; or how the Protestant Church was founded by Luther
and the Devil" [extract].

1833   "Neal Malone" <u>The [Dublin] University Review and
        Quarterly Magazine</u> I, 1 (1833), pp. 151-170.
        — Titles in later editions: "Neal Malone. A Tale of a Tai-
        lor", "The Pugnacious Tailor".

"The Dream of a Broken Heart" <u>The Dublin University
Review and Quarterly Magazine</u> I, 2 (1833), pp.
341-362.

"The Dead Boxer. An Irish Legend" <u>DUM</u> II (1833),
pp. 617-654.

In <u>TS</u>^{2} (1833):
1) "The Midnight Mass", vol. I, pp. 1-150.
2) "Phil Purcel, the Pig-Driver", <u>ibid</u>., pp.
   209-264.
3) "An Essay on Irish Swearing", <u>ibid</u>., pp.
   265-306.
4) "The Geography of an Irish Oath", <u>ibid</u>., pp.
   307-471.
5) "The Poor Scholar", vol. II, pp. 57-298.
6) "Phelim O'Toole's Courtship", vol. III, pp.
   255-433.

— Titles in later editions: 4) "How Peter Connell took the
Pledge"; 6) "The Courtship of Phelim O'Toole".

1834   "The Resurrections of Barney Bradley" DUM III
        (1834), pp. 177-193.
        — Titles in later editions: "Barney Bradley", "Barney Brad-
        ley's Resurrection".

        "Sha [read Lha] Dhu; or, the Dark Day. A Story"
        DUM IV (1834), pp. 426-441.
        — Title in later edition: "The Two Brothers. An Irish Tale".

1836   "Jane Sinclair, or the Fawn of Springvale. A
        Story" DUM VIII (1836), pp. 334-350, 702-721.

1838   "Rickard the Rake. In Three Snatches" DUM XI
        (1838), pp. 364-383.
        — Title in later edition: "The Irish Rake" [extract].

        "Barney Brady's Goose; or, Dark Doings at Slath-
        beg" DUM XI (1838), pp. 604-624.
        — Title variant in later edition: "... Mysterious Doings
        ...".

1839   "The Three Wishes. An Irish Legend" DUM XIV
        (1839), pp. 600-613.

1840   "The Parent's Trial" The Citizen or Dublin Monthly
        Magazine II, 8 (1840), pp. 21-37.
        (= "Records of the Heart" no. 1)
        — Title in later edition: "A Record of the Heart, or the
        Parent's Trial".

        "The Irish Fiddler" IPJ no. 7 (1840), pp. 52-55.
        — Titles in later editions: "Mickey M'Rory, the Irish Fidd-
        ler", "Mickey M'Rory, the Country Fiddler".

        "The Country Dancing-Master. An Irish Sketch"
        IPJ no. 9 (1840), pp. 69-72.
        — Title in later editions: "Buckram(-)back, the Country
        Dancing-Master".

        "The Irish Matchmaker" IPJ no. 15 (1840), pp.
        116-120.
        — Title in later editions: "Mary Murray, the Irish Match(-)
        maker".

"Bob Pentland, or the Gauger Outwitted" IPJ no. 16 (1840), pp. 125-127.

— Titles in later editions: "The Gauger Outwitted", "Bob Pentland, the Irish Smuggler; or, the Gauger Outwitted".

"Irish Superstitions — Ghosts and Fairies. (First Article)" IPJ no. 21 (1840), pp. 164-166.

— Title in later editions: "The Fate of Frank M'Kenna".

"Irish Superstitions — Ghosts and Fairies. The Rival Kempers. (Second Article)" IPJ no. 24 (1840), pp. 188-191.

— Titles in later editions: "The Rival Kempers", "Paddy Corcoran's Wife" [extract].

1840/41   "The Irish Midwife" [parts 1-3] IPJ no. 26 (1840), pp. 202-204, no. 27 (1841), pp. 209-213 and no. 40 (1841), pp. 313-316.

— Titles in later editions: "Rose Moan, the Irish Midwife", "Dandy Kehoe's Christening" [extract], "Corny Keho's Birth and Christening" [extract], "Rose Moan, the Country Midwife".

1841   "A Legend of Knockmany" Chambers' Edinburgh Journal no. 468 (1841), pp. 409-411.

— Title in later edition: "Fin M'Coul, the Knockmany Giant".

"The Misfortunes of Barney Branagan; Showing how he became a Wealthy Man by the Same" DUM XVII (1841), pp. 80-100, 233-244, 319-327, 445-455, 585-598.

— Titles in later editions: "Barney Branagan", "Riches in spite of Ill-Luck".

"Irish Superstitions. — No. III Ghosts and Fairies" IPJ no. 34 (1841), pp. 269-271.

— Title in later editions: "Frank Martin and the Fairies".

"Moll Roe's Marriage; or, the Pudding Bewitched. A Tale for an Irish Wake" The Citizen or Dublin Monthly Magazine III, 17 (1841), pp. 155-161.

— Titles in later editions: "The Bewitched Pudding. A Story told at a Wake", "The Pudding Bewitched", "The Mad Pudding of Ballyboulteen".

"The Foster Brother" IPJ no. 43 (1841), pp. 338-340.

— Title in later editions: "Frank Finnegan, the Foster-Brother".

"The Irish Shanahus" IPJ no. 48 (1841), pp. 378-380.

— Titles in later editions: "Tom Gressiey, the Irish Senachie", "Tom Gressiey, the Irish Senachie, or the Origin of the Name of Gordon".

"The Castle of Aughentain, or a Legend of the Brown Goat, a Tale of Tom Gressiey, the Shanahus" IPJ no. 49 (1841), pp. 386-389.

— Title in later edition: "The Castle of Aughentain; or a Legend of the Brown Goat. Narrated by Tom Gressiey, the Irish Senachie".

"The Irish Prophecy Man" IPJ no. 50 (1841), pp. 393-396.

— Title in later editions: "Barney M'Haigney, the Irish Prophecy Man".

"The Clarionet" in: William Carleton, The Fawn of Springvale, The Clarionet, and Other Tales (Dublin and London 1841), vol. II, pp. 1-191.

1845   In Tales and Sketches, illustrating the Character, Usages, Traditions, Sports and Pastimes of the Irish Peasantry (Dublin 1845):

1) "Talbot and Gaynor, the Irish Pipers", pp. 154-163.
2) "Condy Cullen; or, the Exciseman Defeated", pp. 275-288.
3) "Stories of Second Sight and Apparition", pp. 365-393.

— Titles in later editions: 2) "The Gauger Captured and the Gauger Outwitted", "Condy Cullen and the Gauger", "Condy Cullen and how he defeated the Exciseman"; 3) "Second Sight and Apparition".

1847	"O'Sullivan's Love; a Legend of Edenmore" <u>DUM</u> XXIX (1847), pp. 277-295, 428-446.
	"An Irish Election in the Time of the Forties" <u>DUM</u> XXX (1847), pp. 176-192, 287-297.
1850	"Black and All Black. A Legend of the Padereen Mare. Related on Christmas Eve, by an Old Senachie" <u>Illustrated London News</u>, Christmas Number and Supplement (1850), pp. 494-495.
1853	"The Fair of Emyvale" <u>Illustrated London Magazine</u> I (1853), pp. 17-21, 57-66, 101-107.
1853/54	"The Silver Acre" <u>Illustrated London Magazine</u> I (1853), pp. 221-228, 267-272 and II (1854), pp. 12-16, 47-57.
1854	"Master and Scholar: Being the Wonderful History of 'Sam' and Pat Frayne; or, a Thirst after Knowledge" <u>Illustrated London Magazine</u> II (1854), pp. 198-206.
1855	"The King's Thief" in: <u>Commercial Journal and Family Herald</u> (Dublin), 22.9-13.10.1855.
1856	"Fair Gurtha; or, the Hungry Grass. A Legend of the Dumb Hill" <u>DUM</u> XLVII (1856), pp. 414-435.
1860	"Utrum Horum? or the Revenge of Shane Roe na Sogarth; a Legend of the Golden Fawn" <u>DUM</u> LV (1860), pp. 528-541, 653-674.
	"The Man with the Black Eye. Being a Satirical Allegory upon Life" <u>Duffy's Hibernian Magazine</u> (Dublin), I (1860), pp. 9-21.
1861	"The Miller of Mohill" <u>Illustrated Dublin Journal</u> I, 1-4 (1861), pp. 1-4, 17-20, 33-36, 60-62.

1868   "The Weird Woman of Tavniemore; or Milking the Tethers, a Tale of Witchcraft" The Shamrock (Dublin), IV (1868), pp. 498-516, 529-532, 545-549.

1869   "The Romance of Instinct" The Shamrock V (1869), pp. 340-342, 360-362, 376-377, 392-393, 444-445.

2. FIRST EDITIONS OF THE NOVELS

1837/38   "Fardorougha the Miser, or the Convicts of Lisnamona" DUM IX (1837), pp. 212-230, 251-271, 426-442, 521-546, X (1837), pp. 671-692 and XI (1838), pp. 95-111, 250-276.
— First edition in book form Dublin 1839.

1845   Valentine M'Clutchy, the Irish Agent; or, Chronicles of the Castle Cumber Property. 3v. Dublin 1845.

Art Maguire; or, the Broken Pledge. A Narrative. Dublin 1845.

Rody the Rover; or, the Ribbonman. Duffy's Library of Ireland, vol. 5. Dublin 1845.

Parra Sastha; or, the History of Paddy Go-Easy and his Wife Nancy. Duffy's Library of Ireland, vol. 6. Dublin 1845.

1846   "The Black Prophet — a Tale of Irish Famine" DUM XXVII (1846), pp. 600-623, 739-760 and XXVIII (1846), pp. 75-94, 214-231, 334-359, 466-490, 578-600, 717-747.
— First edition in book form London and Belfast 1847.

1848   The Emigrants of Ahadarra. A Tale of Irish Life. Parlour Library, vol. 11. London and Belfast 1848.

1849 The Tithe Proctor: A Novel. Being a Tale of the Tithe Rebellion in Ireland. Parlour Library, vol. 24. London and Belfast 1849.

1852 The Squanders of Castle Squander. 2v. London 1852.

— Chs. I-IV also printed in supplements to Illustrated London News, 17.1 and 31.1.1852.

Red Hall, or the Baronet's Daughter. 3v. London 1852.

— Title in later editions: The Black Baronet; or the Chronicles of Ballytrain.

1855 Willy Reilly and his Dear Coleen Bawn; a Tale, founded upon Fact. 3v. London 1855.

— An earlier version in The Independent (London), December-January 1850/51.

1860 The Evil Eye; or, the Black Spectre. A Romance. Dublin 1860.

— Two chapters of an earlier version in The Irish Tribune (Dublin), June 1848. An incomplete serialization under the title "Suil Balor; or the Evil Eye. A Romance" in the Weekly Gazette, Incumbered Estates Record and National Advertiser (Dublin), I, 23-29 (1855).

"The Rapparee" Duffy's Hibernian Magazine (Dublin), I (1860), pp. 57-68, 101-106, 156-161, 197-207, 254-263.

— First edition in book form (expanded version): Redmond Count O'Hanlon, the Irish Rapparee. An Historical Tale. Dublin 1862.

1861 "The Double Prophecy; or, Trials of the Heart" Duffy's Hibernian Magazine II (1861), pp. 1-11, 49-59, 97-103, 141-149, 187-196, 237-248 and III (1861), pp. 1-10, 49-56, 97-103.

— First edition in book form Dublin 1862.

1889   The Red-Haired Man's Wife. Dublin and London 1889.

1906   "A New Pyramus and Thisbe, The Battle of Aughrim"
        Blackwood's Edinburgh Magazine no. MLXXXIV (1906),
        pp. 273-277. [Extract from the unpublished novel
        "Anne Cosgrave; or, the Chronicles of Silver
        Burn".]

SELECTED

BIBLIOGRAPHY

1. EDITIONS OF CARLETON'S WORKS

(see Appendix II for details of works not included in
the collected editions listed here)

Traits and Stories of the Irish Peasantry. 2v. Dublin
1830.

Traits and Stories of the Irish Peasantry. Second series. 3v. Dublin 1833.

Tales of Ireland. By the Author of "Traits and Stories
of the Irish Peasantry". Dublin 1834.

Traits and Stories of the Irish Peasantry. A new edition. With an autobiographical introduction, explanatory notes and numerous illustrations (...). 2v. Dublin and London 1843-44.
— This edition is a reissue of the "First complete and fully illustrated edition" published in monthly parts in 1842-43.

Tales and Sketches, illustrating the Character, Usages,
Traditions, Sports and Pastimes of the Irish Peasantry.
Dublin 1845.

The Works of William Carleton. Collier's unabridged
edition. 2v. New York 1880.
— Reissued in 3v., New York 1881; photographic reprint in Short
Story Index reprint series, Freeport, N.Y. 1970.

Stories from Carleton. With an introduction by W.B.
Yeats. London, New York and Toronto n.d. [c. 1888/89].

Traits and Stories of the Irish Peasantry. Edited by
D.J. O'Donoghue. 4v. London and New York 1896.

The Autobiography of William Carleton. With a preface
by Patrick Kavanagh. London 1968.

2. SECONDARY LITERATURE

Adams, W.F. *Ireland and Irish Emigration to the New
World from 1815 to the Famine*. New Haven, Conn.
1932.

Allen, Walter. *The English Novel: A Short Critical History*. 1954; reprinted Harmondsworth 1968.

Anon. "The Didactic Irish Novelists — Carleton, Mrs.
Hall" *DUM* XXVI (1845), pp. 737-752.

———. *Proselytising the Irish: or the Struggles and
Prospects of Protestantism; with Strictures on
Street-Preaching*. By an Observer. Edinburgh n.d.
[1858].

Baker, E.A. *The History of the English Novel*. Vol. VII.
London 1936.

Barrington, Sir Jonah. *Personal Sketches of his Own
Times*. 2v. 1827; second edition, revised and improved, London 1830.

Beaumont, Gustave de. *L'Irlande: Sociale, Politique et
Religieuse*. 2v. Paris 1839.

Beckett, J.C. *The Making of Modern Ireland 1603-1923*.
1966; reprinted London 1969.

Boué, André. "William Carleton and the Irish People"
Clogher Record VI, 1 (1966), pp. 66-70.

———. *William Carleton 1794-1869. Romancier Irlandais*.
Diss. Paris 1973.

Brown, Stephen J., S.J. Ireland in Fiction: A Guide to Irish Novels, Tales, Romances and Folklore. Second edition, 1919; reprinted Shannon 1968.

Casey, Daniel J. "Lough Derg's Infamous Pilgrim" Clogher Record VII, 3 (1972), pp. 449-479.

Clarke, Austin. A Penny in the Clouds: More Memories of Ireland and England. London 1968.

Connell, K.H. The Population of Ireland 1750-1845. Oxford 1950.

Curtis, Edmund and R.B. McDowell, ed. Irish Historical Documents 1172-1922. London 1943.

Curtis, L.P., Jr. Anglo-Saxons and Celts: A Study of Anti-Irish Prejudice in Victorian England. Studies in British History and Culture II. Bridgeport, Conn. 1968.

Davie, Donald. The Heyday of Sir Walter Scott. London 1961.

Dowling, P.J. The Hedge Schools of Ireland. 1935; revised edition Cork 1968.

Edgeworth, Richard Lovell and Maria Edgeworth. Essay on Irish Bulls. London 1802.

Flanagan, Thomas. The Irish Novelists 1800-1850. New York 1959.

Foster, John Wilson. Forces and Themes in Ulster Fiction. Dublin and London 1974.

Foster, Thomas Campbell. Letters on the Condition of the People of Ireland. Second edition, London 1847.

Freeman, T.W. Pre-Famine Ireland: A Study in Historical Geography. Manchester 1957.

Handlin, Oscar. The Uprooted. Boston 1951.

Ibarra, Eileen Sullivan. "Realistic Accounts of the Irish Peasantry in Four Novels of William Carleton". Diss. Gainesville [Univ. of Florida] 1969.

Kiely, Benedict. _Poor Scholar: A Study of the Works and Days of William Carleton (1794-1869)_. New York 1948.

Krans, Horatio Sheafe. _Irish Life in Irish Fiction_. New York 1903.

Leadbeater, Mary Shackleton. _Cottage Dialogues among the Irish Peasantry_. 2v. London 1811-13.

Lyons, F.S.L. "Vicissitudes of a Middleman in County Leitrim, 1810-27" _Irish Historical Studies_ IX (1954-55), pp. 300-318.

MacCurtain, Margaret. "Pre-Famine Peasantry in Ireland: Definition and Theme" _Irish University Review_ IV,2 (1974), pp. 188-198.

MacDonagh, O. "The Irish Catholic Clergy and Emigration during the Great Famine" _Irish Historical Studies_ V (1946-47), pp. 287-302.

McDonagh, Thomas. _Literature in Ireland: Studies Irish and Anglo-Irish_. London n.d. [1916].

McHugh, Roger. "William Carleton: A Portrait of the Artist as Propagandist" _Studies_ [Dublin] XXVII (1938), pp. 47-62.

Maxwell, Constantia. _Country and Town in Ireland under the Georges_. 1940; revised edition Dundalk 1949.

Mercier, Vivian. _The Irish Comic Tradition_. London 1962.

Molua (pseud.). "A Contrast in Public Values. The Catholic Statesman: The Apostate Man of Letters" _The Catholic Bulletin_ [Dublin] XXI (1931), pp. 583-587.

Montague, John. "Tribute to William Carleton" _The Bell_ [Dublin] XVIII (1952), pp. 13-20.

Montgomery, Rev. John. _Popery as it Exists in Great Britain and Ireland, its Doctrines, Practices, and Arguments; Exhibited from the Writings of its Advocates, and from its Most Popular Books of Instruction and Devotion_. Edinburgh and London 1854.

Norman, E.R. *Anti-Catholicism in Victorian England*.
      London 1968.

O'Brien, John. *90 Common Questions about Catholic
      Faith*. 1962; reprinted London 1963.

O'Connor, Frank. *The Backward Look: A Survey of Irish
      Literature*. London, Melbourne and Toronto 1967.

O'Donoghue, David J. *The Life of William Carleton: be-
      ing his Autobiography and Letters; and an Account
      of his Life and Writings, from the Point at which
      the Autobiography breaks off*. 2v. London 1896.

Otway, Caesar. *Sketches in Ireland: Descriptive of In-
      teresting and Hitherto Unnoticed Districts in the
      North and South*. Dublin 1827.

Pomfret, J.E. *The Struggle for Land in Ireland 1800-
      1923*. Princeton, N.J. 1930.

Power, Patrick C. *A Literary History of Ireland*. Cork
      1969.

Redfield, Robert. *Peasant Society and Culture: An An-
      thropological Approach to Civilization*. Chicago
      1956.

Reynolds, James A. *The Catholic Emancipation Crisis in
      Ireland 1823-1829*. Yale Historical Publications,
      Miscellany LX. New Haven, Conn. and London 1954.

Scott, Florence C. "Teg — the Stage Irishman" *Modern
      Language Review* XLII (1947), pp. 314-320.

Shaw, Rose. *Carleton's Country*. Dublin 1930.

Stevenson, Lionel. *The English Novel: A Panorama*. Lon-
      don 1960.

Williams, T. Desmond, ed. *Secret Societies in Ireland*.
      Dublin and New York 1973.

Young, Arthur. *A Tour in Ireland*. 2v. London 1780.